Reading Russian fortunes examines the huge popularity and cultural impact of fortune-telling among urban and literate Russians from the eighteenth century to the present. Based partly on study of the numerous editions of little fortune-telling books, especially those devoted to dream interpretation, it documents and analyses the social history of fortune-telling in terms of class and gender, at the same time considering the function of both amateur and professional fortune-telling in a literate modernizing society. Chapters are devoted to professional fortune-tellers and their clients, and to the publishers of the books. An analysis of the relationship between urban fortune-telling and traditional oral culture, where divination played a very significant role, leads to a discussion of the underlying reasons for the persistence of fortune-telling in modern Russian society.

Faith Wigzell is Head of the Russian Department and Reader in Russian at the School of Slavonic and East European Studies, University of London. She is author of *The Literary Style of Epifanij Premudryj* (1976) and editor of *Russian Writers on Russian Writers* (1994) and *Nikolay Gogol: Text and Context* (1989, with Jane Grayson) as well as numerous articles on early Russian literature and folklore and their creative use in nineteenth-century Russian literature.

CAMBRIDGE STUDIES IN RUSSIAN LITERATURE

Recent titles in this series include

Wagner and Russia
ROSAMUND BARTLETT

Russian literature and empire
Conquest of the Caucasus from Pushkin to Tolstoy
SUSAN LAYTON

Jews in Russian literature after the October Revolution
Writers and artists between hope and apostasy
EFRAIM SICHER

Contemporary Russian satire: a genre study
KAREN L. RYAN-HAYES

Gender and Russian literature: new perspectives
edited by ROSALIND MARSH

The last Soviet avant-garde: OBERIU – fact, fiction, metafiction
GRAHAM ROBERTS

Literary journals in imperial Russia
edited by DEBORAH A. MARTINSEN

Russian Modernism: the transfiguration of the everyday
STEPHEN C. HUTCHINGS

For a complete list of titles published see end of book

READING RUSSIAN FORTUNES

'Fortune-telling', painting by V. E. Makovskii (1912). A gypsy reads palms for village girls.

READING RUSSIAN FORTUNES

Print Culture, Gender and Divination in Russia from 1765

FAITH WIGZELL

CAMBRIDGE UNIVERSITY PRESS

CAMBRIDGE UNIVERSITY PRESS
Cambridge, New York, Melbourne, Madrid, Cape Town, Singapore, São Paulo

Cambridge University Press
The Edinburgh Building, Cambridge CB2 2RU, UK

Published in the United States of America by Cambridge University Press, New York

www.cambridge.org
Information on this title: www.cambridge.org/9780521581233

First published 1998
This digitally printed first paperback version 2006

A catalogue record for this publication is available from the British Library

Library of Congress Cataloguing in Publication data

Wigzell, Faith.
Reading Russian fortunes: print culture, gender and divination
in Russia from 1765 / Faith Wigzell.
p. cm. (Cambridge studies in Russian literature)
Includes bibliographical references and index.
ISBN 0 521 58123 0 (hardback)
1. Fortune-telling – Social aspects – Russia (Federation) – History.
2. Fortune-telling – Publishing – Russia (Federation) – History.
I. Title. II. Series.
BF1861.W57 1998
133.3′0947–dc21 97-18196 CIP

ISBN-13 978-0-521-58123-3 hardback
ISBN-10 0-521-58123-0 hardback

ISBN-13 978-0-521-02479-2 paperback
ISBN-10 0-521-02479-X paperback

We feel that when all possible scientific
questions have been answered,
the problems of life remain
completely untouched.
(Wittgenstein)

The future is certain, only the past
is in doubt
(old Soviet joke)

Contents

Illustrations

Acknowledgements

> Dreaming of writing a book means pain and sorrow (A dream-book of 1794)

The writing of this book caused less pain and sorrow than it might have done thanks to the generous help I received. The British Academy provided the opportunity of a research visit to Russia and the British Council funded two crucial visits under the terms of the SSEES/ Academy Institutes of History exchange. Since the collecting of material about the social history of fortune-telling involved assembling fragments of information, I am particularly grateful to those who provided references, in particular Catriona Kelly, Will Ryan and members of the Study Group on Eighteenth-Century Russia. Gratitude, too, to colleagues at the School of Slavonic and East European Studies who read sections of the manuscript: Roger Bartlett, Bob Service, Natasha Kurashova, Peter Duncan and former colleagues Catriona Kelly, Will Ryan and Georgette Donchin. Their comments were much appreciated, though they are not of course in any way responsible for the book's failings. For help with bibliographies, preparation of the manuscript and negotiations with publishers, my thanks are due to Radojka Miljevic and Caroline Newlove, and for the verse translations to Mary Hobson. Last but not least I would like to express my thanks to the anonymous readers of the typescript for Cambridge University Press, whose comments and suggestions were invaluable.

Introduction

Fortune-telling has been described as 'an invisible religion'.[1] Though the term was originally applied to fortune-telling in contemporary Britain, it has equal relevance for Russia. Not only was fortune-telling before the Revolution both ubiquitous and valued by consumers and practitioners alike, but it was, at the same time, largely ignored by commentators. While the serious study of popular culture in Russia has developed in leaps and bounds in recent years,[2] the study of fortune-telling remains in limbo. My aim in the book is to rescue that history, looking at both domestic fortune-telling and professional practice as reflections of the processes of cultural transmission, assimilation and rejection. While many of these processes have their parallel in Western Europe, where they took place much earlier, Russia presents an interesting case study of a society which, by adopting West European cultural attitudes only in the eighteenth century, telescoped the transition from a pre-modern to a modern society into a mere one hundred and fifty years. At the same time as acquiring fortune-telling books from the West, the country also imbibed the principles of the Enlightenment, which promptly undermined the acceptability of the former. This book examines changes in readership, publishing practices and social attitudes to fortune-telling books as well as the role of fortune-tellers before the Revolution, and then considers their survival in Soviet and post-Soviet Russia. Simultaneously, it casts light on attitudes to foreign culture and the importance of the eighteenth century in the cultural patterns of the nineteenth.

Such considerations may also directly affect our understanding of élite culture in Russia, in particular literature, for fortune-telling and fortune-telling books were a familiar, if not always accepted part of the world of writers such as Pushkin and

Zhukovskii in the early nineteenth century and Zamiatin and Tsvetaeva in the twentieth. Their work is sometimes directly informed by their familiarity with fortune-telling, which in this way must be considered part of the cultural context in which literature operated in pre-Revolutionary Russia.

Apart from its relevance for an understanding of Russian culture at all levels, the study of fortune-telling makes a contribution to the debate about the nature of popular culture conducted over the last twenty-five years or more in Western Europe and America. One area of dispute has been definition. Can it be defined by general characteristics such as its willingness to shock and to reflect ephemeral tastes and concerns? Part of the answer appears to depend on the stage of social development of a given society. Popular culture before the modern period of industrialization, social mobility and commercialization tended to conservatism and the creation of its own tradition with some of the general characteristics of folk culture.[3] On the other hand, modern popular culture from film to novels or song is conventionally viewed as subject to rapid change and development. Such a distinction does not fit fortune-telling, which evidently belongs to the conservative popular culture of the pre-modern period, while surviving, indeed flourishing, in modern society, supposedly marked by dynamism. Indeed the importance of fortune-telling lies precisely in the way it straddles the cultures of a pre-modern and a modernizing society. Such was urban and literate Russia in the period covered by this book – 1765 being the date of the first printed fortune-telling book. This small volume reflected the first glimmerings of a consumer culture based on print, replacing oral tradition and the manuscript culture of the few. Its appearance coincided with the recognition by the rural minor nobility of the value of literacy.

In order to discuss fortune-telling as a conservative element in a modernizing culture, the focus necessarily falls on fortune-telling among the urban and literate population rather than on the rural peasantry. These were groups who were becoming or had become detached from traditional Russian society, in which folk divination formed an integral part of a largely unchanging world view and possessed clearly defined and generally stable functions.[4] Their need for clarification of the future was filled by a variety of mantic skills, almost entirely imports from Western Europe. In the modernizing society in which they lived, the position of fortune-telling was much more precarious. It had to carve out distinct and appropriate rôles as well as strategies for survival, all of which cast light on a range of questions about the nature of popular culture, oral tradition and Russian culture as a whole. In this book, therefore, rural divination is only treated as context and cultural residue, with one chapter devoted to the function of divination in Russian peasant society and its interrelationship with fortune-telling among urban and literate groups.

This is not, however, a study of literate versus pre-literate culture, for such was the phenomenal popularity of fortune-telling in Russia that it formed a secondary oral tradition, not only in the domestic sphere among those who purchased or used fortune-telling books, but also in the practice of urban fortune-tellers. One of the points made in this book is to emphasize the validity of secondary oral tradition in a country which tends to focus exclusively on its rich primary oral tradition. At the same time comparisons and contrasts cast light on conventional assumptions about the conservatism of folklore and the dynamic quality of popular culture.

Another facet of the debate about the definition of popular culture concerns the social class of those who share it, or, more precisely, whether it belongs to all classes except the élite (the binary opposition view) or is open to all, and to what extent it is common in character or particular to one social group. Nineteenth-century Russian cultural historians subscribed to the binary model, which has hung on in Russia,[5] while being seriously questioned in the West.[6] Thus, in his pioneering study of popular fiction in Russia 1860–1917, Jeffrey Brooks showed that, as books reached the peasants, their contents were increasingly tailored to fit their tastes and needs, and, as a consequence, this type of commercial fiction appealed primarily to peasants and poor workers. At the same time, reading material for different classes and groups in late nineteenth- and early twentieth-century Russia became increasingly varied, though the distinction between élite and popular culture remained widely held. By examining the market for fortune-telling books over a much longer period, I examine the validity of these assumptions for a different area of popular publishing.

A further area of debate about popular culture concerns the

extent to which popular commercial literature gives the people what made money for its publishers, while pretending 'to give them what they want'. In the eyes of Marxists of the Frankfurt School, it is therefore a means of keeping the masses quiet, a view supported in slightly different ways by others. Readers of popular literature, according to this approach, are merely passive consumers, who buy what looks attractive or intriguing. Paralleling the focus in literary studies on the rôle played by readers in the perception and interpretation of texts, a new emphasis on the active rôle of consumers has emerged, applicable even, as Richard Stites shows, in a totalitarian society like the Soviet Union, where cultural policy was dictated from above and consumer taste is conventionally assumed to have had no force.[7] Here fortune-telling books again present an interesting case study, since they require active involvement from readers. Discussion of passivity tends to draw questions of gender in its wake, especially in the case of fortune-telling, which is generally considered part of women's culture. In considering the gendered rôle played by fortune-telling, I question the conventional view that fortune-telling reflects women's passive approach to life, and, through a consideration of the readership of fortune-telling books and professional fortune-tellers, postulate its role in women's culture, as well as assessing men's level of involvement.

On a more general level, the study of fortune-telling adds force to the increasingly accepted view that modern societies differ less from traditional societies than has previously been imagined, a point of view cogently argued by Judith Devlin in her book on superstition among French peasants in the nineteenth century. In it she suggests that 'even if one discounts the indications that irrationality flourishes in modern culture, the history of psychology suggests that positivistic assumptions about human nature need to be revised'.[8] My book re-emphasizes this conclusion by focusing not only on a different country but also on urban and literate groups whose lives brought them up against new attitudes.

The reasons for the neglect of fortune-telling require additional elucidation. When in nineteenth-century Russia fortune-telling and fortune-telling literature fell foul of attitudes prevalent among the educated élite, the situation was not in essence different from that prevailing in Western Europe or America. On the other hand,

Western attitudes were as a whole much less strongly felt. The size and social diversity of the educated classes meant that they did not, or did not all, see it as their mission to defend and promote élite culture in the same way as did the Russian intelligentsia, who perceived themselves as a beleaguered minority amidst a sea of ignorance, philistinism or government indifference. Increasingly through the nineteenth century they became hostile to popular culture, because it employed the modern medium of print to promote cultural values which undermined their own efforts to foster an élite culture as a national heritage. Peasant superstition was too close to be regarded with indulgence. The net result was that commentators almost totally ignored fortune-telling when discussing the culture of classes and groups other than their own, except to deride.

In effect, three binary oppositions combined to effect this vanishing trick; not only the polarization of élite and popular cultures as previously mentioned, but also of rural folk and urban popular cultures and perceived male and female qualities. Nineteenth-century Russian ethnographers subscribed to the dominant cultural ideology in their acceptance of at least two of these binary oppositions, in each case placing moral value on one item in the pair. In so far as it was perceived by the dominant male élite culture as a women's preoccupation, fortune-telling was viewed as a demonstration of female empty-headedness and illogicality. Such attitudes were implicit more often than explicit, but certainly contributed to the disdain male observers felt for fortune-telling. They similarly regarded popular culture as either a debased form of élite culture, or a vulgar upstart that should be suppressed in favour of a morally improving artificial implant. In those rare cases where popular culture was deemed acceptable, scholars consistently preferred rural tradition to urban culture. While folk culture could be seen as age-old and colourful, expressing Russian national character, urban popular culture, by contrast, was degraded and degrading. Accordingly, ethnographers would pay attention to, for example, Yuletide divinatory rituals, but ignore fortune-telling in cities and among literate groups, since it possessed neither rural charm nor national appeal.[9] The tiny number of ethnographers who did remark on fortune-telling consistently mingled comment with condemnation. Thus fortune-telling found itself in the negative half of the equation, always despised and neglected. As a consequence, sources are problematical to say the least, being not merely scanty but also prejudiced.

The situation changed little after 1917, since fortune-telling, unlike some facets of pre-Revolutionary popular culture, could not be harnessed to the aims of the new society. As a consequence, the phenomenon achieved little more than passing mention in films or books. Since 1987 and the demise of the old order, long repressed interest has re-emerged in Russia itself. Though early popular fiction has been republished along with some nineteenth-century commentaries on urban life, the study of popular culture is still neglected and bedevilled by problems. The Tartu circle of scholars, headed until his recent death by Iurii Lotman, have made very little use of popular texts despite the purported 'inclusiveness' of their work on the semiotics of Russian culture.[10] Just as their approach reflects the durability of the perceived binary oppositions between élite and popular culture, so too the opposition between rural folk and urban popular culture is still conventional thinking. In the case of folk divinatory beliefs, the dominant approach of modern Russian ethnographers, ethnolinguists and folklorists to oral divinatory tradition still militates against popular urban culture, given that, as in much of the nineteenth century, it concentrates on the degree to which folk belief reflects ancient mythological thinking or ritual. One thinks here of the work of Academician Nikita Tolstoi and other scholars at the Institute of Slavonic and Balkan Studies in Moscow. For example, Tolstoi, writing about the mythological element in Slavonic dream interpretation, mentions the written dreambook tradition only to dismiss it. Oral tradition, he declares in a statement worthy of a nineteenth-century ethnographer, 'differs from the literary layer in its greater genetic purity and integrity as well as its antiquity and stability'.[11] While many forms of divinatory text certainly cannot furnish evidence of ancient beliefs, notions about the instability and antiquity of dreambooks need dispelling. So long as the main aim is, in the words of N. I. and S. M. Tolstoi, 'the reconstruction of the original system of Slav folk culture', urban fortune-telling can never compete for scholarly attention.[12]

The lack of an established term for popular culture reflects these entrenched attitudes. Not only, as Catriona Kelly points out, has the term *kul'tura* failed to acquire the relativistic connotations of 'a world of separate, distinctive and meaningful ways of life' in

Russia,[13] but an appropriate term for popular is also missing. *Narodnyi* has associations with one specific social group or with the nation as a whole, while *populiarnyi* lacks the connotations of its Latin original *popularis*, meaning 'of the people'. Whereas in English the terms 'folk' and 'popular', despite certain problems, can be used to delineate two different types of culture, in Russian this cannot be done so simply. Nikita Tolstoi has recently attempted to solve the problem by using the term 'culture of the "third" type', situated between élite and folk culture, or alternatively, based on the supposed social origin of its consumers, and so calling it *prostonarodnyi* (of the common people).[14] Given the pejorative overtones of the word *prostonarodnyi* in Russian, its use hardly implies the subject is deserving of serious treatment. But even as a term describing the social class of consumers, *prostonarodnaia kul'tura* will not do for modern mass culture, and it even has limited application for the pre-Revolutionary period. Fortune-telling books were not simply the property of the urban proletariat or peasants losing touch with folk culture. It is hard to imagine either that the term 'third culture' can possibly catch on. Neutral it may be, but self-explanatory it is not.[15]

With material even from biased sources so scanty, it became essential to draw on fictional references for the discussion of the reception and readership of fortune-telling books. These, too, are problematical. Firstly, they are composed by writers from an élite milieu, overwhelmingly male. At best, references to fortune-telling evoke a milieu or a mood, but more often the aim is either exposé or confirmation of a (usually female) character's foolishness or backwardness. It could be argued that, embedded in a work of fiction, references to fortune-telling can have little validity as evidence, but Russian fiction often possesses an explicitly documentary character, because passing factual material off as 'fiction' made censorship approval easier. Furthermore, such references do reflect the author's attitudes and often, more widely, society's too. As such they can be very valuable.

In the light of the above, I have relied primarily for basic documentation on the multitudinous editions of fortune-telling texts published 1765–1918. Through them the types and popularity of domestic fortune-telling in Russia can be established and compared with their European counterparts and originals. As the topic grew in scope, it became essential to focus on one particular type of text as a case study. The obvious choice was what may be regarded as the quintessential Russian fortune-telling text, the dreambook. While others went in and out of fashion, dreambooks maintained their spectacular popularity and were the first fortune-telling books to reappear in the 1980s. So popular are they in Russia that the Union Catalogue of eighteenth-century books indexes them separately. Other factors helped determine this choice; firstly, the composition of dreambooks rendered them susceptible to change under local conditions, thereby illumining the relationship between Russian fortune-telling books and their European counterparts, as well as changing social circumstances in Russia. Secondly, the existence of a vivid native oral tradition allowed for useful comparisons and contrasts. Finally, dreambooks provide invaluable material for the study of gender, since they, even more than other types of fortune-telling text, were and still are part of women's culture.

By contrast, I have deliberately excluded theosophy, spiritualism and varieties of occultism from serious consideration in the book. Like alternative medical techniques such as mesmerism and hypnotism, which fuse with divination at their borders, they enjoyed success among small groups of cognoscenti often drawn from the highest levels of society, but, unlike fortune-telling books, either faded from view or failed ever to attract a broader clientèle. Thus the occult and pseudo-sciences are mentioned in this book only where they are relevant to the general discussion.

Even the study of fortune-telling books themselves presents considerable difficulties for the researcher; no specialist catalogue of this material has ever been attempted. What is more, publishers did not always observe the legal obligation to place copies of their wares with the deposit libraries, and when they did, there was no guarantee that the books would be preserved. The proportion missing from the catalogues of major Russian libraries as a consequence of theft, neglect or censorship is astounding, while non-deposit libraries simply never bothered to collect what was regarded by high-minded librarians as rubbish. Even tracking down what remains in libraries requires patience and ingenuity. Apart from the eighteenth century for which the Union Catalogue provided invaluable help,[16] the compilation of an adequate bibliography of dreambooks and other manuals involved my using booksellers' catalogues, nineteenth-century bibliographical surveys, advertisements and references in memoirs.[17] Titles were then rooted out of Russian libraries (Moscow and Kazan' Universities, the Russian State (formerly Lenin) Library in Moscow, the Russian National Library in St Petersburg (formerly the State Public Saltykov-Shchedrin Library), the State Public Historical Library in Moscow and the Academy of Sciences Library in Petersburg). Given the Soviet policy of leaving details of 'unsuitable' books out of the readers' catalogue, finding the titles was a challenge. Although I have not managed to see copies of all the titles of whose existence I am aware, especially from the period after 1830, I have tried, where possible, to examine what sounds like the most unusual, as well as sample the most typical.

Bibliographical problems pale into insignificance compared with the problems of tracing the textual history of fortune-telling books in Russia, thanks to the cavalier attitudes of publishers and editors to cheap commercial books. At no time did they feel inhibited about changing, expanding or contracting either titles or the main body of works. Consequently, identical books may have different names, while identically named texts contain differing material. Nor, in the absence of proper attributions, is it generally possible to know when a given translation first appeared in Russian. Since the same fluid textual situation also occurs in foreign dreambooks, tracing the edition from which a translation was made is beyond the resources of one individual living far from Russia. I have therefore restricted myself to establishing in the first chapter the range and types of Russian fortune-telling books, as well as questions of origin and textual history. Even so, the result serves up a daunting quantity of detail, which, I feel, constitutes an essential framework for the subsequent discussion of social and publishing history.

Writing in English not only permits the use of the term 'popular culture', but also the differentiation of the two terms, 'fortune-telling' and 'divination' (Russian has only *gadanie*). When referring to Russia, I use 'divination' to indicate traditional rural practices, and 'fortune-telling' for divinatory activities among literate/urban groups, though as this sentence demonstrates, the adjective 'divinatory' is used more generally. In so doing, I am not subscribing to the overtones of frivolity and contempt that the word 'fortune-telling' possesses in English. I merely find the terms a useful way of describing cultural activities occurring in different social spheres.

A further problem is the term *lubok*, used to describe not only the woodcut (later copper engraved) chapbooks and pictures of the eighteenth and first half of the nineteenth century, but also the commercial pulp fiction, kopeck dreadfuls and other cheap literature, produced for the bottom end of the market after 1860. I have chosen to use the term *lubok* in its narrower sense as an external term, referring to the manner of production, that is, woodcut or copper engraved chapbooks as opposed to print. Apart from the simple necessity of distinguishing the two types of book in a study partially devoted to publishing history, I also wished to avoid any suggestion that fortune-telling books, whatever the dominance of the peasant market by the late nineteenth century, were not enjoyed by a wide spectrum of the population.

For all my efforts, I am aware that there must be mistakes of fact and emphasis in my book. It seems likely that the history of many aspects of popular culture in Russia will be pursued with energy and without (so much) bias in the coming years. I look forward to research on fortune-telling that can confirm or correct my conclusions.

Titles of fortune-telling books are given in both text and notes in English, but the bibliography contains an initial section which lists all those referred to in alphabetical order in English followed by the Russian title. Titles of all other Russian books are given in English in the main text but in transliteration in the notes and bibliography, on the grounds that Russian readers are those who might wish to pursue the subject further. The only exception to this rule are works of Russian literature, titles of which are everywhere translated.

CHAPTER 1

Dreambooks and other fortune-telling guides

From the latter part of the eighteenth century until the Revolution, bookshops, market traders, and colporteurs all sold books and pamphlets on fortune-telling. Their eye-catching titles promised novelty, mystery and efficacy, their contents attributed to illustrious sages, alchemists, sorcerers and seers. Each declared itself bigger and better than rivals or predecessors. Thus *The New and Complete* . . . was capped by *The Newest and Most Complete.* . . . As printing technology improved during the nineteenth century, booklets targeted at peasants substituted brightly coloured covers for the intriguing titles of earlier volumes. These covers depicted a venerable sage elucidating a young girl's dream or a brightly coloured circle of fate divided into segments (see ills. 1 and 2). Some of these books, notably the first few and the cheap editions for peasants, were very short, commonly consisting of instructions and interpretive key to a single fortune-telling method, though occasionally to more. Others were omnibus editions in as much as twelve parts and three volumes. Computed by the number of titles and editions, they enjoyed spectacular success with readers, rivalled only by songbooks and popular fiction.

This chapter documents the history of fortune-telling texts in Russia, their types, antecedents and evolution. In the virtual absence of any documented material on the subject the chapter opens with a general discussion of the first books and their impact on later versions as well as of the evolution of large omnibus editions. The various fortune-telling skills are then discussed individually, with particular attention paid to the history of dreambooks. The chapter concludes with a survey of the other short texts that appeared in large fortune-telling compendia, excluding those of folk origin which are examined in chapter 2.

The first two Russian fortune-telling books appeared in 1765:

1 The front cover of *The Interpretation of Dreams of Martyn Zadeka*, Moscow, 1885. The illustration depicts both the russification of the Swiss Martin Zadeck, here seen as an old Russian peasant in his peasant *izba*, and gender rôles (young women queuing to receive guidance from an old man whose wisdom lies in a book).

2 A *lubok* lithographed version of *King Solomon's Divinatory Circle* (here just called *A Little Divinatory Book*), produced in Mstera in 1879. Instructions given below the picture explain how to throw a grain of wheat onto the circle, and then look up the resulting number in the key inside the book's covers.

the first, a sixty-six-page volume, entitled *A New Fortune-Telling Method Translated from Arabic*,[1] was of a type called in Russian *orakul* (oracle). It presented tables of the twelve zodiac signs, forty-eight crucial questions about the future and twelve times forty-eight answers grouped according to the given sign. The second, *A Curious and Brief Elucidation of The Worthwhile Sciences of Physiognomy and Chiromancy*, came complete with pseudo-scientific disquisitions, and explained how to work out an individual's character and future from his or her physical appearance or palm. Despite the exotic reference to an Arabic source, the first book, like the second, had been translated (from German). The clue lay in the foreword which begged the reader not to enquire too closely how the editor had discovered the Arabic original. Both were reissued three years later along with the first printed dreambook, *The Interpretation of Dreams According to Astronomy, Occurring According to the Movements of the Moon, Translated from Polish.*

In many respects these three typify all Russian fortune-telling books. Firstly, they are translated from West European originals. Secondly, their categories of fortune-telling, oneiromancy (or dream divination), physiognomy, chiromancy (or palmistry) and oracles of the type described above went on to become, along with cartomancy, the most popular denominations for Russian fortune-telling texts. Only the oracle, as will be seen, failed to survive until the twentieth century. All three were reissued; the oracle ran to four further editions in the eighteenth century, the physiognomy and chiromancy book to ten by 1807 and the dreambook two. Even the illustrations became standardized; the frontispiece in the chiromantic text showing an astrological chiromancer and physiognomer at work reappeared regularly over the next seven decades (see ill. 3). Furthermore, all three books were quickly imitated; the next decades saw the appearance of many translations of rival texts or, indeed, retranslations of the same texts, resulting in myriad variants.

After 1805 translation of new materials stopped, and by 1830 novelty had ceased to hold any attraction. Probably not much more than a dozen new works were translated between 1830 and 1890. When a new translation appeared, its foreign origin was turned into a selling point in an attempt to compete with established titles, whose non-Russian origin was by then ignored or evident only from the allusion to foreign sages in the titles. In the

3 An astrological astronomer and chiromancer at work. Taken from the sixth edition of *A Curious and Brief Elucidation of the Worthwhile Sciences of Physiognomy and Chiromancy*, Moscow, 1789. The picture became popular in Russian fortune-telling books.

quarter century before the Revolution some publishers attempted to introduce new types of translated text, responding perhaps to the fashion for the occult, but these, like foreign sources during the previous half-century, failed to find favour with the average purchaser. Far from desiring anything new, he or she was only interested in tried and trusted predictive methods. From being viewed as exotic foreign novelties, fortune-telling books had moved into the sphere of Russian tradition.

The history of fortune-telling texts in Russia in many ways mirrors that in other European countries, not only in their common store of texts but also in the processes of assimilation and dissemination; conservatism, textual instability, piracy by publishers were all characteristic of European and American popular fortune-telling literature.[2] Yet no history is identical. One of the local features in Russia is the formative role played by eighteenth-century books in shaping later tradition, which has parallels in other areas of Russian popular and élite culture. Just as the collection of folk songs made in the late eighteenth century by L′vov and Prach came to be regarded as the ultimate source by nineteenth-century composers, even though not all the songs were the genuine article,[3] so too eighteenth-century fortune-telling texts established the dominant types right up till the Revolution, coming to be seen as part of Russian tradition.

The eighteenth century left a further legacy in the form of fortune-telling compendia. Most eighteenth-century editions comprised single texts, preceded by disquisitions of a scholarly nature which added an aura of gravity and venerability. Composed at various times from antiquity to Renaissance Europe, these were outdated in terms of contemporary scientific thinking. By the 1780s short divinatory texts, such as coffee-cup reading, bean divination, folk omens, Yuletide divination, astrology, calendar predictions, lists of unlucky days or omens for weather forecasting were being tacked onto the end of the main text. Around 1790 publishers began combining these with more than one main text, as in *The Wizard, No Idle Babbler, or The Genuine Fortune-Teller . . .*, St Petersburg, 1792, which amalgamated cartomancy and an oracle with Yuletide divination and 'mind-reading' of names. A mere two years later, *The Magic Mirror, Revealing the Secrets of Albertus Magnus . . .*, Moscow, 1794, was on its way to being an omnibus fortune-telling compendium with a dreambook, tables of unlucky days, astrological information and charts, discussion of the four humours and physiognomy, as well as a list of conjuring tricks and information about the 'mind-reading' of names. These last two items became the most popular kinds of non-divinatory text in omnibus editions of the next decade. Other very popular types were perpetual calendars, riddles, conjuring tricks, forfeits, trick arithmetic (think of a number . . .), charades or folk remedies. Political prophecy, most frequently the text ascribed to Martyn Zadeka, also commonly featured.[4]

By the second decade of the nineteenth century, the earliest compendia were being reissued with extra texts tacked on; for example, the seventh edition of *The Magic Mirror . . .* (1818) had added chiromancy, an oracle and a much longer name-guessing text.[5] It had grown to twice its original size. Other compendia ran to numerous 'books' and several volumes or parts, containing most if not all the well-known texts. For example, the third edition of *The Ancient Astrologer or Oracle . . .* (1820), which came in twelve books and three parts, included versions of all the well-known texts as well as the prophecies of Giuseppe Moult[6] and Martyn Zadeka, the Bruce calendar, conjuring tricks and guessing games. So popular did compendia become in the period 1800–30 that they temporarily outnumbered single texts.[7] For reasons that will be explained later, a period of decline, 1840–90, was followed by one of vigorous revival, 1890–1917.

DREAMBOOKS

Though dreambooks were not the first type of divinatory guide to appear in printed form, they rapidly made up for lost time. From the late eighteenth century until the Revolution they were treasured by large sections of the population, and familiar even to those who scorned 'superstition'. Of the total of just over a hundred fortune-telling volumes published between 1765 and 1830, eighteen were dreambooks (some of them republications). In addition twenty-one texts were incorporated into compendia, making them the second most popular type of text at this period.[8] As literacy gained ground, and book-buyers multiplied after 1840, hardly a year went by without at least one dream text offering to illumine the future. It required the Revolution to put paid to dreambooks, and all other kinds of fortune-telling text, at least until 1989.

The spread of dreambooks was facilitated by the absence of any conception of copyright. The first printed dreambook, like other fortune-telling literature, went on to be pirated by other publishers who reprinted it with or without adaptations. Cavalier attitudes of this type were commonplace in Russia in the eighteenth and early nineteenth centuries in many sectors of publishing, while in the area of popular literature they continued to be the norm up to 1917. In the 1880s and 1890s, popular publishers competed to capture the burgeoning market among peasants with short dream texts, varying only slightly in title and contents. Any new publishers entering the market simply copied a rival's product or used a handy earlier edition. Divinatory texts were considered common property; compilers (who may have been either editor or publisher) were usually anonymous, leading to the conclusion that republication did not require the permission of anyone other than the censor. Publishers regarded piracy as one of the hazards (and advantages) of their business.

The typical dreambook was sixty-four pages (four signatures or printers' sheets), though in the late nineteenth and early twentieth centuries many were half or even a quarter that length. Longer versions could exceed a hundred pages. The very first omnibus fortune-telling books did not include a dreambook, but by 1800 this had changed, and over the next thirty years nearly three-quarters did. Some compendia, such as the three-volume *A Secret Microscope, Or The Mirror of Magical Secrets . . .* (1817), proffered two different types of dream text, an iconic and an astrological. The former consisted of a list of dream objects and brief interpretation of their significance, the latter regarded the date as significant. Though perhaps eighty or ninety per cent of Russian dreambooks are iconic, attempts to establish astrological guides were also made, notably in the early years of the dreambook's existence in Russia.

Apart from a list of objects, iconic dreambooks sometimes provided interpretations of different forms of the object or actions involving it; for example, in *Soothsay, Do Not Jest, Tell the Whole Truth that Lies in Your Heart . . .* (1808), dreaming of a grey beard is said to predict great honour (*chest'*), a long beard strength and honour, to be shaven means harm and shaving off one's beard signifies loss and dishonour. Bearing in mind that translated dreambooks had yet to develop local features, the temptation to draw conclusions from the above about residual resentment against Peter's forced shaving of his nobles, or of clerical or Old Believer influence should be resisted. These interpretations certainly existed in the West European original.

The first printed dreambook (1768) had been preceded by manuscript versions, which had made their way to Russia as part of the influx of literature translated from Polish in the second half of the seventeenth century. Indeed, indexes of banned books had condemned dreambooks from the earliest times; however, no actual manuscripts from the pre-Petrine period have been found.[9] The first extant, albeit incomplete, Russian manuscript dreambook has been dated by Sobolevskii to around 1700. Two others, dated 1745 and mid-eighteenth century, openly proclaim that they are translations from the Craców editions of 1694 and 1700, that is, of the best-known European dreambook, *Somniale Danielis*, published, as was usual in Poland, together with astrological materials.[10] The scant number of such finds makes it unlikely that manuscript dreambooks were common, a conclusion supported also by the records of library holdings. Although Prince D. M. Golitsyn, the eminent statesman of the Petrine period, owned a dreambook and a *Fortuna*, a divinatory book popular in Poland, it is probable that the dreambook was, like the *Fortuna*, in Polish.[11] The libraries of ten Moscow merchants inventoried in 1738 shows that only one possessed anything approaching divinatory literature and that was an almanac.[12] No other dreambooks have come to light in libraries of the time.

The first manuscript texts drew on the European oneirocritical tradition, which had its roots in the ancient world, in particular Mesopotamia, where dream beliefs were set down in writing in the middle of the second millennium BC.[13] Although both Plato and Aristotle were authorities on the nature and general significance of dreams, the first person to systematize interpretations was the second-century physician, Artemidorus, said to be from Daldis, but actually from Ephesus, whose five-volume *Oneirocritica* was based on materials collected on his travels, from correspondence and wide reading of oneirocritical literature. The study of dreams was regarded as a proper area of investigation which the advent of Christianity did not stifle; after all, prophetic dreams feature prominently in the Old Testament, and in the Christian tradition they became one of the characteristics by which saints could be distinguished from ordinary mortals.[14] The Church adapted classical divisions of dreams to suit its own purposes, dismissing some as meaningless reflections of everyday concerns, while others were held to emanate from a higher reality. In the latter dreams saints and angels acted as mediators. As in the Mesopotamian and Classical Greek oneirocritical traditions, other dreams were seen as evil, that is, in Christian terms, prompted by the Devil. Dreambooks flourished in Byzantium; apart from Artemidorus, Astrampsychus, the Arabic collection of Achmet ben Sirin and a variety of compilations including the *Oneirocriticon of the Prophet Daniel dedicated to King Nabuchodnosor*, an anthology attributed to the Old Testament prophet Daniel, were all extremely well known.[15]

Medieval Europe adopted the oneirocritical tradition with enthusiasm; Artemidorus and Achmet were available in Latin and Greek as well as being translated with enormous success into the main European languages. The advent of printing further hastened their spread, with Artemidorus' *Oneirocritica*, for example, first appearing in English in 1606, and reaching its twentieth edition by 1722. More often than not, his work and that of other great dream authorities were known through compilations and abbreviations. By far the most popular was the pseudo-Daniel dreambook, usually known as the *Somniale Danielis*. Translated into Latin in the seventh century, it survives in hundreds of manuscripts, together with translations into Old and Middle English, Old French, German, Dutch, Italian, Welsh, Polish and the Scandinavian languages.[16] The first printed editions appeared in the late fifteenth century, and led to it becoming the standard dreambook in Poland and Scandinavia; it was, indeed, so widespread that a recent project, sponsored by the Nordic Institute of Folklore, could be devoted exclusively to cataloguing the very extensive traces left by this one publication in the oral milieu of Scandinavia.[17] The enormous popularity of the work stems from its simplicity. Dream objects are grouped according to their initial letter, but are not always listed strictly alphabetically. A brief interpretation follows each object. *Somniale Danielis* underwent innumerable editions distinguished by minor variations in the order, contents and interpretations. It is still published today, though not always with the name of Daniel attached to it.[18]

By contrast with the Polish version of *Somniale Danielis* or the simple alphabetical type of dreambook that later became standard in Russia too, the first Russian printed dreambook was an astrological type, consisting of thirteen columns on each of seven pages, one for each day of the week. Each page contained a list of people or objects seen in the dream with columns containing the various meanings depending on the zodiac sign under which it had occurred. It was reprinted (or possibly retranslated) in 1799 in the guise of the engagingly entitled *The Dreambook, Telling Mother Truth,* with reprints in 1831 and 1838, and an updated second edition in 1829 as *The Newest Dream Interpreter, Telling Mother Truth.* Perhaps because it was so concise, it could also easily be tacked on to other texts, such as the two editions of Martyn Zadeka's prophecy that came out in 1807.[19]

A similar astrological treatment of dreams appeared in 1791 as *A Morning Pastime over Tea, Or a New, Complete and as Far as Possible Accurate Interpretation of Dreams According to Astronomy and in Verse.* Most likely a translation of a West European rhyming dreambook, it lists zodiac signs down the left-hand side of the page, and the dream objects along the top. The reader is then guided to interpretations in couplet form. Dreaming of crawfish, for example, means that:

> Of this you may be truly sure
> Your lover now will step through the door

Unlike the first dreambook, it does not differentiate between dreams on different nights of the week, and thus offers fewer interpretations than the first dreambook.

The disadvantage with any of the variations of the dreambook that listed dreams under tables was that relatively few dream objects could be squeezed into the column of dreams and fitted onto a page. If the user's dreams did not embrace objects from this short list, the book was useless. Furthermore, it demanded a minimal knowledge of astrology, thereby diminishing its appeal to the semi-educated. The astrological dreambook gradually passed out of fashion, featuring in just a few compendia between the 1790s and 1830,[20] but only in addition to an iconic text. The combination of two kinds of dreambooks inevitably produced, in some instances, rival interpretations for the same object, but such concerns seemed almost never to have bothered compilers or publishers, either then or at any other time.

Attempts were made to popularize other kinds of dreambooks in Russia. *The Gypsy Woman, Interpreting Dreams, Predicting to Each Person What May Happen . . .* (1789) (a volume that has no connection with gypsy lore whatsoever) obliged the user to throw three dice in order to work out the general meaning of the dream, rather than picking out key objects in the dream and offering an interpretation of these. The failure of this type of dice-throwing dreambook to catch on may be attributed to various factors. Firstly, dice belonged to the world of men, whereas dream divination was part of women's domain (see chapter 5). Secondly, it was quite alien to familiar folk traditions of dream interpretation; though the use of three dice, the commonest method of making a decision in Western Europe, was well known in Russia, there was no connection between dice-casting and oneiromancy there. It might also be observed that Russian dream interpretation traditionally took place over breakfast, when finding three dice is beyond most people. Although the book nowhere says that it is translated – indeed it suggests the reverse by declaring it is the work of an unknown author – in fact, its contents, which also include a section on divining character with a throw of the dice, and a trick way of guessing names, are all typical of Western divinatory literature. Furthermore, the section on character includes references to mythological figures such as Cupid, clear evidence of its Western origin.

The Gypsy Woman . . . never reappeared; by the end of the eighteenth century alphabetical iconic dreambooks had captured the imagination and pockets of purchasers. But though from then on they predominated, it would be a mistake to assume that they were standardized. Not only were there sub-types deriving from different European dreambooks, but, much as in folklore or medieval manuscript tradition, two books published by rival houses under the same title were never identical. It was even possible for different editions of identically entitled dreambooks issued by the same publisher to vary. Two iconic dreambooks published in St Petersburg in 1784 clearly illustrate the sort of variations that could come about.[21] From the similarity of content and title (both began *A Dreambook or The Interpretation of Dreams . . .* but had different sub-titles), they would appear to be variants of *Somniale Danielis.* Both consist of a semi-alphabetical arrangement of dream objects, followed by brief interpretations. About half of each book is given over to selections from the ancients, including a short table indicating whether dreams will come true according to the hour of the dream and the night in the lunar month. Both also include an astrological *planetnik i zodiachnik* (i.e. a guide to the influence of the planets), a table of unlucky days, a description of the four humours and the writings of Tavernier and Michael Scot on dreams. The contents of the two books are not, however, completely identical; the first incorporates more zodiacal guidance, while the second offers an additional dream text, a chart ascribed to an Indian centenarian. Furthermore, even the main dream texts differ slightly. Though both, for example, list *adskii ogon'* (fires of hell), *angel*, *almaz* (diamond), *arbuz* (water melon) and *armiia* under the letter A, small differences occur in the symbols given under *almaz*, which in one (SK6700–1) offers interpretations for diamonds and other precious stones (riches and marriage), and for a diamond lost from a ring (the loss of an eye or a favourite object). The other gives virtually identical interpretations for dreaming of a diamond found and a diamond lost.[22]

Apart from the variations that existed among Russian editions of the *Somniale Danielis*, a different sub-type, which began appearing in the early nineteenth century, catered for those who wanted more detail and fuller explanations. *A New, Complete and Detailed Dreambook, Signifying the Amplified Interpretation and Elucidation of Every Dream . . .*, published in 1802 and reprinted in 1811 and 1818, proffered, as its title suggested, not only a wider variety of interpretations but also more explanatory detail. Whereas most other dreambooks offer bald assertions such as that 'dreaming of cats means denial or destruction of marriage',[23] this book provides a rationale:

> Dreaming of cats means the breaking of marriage vows by both parties, also of a marriage contract, for just as the cat lies in wait for rats and mice, so the seducer pursues women until he catches them in his net, for women compare with birds on account of their beauty, charm and chattering ways. (p. 134 in the 1818 edition)

Like other dreambooks, this had been translated, most probably from French or perhaps German, and is traceable to an alphabetical compilation derived largely from Artemidorus, but expanding on his dream interpretations: Artemidorus simply observes that 'the cat signifies an adulterer, for it is a bird thief, and birds resemble women'.[24] In its selection of dream objects, the 1802 dreambook reflected its ancient origins; it is hard to imagine that the Russian reader had frequent need of interpreting dreams about eating lizard or camel meat! It is a tribute to the basic stability of dreambooks that such interpretations survived centuries of publication in various languages and environments.

1830 comes as a turning point in the history of dreambooks and fortune-telling books generally, since at this point élite readers abandoned fortune-telling books to the rapt attention of an ever expanding lower-class readership (see chapter 3). By 1830 the iconic dreambook was set to reign virtually unchallenged, both on its own and as part of compendia. The many new readers, scarcely detached from oral tradition, preferred iconic dreambooks to the astrological type which in the form of *The Dreambook, Telling Mother Truth* experienced its swan song in 1838. The loss of an élite readership also meant the demise of the expensive expanded dreambook. *A New, Complete and Detailed Dreambook* . . . (1802, 1811, 1818), for example, came out in a truncated version in 1831, with a final further abbreviated edition in 1839.[25]

In their new simplified form dreambooks gradually became the most popular type of fortune-telling book in Russia, with the sole exception of *King Solomon's Divinatory Circle*, whose distinctive history is discussed later. What came to be the simple Russian dreambook *par excellence* was taken from one of the compendia of the early years of the century, appearing first in 1848 under the title of *The Interpretation of Dreams by the Venerable 106-Year-Old Man, Martyn Zadeka.* Based on the *Somniale Danielis,* though without the prophet's name ever being mentioned, it came out with amazing regularity up until the Revolution. The number of pages varied from one to four printer's sheets with the shortest versions appearing after 1870, when dreambooks began reaching peasants in the countryside with greater frequency. Not much bigger than a modern passport, it was an ideal item for market stalls or colporteurs' boxes. The contents of late nineteenth-century versions differ remarkably little from those of versions published in the late eighteenth and early nineteenth centuries, as a comparison of the entries under the letter A in the 1784 and 1860 Zadeka-type dreambooks reveal. The sole novelty in 1860 is *anushkiny glazki* (pansies), while an edition of 1885 published by Presnov adds only *arshin* (=0.71m.) and *aspid* (serpent). None of these additions were unique, having featured already in other nineteenth-century

Russian dreambooks, and they probably originated in variants of the *Somniale Danielis.* Thus by the second half of the nineteenth century short dreambooks had developed a traditional core, to which new interpretations were added, only scantily, gradually and inconsistently.

Martyn Zadeka's book was not the only small cheap single text. In fact, after 1860 several firms specialized in books of thirty-two or sixty-four pages, all very similar in content, and containing a basic core shared by the Zadeka dreambook. Recognizing that some of their readers had spelling problems, they often grouped together all objects beginning with the letters 'e' and 'ѣ' which were pronounced the same but came at opposite ends of the alphabet.[26] Publishers themselves often had a shaky grasp of orthography, as the phonetically spelt title, *The New Explanitory Dreambook* (1882) indicates. Towards the end of the century, some dreambooks had gone down to sixteen pages; indeed, an eight-page *lubok* version, cut down from the standard cheap printed dreambook, was on sale during the 1860s and 1870s.[27]

Apart from the simplest dreambooks, others were produced to appeal to a wide range of readers, some of them affluent. Although elegant and expensively produced books like the finely illustrated *Newest Dream Interpreter Compiled from the Manuals of Foreign Men Skilled in the Science of Dream Divination . . .*, Moscow, 1829, no longer found a market, publishers increasingly produced books for a socially fragmented urban market. In the last half of the nineteenth and early twentieth centuries the main place for innovations was in books for the more affluent reader.

The simplest form of innovation was in the number of dream objects. Lists could be expanded by fusing two separate lists of dream objects. This was often done imperfectly, without proper alphabetical sorting, occasionally resulting in conflicting interpretations for the same dream object.[28] Evidently, it was assumed that the purchaser would only discover this after acquiring the book. He or she probably simply chose the preferred explanation.

Though the core dream objects persisted from edition to edition, there was a natural tendency to omit the most grotesquely inappropriate entries, such as dreaming of eating lizard meat or wearing a white four-cornered hat, and for others, such as *apteka* (pharmacy) or *arshin,* to become established in their place.[29] By the late 1880s, publishers were vying with each other to augment the traditional selection of dream objects, whether in separate texts or, after 1890, in the revived genre of fortune-telling compendium. For example, *The New Complete Oracle and Magician . . .* of 1912, which in general closely mimics the early nineteenth-century version with a similar title, contains a much fuller dreambook. The list of objects beginning with the letter A includes a number of objects known either in the earliest core edition or established shortly afterwards, such as *ananas* (pineapple), *arap* (Arab), *azbuka* (alphabet),[30] but had added a dozen or so others which had appeared only in the previous couple of decades (*arifmetika, anis, algebra* or *admiralteistvo,* for example).

Among the additions to dreambooks were dream objects reflecting an urban readership and/or technological advance. Initially, these were both few and imported: pineapples, for example, feature first in a dreambook translated from French in 1839, but subsequently appear frequently. By the last years of the nineteenth century, objects such as oranges, Americans, waltzing, watching the ballet, artichoke, planes (*aeroplan*) or chocolate become increasingly common. Some of these, artichokes for example, seem about as likely to populate the dreams of a provincial tradesman's wife as camels! Dreambook compilers did, however, sometimes react to contemporary circumstances. In the early years of the twentieth century some began including an interpretation for 'agitator', which by 1915 had changed to 'Bolshevik agitator'.[31] The meaning given to dreaming of agitators (loss of honour, deception or unhappiness) reflects the conservative sympathies of publishers and purchasers alike. Those who followed Bolshevik agitators in their dream were promised the same miserable future, while just catching sight of them meant something unpleasant would happen shortly. Many Russians might now argue that this is evidence of genuine prescience! With folk interpretations also beginning to find their way into dreambooks (see chapter 2), the Russian environment had finally begun to impact on dreambooks.[32]

Attempts at more radical change generally failed. In 1869 O. Mil'chevskii published a dreambook which added a large number of his own interpretations to a full conventional list (in a rough proportion of one new dream object to two old). Users could find out the significance of dreams about an auto da fé, Armenians (curiosity about the future) or Englishmen (false friends or creditors).[33] That Mil'chevskii's dream book did not run to multiple editions is probably to be attributed both to its excessive novelty and its failure to suggest its origin in the pronouncements of venerable foreign sages (see chapter 7). In fact, it is remarkable how little impetus there seems to have been for both innovation and the promotion of native dream oracles. The sole purely Russian dreambook of the period was the posthumously issued predictions of a St Petersburg specialist: *The Reference Guide and Encyclopedic Lexicon of Dreams. More than 3000 Explanations of the Phenomena of Sleep. Collected over Sixty-Six Years by the Kindly Old Man of Duck Street* . . ., St Petersburg, 1863. In contrast to the empty boasts of later publishers, this book really did contain a very large number of dream objects and explanations; for example, while the average dreambook contained anything from four to twelve items under the letter A, the Kindly Old Man offered seventy-eight. Obviously a high proportion of his interpretations were his own (approximately three quarters). Some of the conventional items in dreambooks such as 'a diamond lost and found' receive the standard interpretation, but others do not; for example, dreaming of pineapples which earlier meant tears here meant joy. Curiously, the objects included do not make any consistent attempt to relate to Russian life. Certainly, *admiral, artel', arestant* (a person under arrest), *armiak* (type of cheap cloth coat), *akusher* (accoucheur), *arkhitekt* or *akademik* fit in with St Petersburg in the 1860s, but what about *astrolabiia, antilopa* or *anisovoe derevo* (an aniseed tree)? The book did not catch on and was reissued only once.[34]

Nonetheless, comprehensiveness evidently was deemed a commercial plus in dreambooks for better-off urban readers, provided it did not include too radical innovations. In the last three decades of the century, rival publishers tried to outdo each other, several producing dreambooks claiming to contain a million dreams, then *Over One Million* . . ., followed by 1,200,000 and finally 1,500,000. Commercial considerations heavily outweighed truthfulness; in the case of the last, interpretations number well under a thousand, though most of the others were somewhat longer. The relaunch of the omnibus fortune-telling book in the 1890s, in the same format as, and with identical contents to its early nineteenth-century predecessors was an alternative publishing strategy, laying claim to inclusivity. Such omnibuses might even include historical curiosities such as the prophecy of Martyn Zadeka, predicting the future of Europe from the perspective of 1769. The pre-Revolutionary purchaser seems not to have been deterred.

The revival of compendia exemplifies a trend at the end of the nineteenth century towards renovation of the dreambook tradition. Well over a century of continuous publication had had two contrasting effects. On the one hand, readers' confidence in dreambooks was reinforced by their traditional contents; for many urban readers this literary tradition had now replaced or become intermingled with folk beliefs. On the other hand, publishers in the cut-throat world of popular books may have felt that the old books were losing their appeal. Given the huge number of dreambooks regularly appearing in the three decades before the Revolution, saturation of the market was obviously not a problem. The attempt to introduce innovations was probably a commercial move on the part of publishers to steal a march on competitors in the less conservative urban market; the less adventurous dreambooks, it may be construed, continued to appeal to the more traditional rural consumer.

Apart from the reintroduction of omnibus editions, the period from 1880 is marked by the launch of a new type of dreambook, organized under categories such as 'birds and insects', 'the moon', 'teeth' etc. Though new to Russia, the organizational principle derives from Western Europe. Judging by the references to Artemidorus, whose *Oneirocritica* also sometimes groups dreams thematically, the first such text is translated, though it hid its origins by appearing as *One Million 500,000 Dreams. . . .* However, organizationally it was quite distinct from similarly named dreambooks, all of the traditional type. A number of other books for the better-off reader adopted the same principle, only one of which, *Sleep and Dreams: A Scientifically Based Interpretation of Dreams, Compiled by the Famous Medium Miss Hussey* (Warsaw, 1912) frankly admitted its foreign origin. The identity of Miss Hussey remains unknown, but 'her' dreambook is a version of the same thematic type of European dreambook, despite its appeal to fashion (the use of the vocabulary of spiritualism) and claim to be 'scientific' (it comes complete with an article by a psychophrenologist).

Another category of books, whose titles at first suggest a manifestation of the desire for innovation and interest in exotic dream traditions, turns out on examination to have little to do with popular fortune-telling. All are scholarly or semi-scholarly publications of non-European dreambooks: *The Turco-Tatar Dreambook*, published by V. Kondaraki in Moscow in 1884 as a supplement to an ethnographic description of the Crimea; P. A. Poliakov's *Dreambook, Ascribed by Muslims to the Old Testament Patriarch, Joseph, son of Jacob*;[35] and P. P. Pantusov's dreambook from Chinese Turkistan.[36] The appeal of these must have been very limited, since, like other non-standard dreambooks, none was republished. They do, however, reflect a scholarly interest in oneiromancy during a period of immense enthusiasm for the occult and irrational generally.[37]

To conclude: by 1917 Russian dreambooks had settled into the steady pattern of an iconic text, based on European originals, but open to considerable variation and expansion. Though essentially conservative, they did evolve, mainly through the accretion of new dream objects, some reflecting social or technological change. The process of adaptation would certainly have continued had official pressure not put paid to their publication. A major enabling factor in their evolution was the lack of any understanding of copyright, which ensured that innovations were rapidly copied, subsequently joining the accepted canon of dream objects.

This survey has perhaps overemphasized the common features of Russian dreambooks, given that the multitude of editions meant no overall consistency in the choice of dream objects, let alone interpretations. For example, a dreambook of 1904 declared that dreaming of apricots meant satisfaction, while another from 1908 suggested that they meant 'an unpleasant event and loss'. But such inconsistencies do not negate the statement that Russian dreambooks acquired a core list of dream objects with generally consistent interpretations, the majority of which appear in every standard dreambook. There was nothing unusual in the evolution of a national 'redaction' of a common European heritage; in Britain, for example, which, like Russia, inherited the Near Eastern and medieval European oneirocritical tradition, the contents of dreambooks show relatively little resemblance to those of Russian dreambooks but a good deal of similarity from title to title within Britain.

Where new dream objects were introduced, it would be interesting to know whether this occurred arbitrarily (the cynic's view) or reflected common dreams. Certainly the additions do not appear to reflect a specifically Russian reality; however, since novel objects and interpretations featured almost entirely in books for the urban reader, whose life did not differ so greatly from her or his European counterparts, this is hardly surprising.

If dreambooks did not reflect users' dreams, perhaps the reverse is true? Were devotees' dreams conditioned by their knowledge of dreambooks? Since the dreamers are now, unfortunately, beyond questioning, the solution to this problem would demand extensive comparative research into the dream traditions of different peoples and places. Some indications do at least suggest that, in the case of those who knew their dreambook well, they could well have done.[38]

ORACLES

The fortune-telling texts whose popularity outstripped dreambooks as well as all others before 1830 were basically geomantic, though astrology or dice might also be required. Texts were variously entitled, but the term 'oracle' will be used here. Within this general category, two kinds existed, both extremely popular in this early period. The first was known in nineteenth-century Britain, America and much of Western Europe as Napoleon's Book of Fate, although as a form of divination that relied on answering certain specific questions it possessed a long history. Russian translations of this type of text predate Napoleon and hence his 'text' and his name never appear in this context in Russia. The user asked a question (will he propose, will my wife recover from illness?), and then by means of a complicated use of dice or calculations made from a series of dots on a page, worked out the answer to the question. It is dubious whether its success was conditioned by the existence of divination with dice and dots on paper in Russia before the appearance of the first printed books, since it is unlikely to have been passed from sorcerers, who specialized in it, to gentlewomen.[39] So popular was this type of text in Russian drawing rooms in the late eighteenth century that numerous local and translated variants were produced, in which the zodiac signs under which questions and answers were grouped were replaced by names of sages, flowers or (largely invented) Slav gods.[40]

The other type of text, known in medieval England as the Book of Fate, later as the Wheel of Fortune, asked the reader to throw grains, dice or wax balls onto a circle divided into segments and by concentric circles, and thereby discover the answer to a chosen question. Segments might be labelled with signs of the zodiac, or in a variety of other ways, as, for example, in the *Astrologer or New Oracle . . .*, 1798, with qualities and properties such as understanding, the soul, work, weakness, need. In this text, there was a separate circle for each question asked, with numbered concentric circles within each. The reader looked up the selected number and segment in an elaborate key to find the answer to her or his question.

Oracles gradually lost their popularity after 1830, perhaps because the type of fortune-telling that could only answer specific questions was unsatisfying for a new readership looking less for entertainment than guidance (see chapter 4). Thus *The New Oracle or An Innocent Sibylline Divination Based on a Random Series of Dots*, translated from German, 1844, was a vain attempt to re-establish what was now an obsolete type of text. One variant, however, the Wheel of Fortune, known in Russia as *King Solomon's Divinatory Circle*, in which participants threw a grain onto a circle divided into segments, flourished defiantly till the Revolution. The biblical figure of Solomon had long been connected with divination, and it is highly likely that both title and text come from Western Europe, though probably before the second half of the eighteenth century.[41] This simplification of the Wheel of Fortune employed only one circle, and also offered answers to questions. Early availability and the visual nature of *King Solomon's Divinatory Circle* (splendid coloured circles were produced for some editions, see ill. 2) may have occasioned its adoption by the *lubok* industry, which produced woodcut pictures and texts for the humblest readers throughout the eighteenth and nineteenth centuries. Prior to 1850 it was the only fortune-telling text to be issued as a *lubok*,[42] while printed editions also began appearing with great regularity from 1830. By the late nineteenth century it was being mass-printed on one sheet for distribution in villages (see chapter 4), and had become so familiar as to be known simply as *Solomon*. For most Russian peasants it was the first printed fortune-telling text they saw. Unlike dreambooks, which retained their popularity among wide sectors of the population, *Solomon* was strictly a 'people's book'.

CARTOMANCY

Cartomancy seems to have evolved from the oracle in the first half of the sixteenth century in continental Europe, when books supplying ways of finding answers to fateful questions using cards rather than dice began appearing. The first set of specially designed fortune-telling cards, produced by John Lenthall in England in 1590, did not inspire imitators; conventional packs continued to be used throughout the seventeenth and eighteenth centuries (although cards with chiromantic and astrological themes were produced in seventeenth-century Germany). The first reference to the use of more than one card dates from 1765, when the jealous Russian mistress of the Italian adventurer Casanova is recorded as deploying several to answer the questions that tormented her. Probably around the same time, cards began to be used more generally to predict fortunes, leading to a craze in late eighteenth-century Europe. The skill was imported into Russia without delay, the first guide appearing as early as 1782,[43] and at least a further twenty-five by 1830.

Some were sold as special fortune-telling packs, usually complete with instructions, despite the fact that the cards were conventional ones. Where the two sometimes differed was in the number of cards per pack, not all the cards in a conventional pack necessarily being used in fortune-telling. We know they were available in 1788, when purchasers of *A Diversion in Times of Tedium or A New Entertaining Method of Reading the Cards* were informed on pp. 51–3 that cards for fortune-telling could be acquired at the house of M. P. Saltykov. Much later, Rovinskii, the specialist on *lubok* pictures, recalled the existence of special cheap fortune-telling cards, produced for children, and purchased from itinerant peddlers of books or toys. This would have been in the 1840s.[44] Special packs, whether for children or adults contained thirty-two, thirty-six or twice those numbers of cards.[45] Some omitted the low-number cards in each suit (two to five or six); one set of instructions, perhaps with the fateful Queen of Spades of Pushkin's story in mind, asserted that spades were not to be used in fortune-telling.[46] By 1848 both printed texts and Tereshchenko's evidence about professional cartomancy suggest that thirty-six- or fifty-two-card packs had become the norm.[47] But as time went on, the thirty-six-card pack increasingly predominated. One can only speculate on the reasons for this; it may be that the Russian craze for the card game préférence, at its most violent in the 1840s and 50s but far from extinct thereafter, made the thirty-six-card pack the norm.

There were also specially designed fortune-telling cards, including from 1843 those ascribed to Mlle Lenormand, which kept the original suits but added symbolic pictures. A new type, also ascribed to Lenormand and known as 'Le Grand Oracle de Mlle Lenormand' (1845), reached Russia seven years later in the second edition of *An Instruction for Fortune-telling with the Fortune-Telling Cards of the Famous Clairvoyant Mlle Lenormand*, Moscow, 1852.[48] These symbolic cards had no numerical values or suits, but divided each picture into four triangles.[49] As with the other types of Lenormand cards, prediction was usually based on the proximity of given symbols to the main card depicting a man or woman according to the gender of the person whose fortune was being told. The numbers in such packs could vary considerably.[50]

According to Tereshchenko, cards were also used in other kinds of fortune-telling. In a variant on traditional Yuletide practices interweaving the two most popular types of fortune-telling, oneiromancy and cartomancy, the four kings were placed under a girl's pillow (four queens under a young man's). She (for it was usually she) uttered one of the magic formulae instructing her intended to appear to her in her dreams. Black kings boded no good – a jealous old man for spades and a widower for clubs, whereas the king of hearts meant a wealthy young man and the king of diamonds her chosen one. A similar custom employing a single card existed in parts of Iaroslavl province.[51] Apart from this practice, a small *lubok* book published in 1860 promoted an archaic form of cartomancy owing a great deal to the popular Wheel of Fortune. The front cover of *The Magic Indicator. Fortune-Telling in the Cards* depicts cards laid out in a circle with kings, queens and aces in the centre. The user was invited to take a grain or ball of wax, throw it onto the circle and then open the book to determine her or his future.[52]

Cartomancy, unlike oracles, never fell from favour in Russia, with aids undergoing regular publication before the Revolution as single texts, in compendia or as packs of cards with instructions. Such was its popularity with a conservative public that tarot cards never replaced ordinary packs, as they did in England for example. Tarot cards had been used for card games from their invention in

Northern Italy in the mid fifteenth century until they were repackaged in France in 1781 as occult cards of a fabled Egyptian origin.[53] In Russia they enjoyed only a brief period of success among the better-off in connection with the general European fascination with the esoteric and occult from the 1880s.[54]

PHYSIOGNOMY AND CHIROMANCY

Though physiognomy and chiromancy will be considered together on the grounds that from the start they almost always appeared in tandem, they are in fact different in essence. Physiognomy, the science of reading character from physical appearance, is not, strictly speaking, a mantic skill but a proto-science, whereas the name chiro*mancy* indicates its connection with prognostication. Both possessed an ancient lineage. Physiognomy was held in esteem in medieval and Renaissance Europe, as major treatises by Giovanni Battista della Porta and Michael Scot in the sixteenth century indicate. At the same time, at the popular level at least, it was already being employed as a divinatory technique.[55] It was introduced into Russia in the early sixteenth century via a Russian version of the pseudo-Aristotelian *Secretum secretorum*, with Scot's treatise translated in the following century.[56] Evidently physiognomy attracted some following in contemporary Russia, judging by the short treatise on the subject to be found in a manuscript of 1730. The combination of physiognomy and various magical and divinatory texts here shows how easily in Russia, as in the West, the skill of character analysis from physical attributes could be confused with divination.[57]

Chiromancy similarly enjoyed a long history (the first printed text dates from 1448), with a high point in seventeenth-century Europe when several treatises were written. From the outset it was employed as a form of divination. When and how it arrived in Russia is unknown, but a Kostroma peasant Romashko Averkiev was tried in 1692 for looking at palms.[58] The practice seems not to have spread far before the first printed text on the subject appeared in 1765. By 1830, however, this had changed dramatically; at least eighteen separate editions and fifteen in compendia had turned the physiognomy/chiromancy combination into the third most popular fortune-telling text in Russia. Its prestige was boosted by attempts to promote physiognomy as a science, as in the 1781 edition of *A New Means of Learning the Characteristics of Each Man from his Physical Appearance: The Work of Michael Scot. . . .* A translation combining physiognomy, astrology and magic, this was probably too complex to catch on, and it was not reprinted. The increased prestige of physiognomy as a protoscience from the 1780s rested on the influential theories of the Swiss pastor Johan Kaspar Lavater, whose monumental treatise *Physiognomische Fragmente* was well known in French and German translation in Russia from the 1780s.[59] A further boost to the subject came after Franz Joseph Gall lectured on his phrenological theories in 1796. At the popular level physiognomy must have reinforced the drawing-room interest in fortune-telling and character divination from palms, heads or general physical characteristics. Lavater's name (and rarely Gall's) were hijacked to help promote fortune-telling books, though the divinatory texts their names were attached to bore little relation to Lavater's descriptive physiognomy or Gall's phrenology.[60] Though some of the titles containing their names may have been translated together with their texts (a further indication of the inertia in the adoption of material from abroad), it is also probable that the frequent mention indicates that their names had some resonance among purchasers at the time. From 1830–80 physiognomy and chiromancy became secondary texts, attached to a longer fortune-telling text. From the 1880s they underwent something of a revival (thirty-five different books published 1890–1915) but only in editions for the more affluent urban market.[61]

FORTUNE-TELLING WITH NUMBERS

Domestic fortune-telling with numbers never caught on in a big way in Russia, even though magic numerology attracted various groups like the Rosicrucians or the Old Believers who were fascinated by 666. The single type of numerological predictor known in Russia was one called 'Arab Kabbalistic'. This asked the user to calculate the number of words in a given question followed by the number of letters in each word, using these to create a triangle of numbers, which, upon recourse to tables, and converted back into letters, produced an answer. A couple of single texts appeared in the eighteenth century, but the method was evidently too slow and complicated to enjoy widespread popularity, though it appeared frequently in early compendia and very sporadically in later ones.

Certain types of fortune-telling only ever appeared as an adjunct to the above, many because they could be summarized in far less space than even the smallest book took up. However, other methods, for a variety of reasons, were not attractive enough to warrant publication on their own. The first of these, astrology, is placed in this section, not because texts never made use of astrology (the astrological dreambook is one), but because it was, with rare exceptions, always secondary to some other fortune-telling method.

ASTROLOGY

One would expect astrology to rank with cartomancy, palmistry or dream divination in popularity and renown, given its long and rich history in the West. In modern Britain zodiac signs and horoscopes are universally familiar if often dismissed as quackery. This is a legacy not only of the great Victorian and Edwardian astrologers, but of a long history stretching back to the Middle Ages, with high points like the early seventeenth century when almost no one doubted the predictions of famous astrologers like William Lilly, and troughs like the eighteenth century when support was restricted almost entirely to the rural and uneducated.[62] In Russia, by contrast, popular fortune-telling is remarkable for the virtual absence of astrology. Certainly Old Russia had heard of it, not only through lists of banned works but also via works such as the legendary account of the life of Alexander the Great and the *Secretum secretorum*.[63] On the other hand, with literacy, let alone mathematical knowledge, at a premium, the impact was minimal. 'Natural' astrology, which examines the astral influences on agriculture, weather and events like epidemics or rebellions, did feature in the first Russian almanac in the sixteenth century, but this was an isolated instance. Almanacs caught on only in the reign of Aleksei Mikhailovich in the second part of the seventeenth century, simultaneously with the first stirrings of an interest in judicial astrology (a set of rules for evaluating the positions of the planets at an individual's birth, leading to the construction of a horoscope).

In eighteenth-century Britain, natural astrology enjoyed prestige only among country folk, who used it for calendrical or meteorological predictions, while the judicial variant was confined to small numbers in the professional and middle classes.[64] Nonetheless, a longstanding cultural residue remained at all levels of society. In Russia, by contrast, the lack of any widespread familiarity even at the most superficial level made its long-term adoption outside élite circles unlikely. A small amount of natural astrology was incorporated into eighteenth-century calendars, though less than in their European equivalents (see below), while divinatory manuscripts of Byzantine origin containing elements of astrology and known in medieval Russia continued to be copied.[65] But a more serious attempt to discuss astrology was not made until early years of the nineteenth century, when the heavyweight publishers Kriazhev and Mei put out *The Astronomical Telescope . . .* (1804), a non-divinatory book on astronomy and astrology. Its subsequent fate illustrates the rapid descent of astrology from a position of respectability. Reissued by various popular publishers in 1814, 1815, 1818, 1819 (*A New and Complete Astronomical Telescope . . .*), 1821, 1823 (title as in 1819), 1829 (twice under slightly different names) and 1839 (as *The Newest and Most Complete Astronomical Telescope . . .*), it soon reflected the confusion between science and divination in popular publishing circles. Fortune-telling texts were appended, at first usually the pseudo-sciences of physiognomy and chiromancy, but in 1815 a dreambook, and by 1839 the predictions of Martyn Zadeka, a list of unlucky days and the Bruce calendar. All of these in varying degrees laid claims to be scientifically based, and no edition ever included cartomancy or coffee-cup reading. The critic Vissarion Belinskii commented that the 1839 edition was just a joke, but knew only too well that its semi-educated readers viewed it as a serious 'scientific' work. He would have been appalled to know that it was still being published nearly half a century later in 1874 and 1883 in an abbreviated form with physiognomy added in the former case, and in the latter also the Bruce calendar.

Another astrological fortune-telling guide was published in Smolensk in 1802 by a certain Ivan Stolb-Rapinskii, who clearly took the subject very seriously. Its relative complexity and obscure provenance ensured that it was not reprinted, and it remained outside the general development of fortune-telling books.[66] The only other astrological text was a planetary and zodiacal guide which appeared in the various editions of *The Magic Mirror . . .* (1794, 1799, 1801, 1808, 1816, 1818). As fortune-telling books descended the social scale, astrology disappeared with the last compendia of the 1840s, and continued to exist only in the form of passing references in descriptions of other fortune-telling methods. Various oracle texts assumed a knowledge of the names of planets and signs of the zodiac, a dim reflection of horary astrology, which looked at the position of the planets at the time a question was asked of the astrologer. As already noted, the earliest dreambooks linked interpretation to zodiac signs, but little more than a token familiarity was required. So slight was the general knowledge of astrology that the words *astrolog* and *astrologicheskii* tended to be used as synonyms for 'divinatory', as in *The Astrologer or New Oracle . . .* (Moscow, 1794 and later), a book in which astrology played a peripheral role. What is more, a picture of an astronomer with his sphere (see ill. 4) was copied from eighteenth-century originals into various fortune-telling books in the first half of the nineteenth century regardless of their contents. The serious study of judicial astrology only re-emerged in Russia around 1900, as a local reflection of the revival of astrology throughout Europe, but even then never made a big impact on the popular market for fortune-telling books.[67]

CALENDARS AND CALENDAR PREDICTIONS

At first sight, almanacs would not appear to belong in the category of supplementary texts, given that they were, firstly, primarily independent texts and, secondly, not divinatory publications. Mainly translated from German they were (together with religious almanacs) 'in all probability, the most widely circulated Russian publications in the 18th century' (259 calendars and Church calendars) and they remained extremely popular up to the Revolution.[68] Though similar to popular continental European almanacs of the sixteenth and seventeenth centuries, the Russian versions, in line with high-minded Academy policy, lacked the 'heavy dose of astrology' to be found in these;[69] they relate to divinatory literature proper only in so far as elements of 'natural' astrology crept into the astronomy sections, and above all, into the immensely popular weather predictions for the coming year.

4 An astronomer with his sphere. Frontispiece for *The New Predictor, The Sorcerer or Fortune-Teller* . . ., St Petersburg 1795. A book typical of its time in its use of some astrology for divinatory purposes.

When, in 1728, attempts were made to delete weather predictions and other divinatory sections on the grounds that 'they never make true predictions except by chance', sales fell and they were brought back the following year.[70] From time to time, sections from calendars were printed in fortune-telling books, where they may have helped develop the minimal knowledge of astrology necessary for using astrological fortune-telling texts.

Much more influential was the famous Bruce calendar, so-called after General James Bruce, under whose supervision the first edition began to appear in 1710. Strictly speaking, this was not a divinatory text but a perpetual calendar providing information for a hundred years ahead.[71] Apart from calendrical computations, it contained elements of astrology and weather prediction, helping to blur the lines between science, pseudo-science and fortune-telling. Rapidly becoming a 'people's book', that is, beloved of the simple folk, it came out regularly in *lubok* form until 1875.[72] Often adapted by publishers and editors, it was published repeatedly on its own as well as in all manner of fortune-telling books. Its popularity can be measured by noting that there were five editions in the years 1883–6 alone, and at least three in 1917.[73]

The weather predictions that made calendars so attractive caught on because Russia, like most pre-literate and semi-literate societies, relied on traditional oral weather forecasting based on observation, as well as signs linked to the calendar cycle in which the rational and irrational were combined. Pre-Petrine Russia also possessed manuscript versions of Byzantine divinatory texts such as the *Brontologion* or thunder divination, which by the eighteenth century may well have been circulating among those interested in magic.[74] The way prepared for popularity, weather predictions prospered despite climatic differences between Western Europe and parts of Russia which certainly rendered them less reliable than their oral counterparts. By the end of the eighteenth century, weather predictions were also being incorporated into 'scientific' compendia, a clear indication of widespread authority.[75] From the same period right up to the early twentieth century they were also included in fortune-telling books, especially omnibus editions.[76]

TABLES OF SIGNIFICANT DAYS AND HOURS

The idea that some days in the month are auspicious while others bring ill luck is an ancient one. Although some of these tables appeared in translated Slavonic manuscripts, like other kinds of divinatory text they only became widely known in Russia via fortune-telling books and translated European almanacs. Two different tables were known in Russia. The shorter text was unattributed and usually tacked onto dreambooks or dream sections in compendia. The longer was also linked to dreambooks, and when both were included, one preceded and one followed the main text. Such combinations had certainly occurred before the texts reached Russia.

The longer, commonly attributed to the Danish astronomer Tycho Brahe, was usually headed by a statement, similar to the one that appeared in *The Magic Mirror* . . . of 1794:

the table was left in the stone wall of Saint Ibb's Monastery on the island of Ven by the famous European astronomer Tycho Brahe in the year 1600 and discovered in 1660. In which he writes that there are thirty-two days in the whole year when nothing important should be undertaken or brought to fulfilment.[77]

The unlucky days were 1, 2, 4, 6, 11, 12 and 20 January; 11, 17 and 18 February; 1, 4, 14 and 24 March; 3, 17 and 18 April; 7 and 8 May; 17 June; 17 and 21 July; 20 and 21 August; 10 and 18 September; 6 October; 6 and 8 November; 6, 11 and 18 December. A birthday on any of those days condemned the hapless person to poverty and a short life, while anyone falling ill on those dates would experience protracted convalescence. Others would have ill-luck if they moved houses or changed jobs. Though the list was usually attributed to Tycho Brahe, occasionally it appeared anonymously. More rarely, the number of days was said to be thirty-three and the author Albertus Magnus.[78]

In the shorter of the two tables, the dreamer was invited to start counting from the date of the new moon, and then consult the table for the particular day, or rather night, to see whether her or his dream would come true. For example, a dream occurring on the third night after the new moon was meaningless, while those that occurred on the twelfth night would come true in a week. This table was extremely common in dreambooks before 1830, but less so later in the century. The short simple dreambooks peddled to the peasants had no space for such niceties, though it continued to be a popular component of omnibus editions up till the Revolution. As with dreambooks, texts varied slightly from edition to edition, either in wording, or in the significance accorded a given day. Nonetheless, this was a relatively stable tradition, evidently much more so than in Western Europe, since the new thematic type of Russian dreambook, *Sleep and Dreams* (Warsaw, 1912) which was attributed to 'the famous medium Miss Hussey' also included such a list. Though obviously from the same ultimate source, it contains far wider variations (either in the order of predictions or in their form) than anything found in what had become the conventional Russian type of dreambook. *Pearson's Dreambook*, published in London in numerous editions in the twentieth century, contains yet another variant, differing considerably both from the Warsaw version and the usual list in Russian fortune-telling books.

Dreambooks also sometimes contained a third table, this one concerning the hour when the dream occurred. Night dreams were divided into those occurring from 9pm till midnight, from midnight to 3am and 4am to morning. The first would come true in nine, ten or fifteen years, those in the middle of the night in two to four years and early morning dreams in ten days, ten months or a year. Daytime dreams were the only ones that might come true in a short space of time (a week), though they could equally turn out meaningless.

No attempt was made to reconcile contradictory interpretations in these last two tables. The relative rarity of the table of meaningful hours probably results either from widespread familiarity with folk beliefs which placed different interpretations on the meaning of the various hours or from dreamers' impatience with advice to wait up to fifteen years to find out whether their dreams were truly prophetic.

READING THE COFFEE GROUNDS

In Russia coffee, rather than tea, was used for fortune-telling because the manner of making tea in Russia (making a strong brew in a small teapot and mixing it in a glass or cup with liberal amounts of hot water) does not produce enough tea leaves at the bottom of cup or glass for a person's fortune to be read. Coffee was first imported into Russia in the Petrine period, but in quite small quantities. It was not until the 1740s that consumption increased, rising steadily through the eighteenth century, though it remained, like tea, a luxury drink.[79] By the nineteenth century the urban poor in large cities, especially St Petersburg, had taken to drinking coffee.

The first guide to reading coffee cups was published in 1789 in *The Little Divinatory Book Known as a Geomantic Oracle*,[80] but the skill was known earlier, probably imported by foreign residents or Russian visitors to Europe. Too brief to warrant independent publication, the text was appended to both compendia and single texts, becoming an established feature of Russian fortune-telling books (nearly twenty appearances by 1830, and many more after). As an entertaining and perhaps rewarding conclusion to a cup of coffee with family or friends, the appeal of coffee reading to a genteel society was obvious. Since the instructions gave only a few possible interpretations of the shapes left by the coffee grounds when the cup was upturned, coffee divination was easily committed to memory; hence it survived the ban on fortune-telling books after 1917 to become one of the most widely known fortune-telling methods in Russia today.

BEAN DIVINATION

This geomantic method of telling fortunes divided forty-one beans into three unequal piles, then subdivided them into fours as far as possible and arranged them in three rows. Significance was deemed to rest in the number of piles in a row, the position of a given pile in a row, and whether it was next to a pile containing an uneven number of beans. The top row was connected with the head, the next with the heart. Instructions were very brief, and almost invariably coupled with guidance on reading coffee cups, though the latter could appear on its own. On this basis one would assume that bean divination was an imported skill, since it is well-known elsewhere, but seventeenth-century references to the use of beans for divination in circles unlikely to have been exposed to Western influence suggests otherwise.[81] By the eighteenth century, it was widely used by professional fortune-tellers (see chapter 6). Given that Western fortune-telling books do not normally include bean divination, the method may have been imported before 1600 (through a now forgotten text, perhaps of Eastern origin, or by, say, merchants visiting Russia or merchants from Russia who had travelled abroad), passing then into oral currency. Alternatively, it may just possibly stem from an indigenous folk tradition of considerable antiquity. Suffice to note that printed instructions coincide closely with oral tradition as recorded in the 1830s. This type of divination appears to have been less popular as a form of genteel fortune-telling, perhaps because it was so well known orally, or because, unlike coffee, the basic equipment did not naturally appear in drawing-rooms. Fortune-telling in beans was still known in Russian villages after the Second World War, but nowadays seems largely forgotten.

NON-DIVINATORY SUPPLEMENTARY TEXTS

The non-divinatory texts that went into fortune-telling compendia fitted into two categories, that were by no means mutually exclusive. Either they stood on the borderline of divination and magic (and were hence probably regarded as divinatory by editors and, no doubt, also purchasers), or they reinforced the designation of fortune-telling books as light entertainment (see chapter 3). Forfeits, riddles or charades all added to the fun of the book; hence, these gradually went out of favour as fortune-telling books stopped being produced for the leisured classes. Trick arithmetic, conjuring tricks and mind-reading of names, on the other hand, were all, on the surface, close to magic, especially as far as the audience was concerned. For example, mind-reading of names, in which the name of someone's secret passion was elucidated, verged on onomancy (name divination), and was extremely popular from the time of its first appearance in 1786 until the 1840s, after which it fell largely into oblivion.[82] The method used was to ask the subject to say in which numbered columns the name of the beloved appeared. By adding up the total of the columns the name could be found in a key. Like card tricks, which became very popular in Russia between 1830 and 1860, to those not in the know it looked like magic. Its connection with divination was enhanced by the common attribution of the text to a fortune-teller, as in *The Honest Fortune-Teller, or A True and Complete Method of Guessing a Name . . .* (1787, 1792, 1793), and the popularity it soon attained may owe something to the Yuletide folk custom in which unmarried girls tried to learn the name of their future husbands (see chapter 2).

In conclusion it should be noted that the most popular types of divinatory text in Russia between 1760 and the Revolution overall were dreams, cards and *Solomon*, though these were outnumbered in the eighteenth and early nineteenth centuries by geomantic question/answer texts. Most other forms of text (chiromancy, physiognomy, Yuletide divination, weather predictions, omens, beans and coffee grounds) were usually published along with a more important text (e.g. as a supplement to a dreambook) or in compendia.

While, as works translated in the eighteenth and nineteenth centuries, Russian fortune-telling books are not part of ancient folklore, it is certainly the case that these enduringly popular books acquired their own local features and their own tradition. Russian divinatory literature, for all its ultimate dependence on Western European texts, is not identical with, for example, its French or British counterparts. Not only, as already noted, did astrology not take root in Russia, but neither did divination from moles (of the dermatological kind), which was extremely popular in England, nor scrying (crystal-ball gazing), at least until the spiritualist craze of the 1860s, and then it hardly impacted on popular fortune-telling tradition. The extent to which this is due to Russian folklore is considered in the next chapter. But, apart from the books themselves coming to be seen as 'traditional', their contents naturally and inevitably passed into family tradition. Even if they began as foreign imports, fortune-telling books were embraced so warmly by their Russian readers, becoming for generation after generation a part of their lives, that they can with good reason be described as both Russian and traditional.

CHAPTER 2

Divination in Russian traditional culture

In traditional Russian culture, as in other pre-modern societies, divination performed an important social function for the community as a whole; in an uncertain world ruled by supernatural power, there was a natural wish to placate maleficent forces and thank benign ones. Russian peasants viewed the world as a hostile place, where the correct ritual or reading of signs was believed to make the difference between life and death, success and failure. Divination, various in character and function, played an all-encompassing role in daily life as a means of grasping the significance of events and phenomena and offering glimpses into the future. At the same time it performed important social functions. In this chapter I highlight those features of divinatory practice relevant to an understanding of the rôle of fortune-telling among urban and literate groups before considering the interrelationship between the two traditions.

In general, the most significant matters for divination were connected with the fate of individual or family, especially the crucial stages in life. By far the most common concerned marital prospects, but others were conception, birth and life expectancy. Even the likelihood of recruitment belongs in this category, since the absence of a male family member on military service lasting from fifteen to thirty years depending on the period was equated with death. It was a bitter blow in both economic and emotional terms. Little wonder that peasants sought to be forewarned.

The most convenient way of categorizing rural divination is by dividing it into calendrical and non-calendrical. The former was connected with specific days or periods such as Yuletide, whereas the latter was performed whenever need or occasion arose, such as a birth, a weather phenomenon or a disquieting dream.[1] Certain divinatory skills, of which oneiromancy was the chief, belonged in both categories. Calendrical dream divination differed from non-calendrical not only because of the specific dates designated for it, but also because it was accompanied by ritual actions.[2] A magical object (for example, herbs gathered on a particular day, or a bridge made of twigs) was placed under the pillow or near the bed in order to produce prophetic dreams.[3] Non-calendrical dream interpretation, by contrast, responded to dreams as they occurred.

The most significant rituals were concentrated round the great divisions in the annual cycle, the winter and summer solstices, and, to a lesser extent, the spring and autumn equinoxes. The favourite time for ritual calendrical divination was the first of these, Yuletide (*Sviatki*), which lasted from 25 December to 5 January. It was believed that the unclean force was at its most active when cold and dark had stifled nature, the sun was feeble, and yet the world was on the threshold of renewal. During this period as on St John's Eve (23/4 June), unmarried girls and, to a lesser extent, the young men of the village were involved in a large range of divinatory activities about their marital prospects.[4] Trinity Thursday (*Semik*) and Sunday, along with Easter and St Andrew's Day (30 October) were also favourite times.[5]

The importance of the specifics of time and place for calendrical divination further emphasizes its liminal significance and its danger. In order to receive a reliable prediction, participants had to make contact with the other world. Yuletide divination took place in the evening, most commonly at the witching hour of midnight, when contact with the 'unclean force' was easiest, especially if the right place, the bathhouse, the crossroads, the threshing barn, was selected. In order to receive a sign or provoke an encounter, anything that normally protected participants from the *temnye sily* or dark powers (crosses, belts, braided hair) had to be removed or undone. Those awaiting enlightenment waited alone in the dark, aware of the terrible consequences – death was a distinct possibility – for anyone who failed to perform the ritual correctly. In essence non-calendrical divination was equally dangerous; sieve and needle prognostication, for example, were considered too hazardous for unmarried girls.The former, which is described in chapter 6, was connected with thief detection, the latter, which focused on the reaction of two grease-smeared needles to being dropped in a tumbler of water, was about a girl's marital prospects, divined by whether the needles sank, rose, moved together, apart etc. Girls would summon older women to perform this ritual.[6]

Despite the element of fear, such rituals were part of festivities which placed an emphasis on merry-making. Most Yuletide divination was not a solitary affair but a group activity, performed mainly by girls, who looked forward eagerly to their favourite time of year.[7] For them Yuletide represented fun spiced with danger, in the course of which they would discover the identity, age or character of their intended. Even the possibility of learning of distressing events such as spinsterhood, illness or death failed to quench their enthusiasm. Girls gathered in houses or outside in the street to try a selection of the numerous rituals known in their locality. They poured melted wax or tin into water and scrutinized the resulting shapes, or brought a chicken into the house, and waited to see whether it chose to peck first at water, grain or a ring, and from that predicted the type of husband and quality of married life. Out on the street, the name of the first man a girl met would be taken as that of her future husband. In many of these rituals any consciousness of a dangerous encounter with the supernatural had been lost, though hints remain in the symbolic ritual use of ashes, water, bread and grain, and in the Russian equivalent of ghost stories about ritual appeals to mythological figures.[8]

If a problem was worrying a villager, he or she consulted a local specialist.[9] This accorded with the social system in the Russian countryside that assigned special rôles to community members; for example, people who had assimilated all the lore pertaining to the folk calendar were highly respected by the surrounding population who resorted to them in cases of need.[10] There existed various kinds of divinatory specialist with overlapping functions, but divisible primarily into white- and black-magic practitioners.[11] The first included dream interpreters, fortune-tellers and diviners specializing in the retrieval of lost or stolen property. Midwives also interpreted dreams and made predictions about a new baby's future. Best known in the category, though, is the folk healer whose skills included knowledge of folk medicine, curative charms and love spells as well as divination.[12] So long as folk healers were perceived to offer efficacious cures and wise predictions, they enjoyed the respect of the community, and even wider fame. Their name in Russian, *znaiushchii* (the knowing one) or *znakhar′* (or, for women, *znakharka*) implies the possession of special knowledge and skills. They were believed to derive their knowledge from the other world, perhaps originally from dead ancestors, though over time this was transmuted into God and his saints. Their use of spells, whose Christian invocations or endings lent them the status of prayers, reinforced this view.[13] Black-magic practitioners included sorcerers and witches, who embodied supernatural powers within themselves; they could cause 'spoiling', that is, induce crop failure, sickness or death to man and beast.[14] They also made predictions, some of them unwelcome. Consulting them was dangerous because of their powers, but a sorcerer's predictions were thought particularly valid for this very reason. Folk healers, by contrast, did not embody supernatural powers, but acted as mediators with the unclean force. Part of their rôle was to nullify the harmful magic of sorcerers, and in this respect they resemble the 'cunning folk' of England, or the counter-sorcerers of France, though in Russia the categories could blur, sometimes depending on the commentator's own views on the occult.[15] Both types of specialist needed to be treated with care because of their supernatural associations and ability to cast spells, but generally the sorcerer was feared while the folk healer was respected.

Although both sexes and all ages took part in various kinds of divination about personal fate, it was usually women who possessed interpretive skills. White-magic practitioners were more often women,[16] though gender representation was reversed among their black-magic counterparts. Apart from sorcerers and male witches, rural men's *active* interest in divination mainly focused on the economic fate of the family and community (such as predictions about the weather, the harvest or the livestock).

Traditional divination was regarded with seriousness not only because the most effective kinds involved recourse to powers beyond normal human control, but also because it was a valued part of a system of magic rituals of a propitiatory, prophylactic or divinatory character, that aimed to increase humanity's chances in a world over which it had little control. That some of these rituals offered the participants fun, hope and a welcome release from daily drudgery does not negate their underlying seriousness and value for the community. The social functions of calendrical divination encompassed not only these rôles, but also, like other rituals, helped bond the community. Non-calendrical prognostication, which responded to a need or occasion, emphasized some of these more than others. Here emotional support for the individual, together with his or her sense of some control over life, took precedence over community bonding and the element of jollification. Dream interpretation serves to illustrate this point.

Not all dreams were traditionally considered meaningful;[17] Russian peasants attributed prophetic value to exceptionally vivid and disturbing dreams, in particular those which caused the dreamer to wake in the middle of the night. These were viewed as a symbolic warning of future events of major importance in the dreamer's life.[18] The most troubling and enigmatic dreams were taken to the local specialist interpreter. Thus the decision as to which dreams were premonitory and needed interpretation relied primarily on dreamers themselves, and the resulting visit to the specialist acted as a form of therapy. The function of the visit was not simply a request for information, but an expression of the individual's need to tell her or his dream – in effect, a form of purification, the discharging of the dream's power over the dreamer.

Dreams that were less troubling but still powerful or enigmatic were discussed in the family, mainly at breakfast, when an older woman usually presided.[19] Breakfast dream-telling, a formalized procedure in many societies, performed functions beyond interpretation. It helped the individual understand his or her own desires and impulses. At the same time the informal morning custom served as a form of social bonding within families and more particularly among women (see chapter 4). Its longevity and social importance are demonstrated by the survival of the custom today in traditionalist Russian families.[20] The implication is that discussion of the dream with others was a valued activity, whether the aim was to rid oneself of the lingering spell of a disturbing dream, legitimately gain the attention of others, join in a family activity or any combination of these.

As Russians moved to the city or became literate, they inevitably began to lose touch with the ritualized structure of traditional life. Some aspects of that life, for example the many rituals and activities connected with ensuring a good harvest, ceased to have any meaning in an urban environment. More importantly, the whole basis of the rural world view was challenged by the demands of urban life. In Russia as elsewhere in pre-modern Europe the traditional agricultural world was structured by a cyclical ritualized view of time, which conceived of a regular procession of seasons, marked by celebration and ritual, combined with a series of ordinary days punctuated at irregular intervals by holidays. Within the periods of ordinary days, there were further sub-divisions; for example, the various days of the week were given symbolic meanings. Sayings 'encoded information about when to undertake tasks, but also when not to work, when it was necessary to perform symbolic actions, take part in rituals and compulsory celebrations'.[21] Urban life at any social level weakened or destroyed these; regardless of whether the folk calendar dictated that certain actions, work included, were banned on a given day, the factory worker had to turn up as usual. With work transformed into a methodical, regular activity, so leisure was dominated by the working week rather than the old calendar. One facet of traditional life that suffered as a consequence was calendrical divination.

Only the festivities associated with *Sviatki* or Yuletide (divination included) survived the disintegration of the old calendar in the new urban and literate environment. One of the most colourful and enjoyable facets of national culture, it retained its popularity with the élite classes, even as they lost touch with living tradition. For them, printed accounts supplemented fading memories, beginning with the only eighteenth-century reference guide to folk belief, Chulkov's *Dictionary of Russian Superstitions* (1782).[22] By 1825 Yuletide customs had been republished at least eight times in various fortune-telling books, and additionally in a dedicated volume, *Russian Yuletide, or Diverting and Pleasant Amusements from 25th December to 6th January for Amiable Girls, Delightful Young Married Women and Bachelors* (Moscow, 1814–15). But this was not a very high number compared with, say, cartomantic or chiromantic guides, suggesting that the familiarity of the upper classes with Yuletide customs at this point may have depended less on print than on the presence of figures like Pushkin's old nanny, women of peasant origin living in noble households even after their charges had grown up. It was they who acted as the main conduit for folklore to the upper classes.

Literary pre-Romanticism and Romanticism smiled upon both fortune-telling rituals and the special Yuletide divinatory folk songs known as *podbliudnye pesni*, and this seems to have had a lasting impact in softening criticism, such that, unlike most other forms of fortune-telling, Yuletide divination attracted less rather than more criticism as time went by. In 1812, the poet Zhukovskii, whose heroine Svetlana practises Yuletide rituals, could not resist debunking them in the concluding lines of the poem, whereas Tat′iana's involvement in Yuletide rituals in *Eugene Onegin* (1825) is presented as an expression of her Russianness. Six years later, Bestuzhev-Marlinskii opened his story, *A Terrible Prophecy* (1831), with a description of colourful and jolly divinatory rituals in the peasant hut where the officer narrator has arrived by chance. The plot concerns an attempt to evoke the 'unclean force' through the terrrifying ritual of sitting on a wolfskin in a graveyard at midnight. Unlike Zhukovskii, Bestuzhev-Marlinskii does not indulge in moralizing about superstition. While implying that such efforts are futile (the encounter with 'the cunning one' turns out to be a dream), he wards off potential criticism by showing that the officer's dream served as a premonitory warning. Both the admiration of colourful group rituals and the ambivalent attitude to the invocation of the devil reflect educated as well as Romantic attitudes.

Blessed by the intelligentsia, Yuletide divination continued to be popular at all levels of urban and literate society as the nineteenth century progressed. No stigma was attached to them, judging by the poet Fet's two poems of 1842 called 'Divination' (I and II) written in the female voice from the point of view of the participant without any authorial condescension. As Tereshchenko remarked in 1848, 'not only the nobility, living in towns and villages, but even inhabitants of the capital love to immerse themselves in Yuletide pleasures'.[23] On 2 January 1854 the Tsarevna is recorded as taking part in traditional Yuletide tin-pouring and chicken oracles.[24] Yuletide divination thus became an activity shared by all social groups in late Imperial society; for example, in the household of wealthy Jewish business people in which Tamara Talbot-Rice grew up, both servants and girls indulged in traditional fortune-telling on Twelfth Night.[25] Families took the customs with them into emigration; Maria 'Missie' Vassiltchikov, writing of life in Berlin, notes in her diary that, on 1 January 1940, 'Tatiana and I spent the New Year quietly . . . We tried to read the future by dropping melted wax and lead into a bowl of water.'[26]

In passing into urban life, Yuletide divination was reduced to harmless fun. Rituals designed to force an encounter with the 'unclean force' were dropped, and others lost their serious point. Despite this social pressure, many young girls, like Pushkin's Tat'iana, probably continued to believe or half-believe that they might learn the identity of their husband at Yuletide. Trivialization seems to have begun in sophisticated households in the late eighteenth century before spreading to other social groups. In St Petersburg, a less traditional place than the old capital, Moscow, it may have reached humbler urban households as early as 1820, depending upon the interpretation placed on the complaint of the old man in V. Markov's poem, 'Yuletide or Today's World' (1821). He laments that Yuletide customs are dying out among younger townsfolk. It may be that without recourse to village grandmothers or books (too expensive before the 1840s for most), these customs may indeed have been in decline at that point in time in these circles. However, by mid century, thanks to cheap fortune-telling books containing Yuletide customs, the decline had been reversed among all social groups. As books became more affordable for ordinary townsfolk, *podbliudnye pesni* and a list of rituals (mainly the same as in Chulkov) began regular appearances.[27] On the other hand Markov may have been referring not to the disappearance of the customs but to young people's dismissal of them as silly. Whatever interpretation one chooses, their survival among urban dwellers in pre-Revolutionary Russia seems to have been assisted by printed guides. When officialdom banished fortune-telling books after 1918, Yuletide customs all but vanished among urban dwellers, surviving at the cost of being trivialized; girls, to the disapproval of their grandmothers, now see them simply as light entertainment, a party game associated with the contemporary celebration of the New Year.[28] To some extent trivialization is a natural effect of shifting educational levels, but a regime more tolerant of national 'superstition' would probably have fostered rather than condemned Yuletide customs.

In principle, since occasional divination was not tied to particular calendar festivals, it should have found survival in the urban context rather easier. In fact, it fared less well than Yuletide divination. Without such an obvious association with fun, it appears that village forms of divination, mostly those regarded with considerable respect, were rapidly replaced by books. The only type to survive was psalter divination, which, at least in the 1830s, was as much an urban as a rural skill,[29] and therefore did not have to make any kind of transition. Using a psalter for prediction probably arrived in Russia from Byzantium, judging by the existence of special divinatory psalters in manuscript in medieval Russia. The connection with scripture enhanced its authority (psalter divination was begun with the singing of a psalm), and may well have helped maintain its authority in an urban setting.

Other types of divination that did not require the use of books were replaced by fortune-telling books, which, for over a century, were almost completely dependent on imported material. Folk omens were the only traditional material of the non-calendrical type to make the jump into print, appearing first in Chulkov's dictionary of superstition. They next turned up in the engagingly entitled 'Old Wives Philosophy', a short section in *An Ancient and Modern Permanent Divinatory Oracle* . . . (1800 etc.), consisting of predictive signs together with prophylactic magic and primitive advice about domestic problems. Along with the portents, the reader was advised that placing a baked apple in the mouth of a new-born babe before putting him to the breast would ensure he did not grow up a drunkard, a constant maternal fear in Russia.[30] Magic and practical advice stood side by side: thus, to stop a cat running away, seize it by the ears and drag it round the room three times. If this did not appeal, then instead wipe its paws with butter for three consecutive nights.[31] The first solution, an adaptation of the concept of the magic circle, probably only appealed to sadists.

It is unlikely that these words of wisdom came from a translated text, which had all been selected for drawing-room suitability. More credible is the idea that they came from Russian oral tradition, albeit indirectly. Publishers of fortune-telling literature were never interested in collecting their own material in the field, preferring to take their material from printed or manuscript sources. One may postulate that the material first appeared in a book of medical remedies. Despite the popularity of the host volume, the household hints in 'Old Wives Philosophy' did not find their way into other fortune-telling books. The reason is probably not only that they were not divinatory in character – after all, fortune-telling books contained a variety of other material – but that they were too crude for the genteel reading public of the first two decades of the nineteenth century.

By contrast, the predictive omens, which clearly fitted the character of fortune-telling books, continued to appear with some regularity throughout the nineteenth century. But while folk tradition knew vast numbers of portents, fortune-telling books printed the same ones, based on Chulkov's brief selection, over and over again with only minor variations.[32] They often came combined with a dreambook, such as *The Most Complete Dreambook and Interpretation of Various Portents*, a sixty-four-page cheap volume running to multiple editions towards the end of the century. The juxtaposition is, perhaps, not accidental, since the meanings assigned to portents and dream objects in various traditions are often close if not identical.[33]

Other types of folk belief and folk magic finally began to appear in fortune-telling books at the very end of the nineteenth century. Not only did dreambooks belatedly take note of the folk oneiromantic tradition by including more obviously Russian items such as snow, rye or mushrooms in their lists of dream objects, with accompanying interpretations drawn from oral tradition, but the newly revived compendia now might include sections on folk magic, sorcery, spells and remedies. The next stage, occurring in the early twentieth century, made the folk origins of the material a selling point; *Folk Healing or Russian Folk Charms and a Complete Collection of All Manner of Beliefs, Superstitions and Sorcery for All Occasions* (Moscow, 1911) offered folk dream rituals, aphrodisiac recipes, spells and a standard dreambook. Nonetheless, folk belief possessed limited appeal. Although ethnographers had been collecting and theorizing about folk magic and medicine for several decades, publishers were probably aware that ordinary townsfolk tended to sneer at the homespun wisdom of the peasants. A better sales strategy was to rely on written traditions, as in the very popular book which had a strong divinatory component, *A New Book. Household Remedies. The Bruce Calendar for 200 Years. A Course in Folk Healing. Magic, Sorcery and A Complete Collection of Russian Folk Spells*, Moscow, third edition 1916, fourth and fifth editions 1917.[34] This spuriously claimed to have been taken from ancient manuscripts. Thus, despite publishers' desire to revitalize the contents of their wares and contemporary fascination with the occult, material from folk tradition, whether of a divinatory or non-divinatory character, remained a minor element in the composition of fortune-telling books. Most continued without any Russian folk material except that with a long printing history like omens and Yuletide rituals.

Oral divinatory tradition and fortune-telling books therefore lived largely separate lives. But even if direct influence was limited, long familiarity with native traditions, albeit weakened by cultural or geographical dislocation, must have conditioned the acceptance of fortune-telling books, and may have affected the relative popularity of certain types of translated text. For example, folk methods of divination from groups or patterns of small objects may have reinforced the popularity of certain types of oracle. Physiognomy and chiromancy were readily comprehensible to people familiar with omens deducing character and fate from appearance, such as that birthmarks mean happiness or wiry hair means a short temper. It is easy to postulate a dependence of printed text on oral belief when the two are alike; thus, both printed texts and oral sources agreed that the significance of dreams depended on which of three periods of the night the dream occurred, but placed differing interpretations on them. Whereas dreambooks suggested that the time of night affected the length of time before the prophecy was fulfilled, oral belief held that evening dreams were not worth bothering about, morning dreams were meaningful mainly for young couples in their first year of marriage, and only dreams in the middle of the night warranted a visit to the specialist.[35] It was also widely believed that 'holiday dreams come true before dinner'.[36] Those who were replacing oral tradition with books because of social and cultural dislocation would not have had much problem transferring their allegiances.

The popularity of lists of propitious days in dreambooks probably also rested on oral beliefs, but the link here is less clear. In view of folk ignorance of judicial astrology, the idea that propitious dreams could depend on the date in the lunar month naturally did not exist. Nor did the tables of lucky and unlucky days of the month have a direct correspondence in folk belief, given that the peasants did not think of time in terms of months. However, the concept of unlucky days as such is embedded in folk belief, but applied to days of the week; Friday was regarded as especially unlucky, partly because the crucifixion took place on a Friday, though the belief is certainly pre-Christian and clearly represented in the syncretic cult of St Paraskeva-Piatnitsa, who, it was believed, forbade weaving on a Friday, exacting revenge on the disobedient.[37] Other beliefs attached to Monday and Wednesday.[38] In addition, the traditional world view was familiar with the concept of days on which dire consequences followed the undertaking of prohibited activities. It would have been enough to facilitate the adoption of similar lists by the reading public.

Since dreambooks achieved stunning popularity with book purchasers and dream divination played a significant rôle in village life, oneiromancy provides an excellent focus for an investigation into the relationship between the two traditions. Is it simply that folk oneiromancy underpinned the shift to a new imported method of dream interpretation, or are there closer links? In answering this question, it is essential to establish that East Slav oneiromantic traditions were not contaminated by textual imports prior to the influx of translated texts. The problem is complicated by the numerous features common to oneiromancy among the Slavs and other peoples, stemming undoubtedly from common features of the human psyche. These resulted in shared traditions, though cultural diffusion may account for some parallels. It may be reasonably assumed that the East Slavs practised dream divination from the earliest times, and that they did so in a form largely unaffected by outside influences, even though we have no evidence of actual folk dream beliefs in Russia before Mikhail Chulkov inserted a few into his *Dictionary of Russian Superstitions* in 1782. Evidence for a belief in dreams is mainly indirect. With the conversion to Christianity, the East Slavs gained access to the many accounts of prophetic dreams in the Bible and ecclesiastical literature as well as to secular literature containing dream reports.[39] Christian tradition, imitated by Russian hagiographers, recognized dreams in which the dreamer (usually God's chosen one) either had a vision of a future happening or received instructions or prohibitions in a vision or from a heavenly voice.[40] These types of vision, according to Artemidorus and Greek tradition, differed from enigmatic dreams, in which the meaning was veiled, and only became apparent after interpretation. Warnings were issued against placing one's faith in such dreams, suggesting there was a belief to combat.[41]

Yet, though the presence of enigmatic dreams in *translated* literature may partly explain the popularity of some texts and hence provide evidence of Slav interest in dreaming, it cannot serve as evidence of native Slav beliefs about dreams. Unfortunately, original Russian literature furnishes few examples of portentous dreams: the best known is Sviatoslav's dream in the late twelfth-century epic, *The Tale of the Campaign of Igor'*. In an early example of the Slav custom of dream-telling upon wakening, Prince Sviatoslav summons his boyars to elucidate the meaning of his ominous dream. They unravel it, symbol by symbol, warning him of the danger that attends Rus' because of Prince Igor''s foolhardy attack on the Polovtsians. The difficulty of deducing too much from a single problematical example is self-evident,[42] but parallels with prophetic dreams in Russian narrative folk songs, where dreams are unravelled in this way and which can reasonably be assumed to be centuries old, confirm the *Tale of the Campaign of Igor'*'s evidence. We know also that Russian folk dream divination focused on the totality of a complex dream, though this is not a feature unique to the Slavs.[43] Furthermore, dream divination was sufficiently well known to attract condemnation in the sixteenth-century guide to household management, the *Domostroi*.[44] Perhaps the strongest argument is that folk dream beliefs recorded in the eighteenth or nineteenth centuries from groups who could not have had access to dreambooks reflect a stable common core in a wide variety of locations, suggesting considerable antiquity.[45] Whether some of these beliefs were acquired from peoples with whom the Slavs came into contact or not is irrelevant. The conclusion must be that the Slavs possessed an indigenous tradition, little touched in historical times by outside influences, and retained in rural lore.

This tradition was, as already remarked, iconic, but the expert interpreter wove the accepted meaning of symbols in their current configuration into an integrated interpretation. This method, too, had parallels among the ancients; the manner of presentation in dreambooks of symbol followed by laconic explanation presents only the skeleton of ancient oneiromantic tradition.[46] In the printed dreambooks which present the version in which ancient tradition reached Russia, guidance on how to combine the disparate symbols into one explanation was absent. Nonetheless, it is highly likely that owners of dreambooks followed the lead of rural and urban specialist dream interpreters in elucidating whole dreams on the basis of their dreambooks, just as countryfolk did with oral beliefs. In this way they were applying traditional folkloric techniques to a new body of material.

The shared features of dream divination over the whole of Europe also include the principles underlying the relationship between dream object and interpretation.[47] Close parallels of this kind make the task of differentiating Russian oral oneirocriticism from its 'literary' counterpart more complex, but, on the other hand, provide a convincing explanation for the enduring popularity of dreambooks. In both folk and literary oneirocriticism, similarities of shape or of perceived qualities often connect symbol and interpretation. In Iaroslavl province dreaming of pancakes means a letter (both are thin and flat), while blood means relatives.[48] In the standard dreambook text dreaming of hares means 'fear' (in a dreambook of 1794), a fox means deception (an 1885 dreambook), both topoi of European folk animal tales. A windmill means flighty friends or a gossip (1885).[49] The only difference seems to be that in dreambooks, interpretations based on external similarity are much less common than those resting on perceived shared qualities. Also similar are interpretations constructed on metonymy and metaphor, such as a saddle meaning a journey (1885) or ink signifying a letter (Iaroslavl province). Banal interpretations are relatively rare in both folk and literary dream divination, and usually possess some symbolic connotations. Thus in a dreambook of 1811, under 'beer' the dreamer learnt that going to the tavern in one's dreams leads to poverty, an interpretation with which few would disagree. Similarities should not obscure the few differences. Firstly, especially in the literary tradition, connections are sometimes far from obvious. Why should dreaming of having large ears mean an illness (1794)? The original rationale for such conclusions has been lost, either when the explanations of specialists such as Artemidorus were axed from popular texts, or as a result of the processes of translation and cultural transmission. Who knows how many different European cultures had placed an imprint on the text of the 1794 dreambook before it reached Russia? Other apparently unconnected interpretations may have arisen as a direct result of translation, when an interpretation based on the similarity of sounds could not be rendered into another language. In folk tradition, interpretations such as a *reka* (river) meaning *rechi* (speeches), *devitsa* (girl) meaning *divo* (a wonder) (both recorded by Chulkov) or *gora* (a mountain) meaning *gore* (grief) are common. Linkages of this kind are lost completely in translation.

One type of relationship between object and interpretation, sometimes mistakenly cited as a characteristic of Slav dream divination, deduces the dream to signify the reverse of its surface meaning. In fact, the universal belief that dreams can be deceptive has everywhere prompted such interpretations. In the 1794 dreambook, laughing or kissing in one's dream means sorrow, seeing oneself as the devil means honour and a coffin means marriage, while in the 1885 dreambook dreaming of worms means riches. In oral tradition, a fire means frost, and dreaming of being ill means that a relative will recover from illness (Iaroslavl province).

One can go further; a number of these interpretations are identical in both traditions. Both folk and literary traditions hold that excrement means gold, money or treasure,[50] a horse means an enemy, and lice, money. When these are added to other parallels and similarities, such as cats always having a negative meaning and dogs a positive one, or rotten teeth being connected with quarrels with relatives or their demise, it is clear that they have much in common. Were it not that numerous folk dream objects plus the overwhelming majority of folk interpretations do differ sharply from those in printed books, the question of contamination might arise. As it is, common psychological processes offer the only credible explanation. Some of the differences in the corpus of dream objects are a product of the environment in which they circulated or were produced. Both reflected everyday life (though, as remarked in chapter 1, longer dreambooks contained numbers of alien and absurd objects). Rural dreamers do not appear to have dreamt regularly of libraries or pineapples, nor townsfolk of grain fields. But how far dream objects in each environment conditioned actual dreams cannot unfortunately be measured.

The view of the folk tradition as stable and the literary tradition as in a permanent state of flux does not stand up to scrutiny. Despite a common core of interpretations, regional, local and even family variants abound. Furthermore, when countryfolk became familiar with such items as ink or playing cards, these entered oneirocritical tradition. There they were elucidated according to the usual principles. Thus, in Iaroslavl province around 1890, dreaming of *chai* (tea) meant *ne*chai*annost'* (the unexpected). Since tea was a relatively recent arrival in villages, the belief was recent. The number of additions to the folk corpus was small but not significantly less than in the basic cheap dreambook. Even though books for more affluent readers embraced innovation much more whole-heartedly, both traditions inclined to conservatism.

It may be concluded that the considerable parallels between folk and literary dream divination, whether in the types of relationship between object and interpretation or in similarities of interpretations, assisted the adoption of dreambooks among those who had lost touch with native beliefs. The age-old custom of discussing dreams over breakfast and trying to read the dream as a whole were carried over into a new environment and further helped the imported dreambook to become a treasured part of many lives.

As literacy spread to the countryside with fortune-telling books in its train, the possibility arose of the reverse process occurring, that is, for print to influence rural folklore. It took about a hundred years before the books began reaching the countryside with any consistency, and till the 1880s before they did so in real numbers. The one text that arrived earlier was *Solomon*, whose massive popularity is undeniable. It possessed great authority because of its perceived connection with the scriptures. Some of the interpretations are drawn in part from liturgical and biblical sources and are all written in Church Slavonic, the language of the scriptures. For example, the interpretation for the number twelve on the circle read: 'The Lord will grant you the great gift which you await; much good have you done, o Man, God will grant you all blessings.'[51] The scriptural flavouring, together with the incongruous mixture of fortune-telling and religion, lent *Solomon* an especial authority, but one based on the written word. It may have been this that stopped it entering oral tradition, thereby sustaining huge sales in pre-Revolutionary Russia.

It is tempting to postulate that the contents of dreambooks may also have influenced folk dream interpretation in villages by the end of the nineteenth and early twentieth centuries, but the subject is far too little recorded or studied to allow for conclusions. Certainly, oral tradition proved resistant in some places; in the

Gzhatsk area of Smolensk province, for example, people did not hold by dreambooks because they had their own dream interpreters.[52] In the absence of any research on this subject, and given the complications arising from the similarity between some folk interpretations and printed ones, speculation is pointless.

However, even if the influence of fortune-telling books on rural folk traditions was negligible or unprovable, some printed fortune-telling skills entered a different kind of oral tradition existing among urban and literate groups. As books circulated from the late eighteenth century on, their contents were transmitted within families and to friends, creating a secondary oral tradition which was to become more important after the Revolution when fortune-telling books were suppressed (see chapter 8).

The only types of fortune-telling to catch on in the countyside during the late eighteenth and nineteenth centuries were cartomancy and bean divination, of which the former was by far the most popular. Probably because there was no similar divinatory activity in villages, and also because the interpretations of the various cards were easily learnt, reading the cards had become a common feature of village life by the late 1840s.[53] Factories producing hand-painted papier-maché boxes recognized this by making a picture of a peasant girl reading her fortune in the cards a common motif. Tereshchenko also remarked in 1848 that cards had even become part of Yuletide customs, though he did not specify the area to which he was referring. Each girl was allowed three goes in any one evening (presumably in the expectation of eventually getting the right result). Even more revealing of the acceptance of cards in divination is his account of the inclusion of cards among the magic objects placed under the pillow at Yuletide to produce dreams of a girl's intended.[54] By the end of the century in Karelia at least, cartomancy was enormously popular year round in the country, especially with girls who, according to M. Georgievskii: 'lay out the cards thousands of times a year, learning one thing one day and the opposite the next. Other [fortune-telling] methods hardly feature at all in the course of the year.' In contrast to Tereshchenko, Georgievskii says that cards are put away at Yuletide.[55] It may be assumed that practices varied in different localities, but, whether cartomancy was or was not practised as part of calendar rituals, its penetration into the countryside is indisputable and evidence of the ability of folk tradition to adapt to social change.

Sakharov observes that house serfs who accompanied their masters to the city for the winter or longer picked up the habit of reading the cards, and then practised their skill on return. Rather than bringing printed instructions back with them, they almost certainly learnt them by heart. So widespread did reading the cards become in the countryside that printed instructions were superfluous. Colporteurs' boxes at the end of the nineteenth century did not contain cartomantic guides,[56] and cheap multi-text fortune-telling books did not bother with them either. It may be concluded that cartomancy probably entered rural oral culture not directly from fortune-telling books, but via the secondary oral tradition of towns before fortune-telling books reached the countryside in any numbers.

In the case of bean divination, the rôle of fortune-telling texts may well have been even less than with cartomancy, given that the skill had been known in Russia since at least the early seventeenth century. By the time of the first printed texts, bean divination already existed as an established part of the urban fortune-teller's repertoire. Sakharov states that the skill was orally transmitted,[57] observing that nannies and housekeepers, who migrated with noble families between towns and the countryside, were the only rural dwelling peasants to practise bean divination.[58] The possibility that they acquired the skill from a text cannot be excluded, but urban lore is the more likely source.

Divination formed a rich and vital part of traditional Russian culture, in the form in which it had been preserved among Russian peasants. Its rôles were various, but though they included the injection of pleasure into hard lives, serious social functions predominated in a society that believed in magic. The shift towards trivialization, once divination was taken out of its traditional context and placed in a literate or urban environment, is examined in more detail in chapters 3 and 5. Here it has been argued that traditional attitudes to divination underlay the enthusiasm for fortune-telling books in Russia, as elsewhere in Europe. The huge popularity of dreambooks and associated lists of propitious days seems to owe a good deal to comparable beliefs widespread in rural society. Folk belief influenced the literary tradition, in the main, indirectly; its direct impact was limited to Yuletide customs and folk omens, with folk material reaching dreambooks only at the end of the nineteenth century. In the eighteenth century the zest for all things foreign brought popular fortune-telling books from France, Germany and Poland to newly literate Russian readers. Their success depended also on the desire, common among new readers, for something fresh, with the authority of print but not too unfamiliar. Knowledge of folk divination, albeit fading, combined with a sense that printed books *per se* must contain a modicum of truth. Of course, where Russians still cherished folk beliefs, their attachment to these clashed with a desire for novelty and the view of print as authoritative, but as the nineteenth century passed, urban life and Westernization prised more and more people away from traditional beliefs.

Urban and literate groups formed their own divinatory traditions, almost all of the non-calendrical occasional type. Had anyone ever bothered to record them, domestic divinatory beliefs and practices in the urban context would very probably have revealed an intriguing combination of literary and folk elements. The limited evidence we have shows that urban dwellers adopted and circulated the imported mantic skills of reading the cards and divining from rows of beans. These were then transported to the countryside where they took root. The interplay between imported fortune-telling skills and folk beliefs was much more subtle and complex than appears from the initial statement that fortune-telling books in Russia were all translated, and reflected both the tangled nature of cultural assimilation and change, and the danger of assuming that folklore is static while popular printed culture is dynamic.

CHAPTER 3

Readers and detractors

Pushkin's heroine Tat'iana acquired a copy of Martyn Zadeka's dreambook from a passing pedlar. This book then became her greatest treasure:

> . . . Martyn Zadeka's spell
> bewitches Tania . . . he is able
> to comfort her in all her woes,
> and every night shares her repose.
>
> (Pushkin, *Eugene Onegin*, V, xxiii)[1]

Six decades later, E. Nekrasova's reaction to another version of Tat'iana's favourite volume was a direct contrast; in her view, *The Newest Complete Dreambook by Martyn Zadeka* was no more than 'hideous gutter trash'.[2] Tat'iana's attachment and Nekrasova's contempt are typical of reactions to fortune-telling books among users on the one hand and commentators on the other. In this chapter, I consider the readership of these books by class or social group, as well as the climate of hostility in which they defiantly flourished. How far did patterns of social acceptance and rejection change over the period from 1765–1917? What strategies did publishers adopt to render their books acceptable, and how far did these change over time? What kind of reaction did they produce in critics, and what were their specific objections? While the processes involved in the adoption and assimilation of popular books in Russia have much in common with those in other countries, some differences inevitably result from the particular circumstances of Russia, a country where the initiation of print culture was contemporaneous with the first major wave of European influence, the development of a commercial literature coincided with the impact of the Enlightenment, and illiteracy was still the norm in 1917.

At the beginning of the eighteenth century a tiny percentage of the Russian population, the upper nobility, were forced from traditional ways into Western dress and customs, a violent jolt forward in a process already slowly under way in the previous century. Cultural attitudes, however, cannot be adopted as rapidly as clean-shaven faces and low-cut dresses. Though Westernization alienated the upper nobility from the oral-based folk culture of the bulk of the population, the gulf between the two, being so recently established, was for a number of decades more apparent than real. Western dress, wigs, beauty patches, new norms of social behaviour and entertainment disguised the old with show of the new.

What is more, for the first half of the eighteenth century, Europeanization reached no further than court circles and those nobles with the inclination and means to spend at least part of the year in St Petersburg. The rural nobility living on their small and medium estates did not abandon traditional ways until the 1760s, their lifestyle differing little from that of the merchants, one of the most socially conservative groups in Russia.[3] Literacy beyond a very basic level was still a rarity; books, where they existed, were mainly religious and too much reading was thought to drive one mad.[4] The culture of the lesser nobility was based on oral tradition with its calendar rituals and folk beliefs. As a disapproving nineteenth-century commentator put it, country gentry were extremely superstitious, 'believing in all kinds of omens, dreams and divination'.[5]

In the 1760s the social composition of the book-buying public was thus extremely narrow. Books were luxury items, scarcely obtainable outside the cities. In effect only educated nobles, usually those resident in town for at least part of the year, had the means, the inclination and the opportunity of acquiring them. Book-owning among the lesser rural nobility or among urban groups like craftsmen and tradesmen was a rarity.[6] The few merchants and priests who owned books inclined, like the country nobility, to religious texts or perhaps handy reference guides like calendars.[7] Though Russia was still overall a manuscript culture at this period, manuscripts, both secular and ecclesiastical, were, as a rule, kept only by the higher nobility, Church hierarchy, better educated parish clergy and Old Believers.[8]

In general, the rural clergy were unable to function as a source of enlightenment, since all too often barely literate priests were fettered by prejudice and superstition.[9] For the poorly educated priest, just as for his illiterate flock, there can have been little difference between prayers for intercession offered in Church services and incantatory folk charms with their prayer-like invocation to Mary, Mother of God, and concluding 'amen'. The folk healers who used these spells were the same people who told fortunes, so it was not surprising that, conversely, priests were approached by their parishioners to make prognostications, especially as they might have recourse to a divinatory manuscript of Byzantine origin, and certainly to a psalter.

Books began to make their way to the country in increasing numbers in the 1760s. The reasons are unclear, but likely explanations are that they were either brought back home by newly retired (and sometimes book-loving) ex-servitors after the nobility had been released from their service obligations in 1762 and could retire to their country estates; or else petty service-avoiders had by themselves begun to perceive the value of reading.[10] Even so, in 1767 only five sixths of all nobles in some areas were literate, a figure that includes those able to do no more than sign their own names. A couple of decades later, by contrast, the rural nobility had discovered European manners, along with respect for literacy and education and scorn for their former state of superstitious ignorance.[11] Thus it took until the last quarter of the eighteenth century before the nobility as a whole embraced Westernization, and even then, as with the élite in the decades after Peter's reforms, changes were inevitably superficial, especially in more remote areas or less affluent circles. By the end of the century the general respect for literacy had encompassed the rural clergy, with urban groups like the merchants and the lower-middle classes (*meshchane*) beginning to discern its advantages. The circle of people who were literate and had some access to books was expanding, even if their world view was still rooted in tradition.

With better book distribution and the belated appearance of commercial publishers in the 1780s the number and range of books on the market immediately increased (see chapter 4). For the first time, books were produced without one eye on moral improvement or the moralizers, in other words, for profit. The development coincided with the nascent interest in book acquisition among the newly educated and led to a rapid expansion in the market. Fortune-telling books occupied a significant place in this process.

Just as it was argued in chapter 2 that traditional beliefs from a still vivid oral culture conditioned the choice of fortune-telling texts, so, too, a traditional world view, fragmented but not expunged, facilitated the reception of those texts among people newly divorced from traditional culture. In any case, even when the move towards literacy, rationality and a scientific view of the world is of much longer standing than was the case in eighteenth-century Russia, the replacement of one belief system by another does not eradicate deeply ingrained attitudes. Fragments of belief systems can, and indeed do, exist within one individual; witness the large number of serious devotees of astrology in modern Britain or of a variety of divinatory skills in Russia today (see chapter 8). The replacement of 'superstitious' beliefs about the functioning of the world by rational explanation of phenomena does not proceed in a straightforward manner, nor is it necessarily an ongoing process. The adoption of rational ideas, as Charles Stewart has argued, comes about more by social pressure than the individual's considered appraisal of the superiority of empirical observation. Most people acquire scientific knowledge by learning what experts preach, rather than by testing for themselves.[12] Consequently scientific knowledge and traditional belief knowledge are acquired in much the same way, and may not always be clearly differentiated. Pseudo-sciences such as astrology or physiognomy enjoyed a period of popularity and respectability as a consequence of the conviction that they were scientifically based, no firm distinction generally being drawn between scientific deduction and divinatory prediction. Subsequently discredited and rejected by the enlightened classes, they tended to turn into aids to fortune-telling, adopted by the semi-educated. Equally, fragments of earlier belief systems can easily coexist with a scientific approach to life. The world remains an uncertain place for the individual who may frequently feel that he or she has little control over personal circumstances leading to happiness and fulfilment. Fortune-telling and other aspects of an attachment to the irrational may answer this need by offering guidance and support.

The eighteenth-century fashion among the élite classes of Western Europe for the occult may be seen not only as a specific reaction to the over-emphasis on reason, but also as a manifestation of a general human tendency. At the same time, the complex and esoteric forms that this fascination took (Masonry, Rosicrucianism, Mesmerism etc.) reflected the desire for a new intellectual and spiritual challenge and a means of deciphering the unknown. Since divinatory practices of long standing had passed in Western Europe beyond the élite into the custodianship of the lower strata of literate society, and from the male sphere to the female, they could no longer be regarded as respectable or challenging.[13] Hence the attraction of both occult and pseudo-sciences. In the Russia of the 1760s, by contrast, books *per se* possessed an aura of enlightenment regardless of content, and, for a brief period at least, little distinction was made between down-graded pseudo-sciences, divinatory skills and even fashionable occult sciences, except among a sophisticated few. In this context, it is not surprising that translators and publishers, who in the 1760s and 1770s were almost all drawn from the nobility, should have chosen to translate the types of fortune-telling texts discredited among the intellectual élite of Western Europe. At least initially, they were unlikely to have been aware of their low reputation.

A tiny élite, including the future tsar Paul and particularly his wife, Maria Fedorovna, the Moscow Masons and writers like Karamzin, Radishchev and Zhukovskii took a lively interest in the physiognomic theories of the Swiss pastor Lavater, who had visited Russia and then maintained a correspondence with various people in court circles.[14] While they were capable of distinguishing Lavater's disquisitions from popular physiognomy, others very probably were not, finding Lavater's theories above them. The considerable degree of respectability and influence these theories enjoyed in the first part of the nineteenth century may be gauged from Mikhail Lermontov's use of physiognomy in the description of Pechorin in his novel, *A Hero of Our Time* (1841).[15] But outside this small group, readers preferred the absorbing, varied but relatively short fortune-telling texts, just as they appreciated the potpourris of little-known and interesting facts in eighteenth-century journals. Accordingly, it appears that, while many literate Russians were drawn to beliefs in the irrational, the specific focus of their interest was conditioned by educational and social factors specific to Russia of the time.

As already mentioned, the price of books and widespread illiteracy meant that in the eighteenth century sales were largely restricted to the upper classes, and more to the urban gentry than their country cousins. The upper-class readership of fortune-telling books is indicated by appearance and content. The format, title and verse presentation of *A Morning Pastime over Tea, Or a New, Complete and as Far as Possible Accurate Interpretation of Dreams According to Astronomy and in Verse* (1791), all reveal a book designed for gentlefolk. Only an upper-class reader took morning tea and would have had enough prior knowledge to cope with the astrological treatment, albeit simplified, of the subject matter. A more important disincentive factor in the spread of books was cost; items such as lavishly produced packs of fortune-telling cards and large divinatory compendia produced between 1790 and 1825 would have been out of reach of the poorest readers, and even single texts were relatively expensive.[16]

Some of the first fortune-telling books may have been bought out of curiosity; Ivan Petrovich Annenkov, who was unusual in being a country gentleman with a large library, bought a fortune-telling book in the 1760s. Set against his largely heavy-weight collection, it stands out as an oddity, and was a one-off purchase.[17] While Annenkov was obviously not impressed, the volume of sales suggests that less sophisticated readers did not share his indifference or disdain. After 1780 changes occurred within the predominantly upper-class readership, as oracles, dreambooks and the like found their way into the 'libraries' of the lesser rural gentry, while at the same time becoming more clearly part of women's sphere.[18] Two satirical fictional portraits, referring to the first years of the nineteenth century, one by the writer A. E. Izmailov, the other by the novelist Ivan Goncharov, both depict unsophisticated country landowners whose tastes run to fortune-telling guides. Izmailov's landowner and titular counsellor, Nevezhin (Mr Ignoramus), owns a selection of books ranging from popular novels by writers like Mrs Radcliffe or Fedor Emin, to *lubok* editions of the medieval chivalric tale *Bova Korolevich*,[19] an illustrated folk tale about Ivanushka the Fool, and a dreambook.[20] The comic portrait of the Oblomov family in the dream section of Goncharov's famous novel, is, despite exaggeration, probably not far from the truth in its depiction of the backward rural gentry around 1810–20. The lives of the inhabitants of Oblomovka, gentry and peasants alike, are circumscribed by ritual and tradition. Books, it might at first appear, have made an impact on life at Oblomovka with volumes by Kheraskov, Sumarokov and Golikov in the library, but, like Nevezhin's collection, it contains a fortune-telling work, *The Newest*

Dreambook. Furthermore, Goncharov makes it clear that this 'library' is no more than a rarely touched heap of books bequeathed to père Oblomov by his brother. Both writers are using dreambooks as a symbol of the backwardness of the country bumpkin, relying on their noble readers' familiarity with the genre.

Perhaps the educated élite would have ceased to take any interest in divinatory books by the 1820s had it not been for the influence of Romanticism, with its fascination for the irrational. In Antonii Pogorel'skii's *The Double* the narrator is startled that his double (with whom he spends his evenings talking) does not believe that cards and coffee grounds can predict the future. Surely, he asks, you agree 'that sometimes cards can predict the future?' As befitting a double, his interlocutor disagrees.[21] This fictional debate probably mirrors real-life discussions among those influenced by Romantic ideas. The Romantics' sympathy was primarily directed towards folk belief because it embodied national character,[22] or so it was believed, but the differences between folk and literary traditions were perceived less clearly than they were later in the century. In 1827 a dreambook was seen on the poet Pushkin's desk at Mikhailovskoe and his Petersburg library contained a cartomantic guide. Were these simply research material for the fifth canto of *The Queen of Spades* and *Eugene Onegin*? Certainly, Pushkin's treatment of Tat'iana's attachment to her beloved Zadeka dreambook suggests a highly ironic attitude. On the other hand, he himself was very superstitious, and, like many creative artists of his generation in Europe, believed that dreams might be prophetic.[23] Like the Decembrist poet Ryleev, he had consulted a professional fortune-teller. Even if he trusted folk belief more than printed guides, his interest in the irrational ensured that references in his work to fortune-telling books are ambiguous or serve to characterize a milieu, rather than being condemnatory. With other writers from Zhukovskii to Venevitinov using motifs from folk belief in their poetry, folk divination and urban fortune-telling enjoyed a degree of intellectual respectability.

Though literacy levels were low, readers from other social groups did exist. By the 1770s, the number of non-aristocratic urban readers was growing, though they were still far from common. A common assumption, based on the situation obtaining around 1825, has been that such people bought only the Russian equivalent of chapbooks, the cheap woodcut books produced by the rapidly emerging *lubok* industry. In fact, the division between the readership of the two types of books was only just beginning to emerge at this point.[24] For educated people of Pushkin's generation as well as those of a generation earlier, the classic heroes of *lubok* fiction, Eruslan Lazarevich, Bova Korolevich, Milord Georg and Frantsyl Ventsian, were familiar names, albeit assigned to childhood.[25] The references to them in Pushkin's own works would have struck a chord with his largely upper-class readers. Conversely, according to the writer and journalist, Nikolai Novikov, almost any printed book that ran to three or more editions included the urban lower-middle classes among its readership.[26] A number of fortune-telling books fell into that category. In the preface to the fourth number of his journal *The Painter*, Novikov explains that the 'low reader and despised urban lower-middle classes' ('prostonarodnyi chitatel′ i prezrennoe meshchanstvo') had their own favourites. He noted that they also read his journal, though for the not altogether flattering reason that their ignorance of foreign languages seriously limited the range of available reading matter. By 1802, as the writer Nikolai Karamzin noted, merchants and the urban lower-middle classes were clubbing together to buy newspapers.[27] The same people were also potential buyers of fortune-telling books. Evidence that they made such purchases comes from book inscriptions. One in a dreambook of 1807, also containing Martyn Zadeka's famous prophecy and a section on conjuring tricks, notes that the owner, one Vorontsov, is a clerk (who ironically cannot spell the word!), who had purchased the book in 1818 from a merchant. About the same time, a semi-literate merchant's son from Moscow proudly declared himself the owner of a fortune-telling compendium, *A Secret Microscope . . .* (1817).[28] Some clerics, too, valued divinatory literature; in 1825 a seminarist from the south of Russia went to the effort of copying a printed dreambook by hand, presumably for want of ready access to a printed version of his own.[29]

With the expansion of publishing at the end of the eighteenth century, therefore, not only the country gentry, but also some minor officials, priests, lower-middle-class urban dwellers, house serfs and serfs on the *obrok* system (those paying their dues to the landlord in money rather than kind) all began to buy books.[30]

Despite evidence of the interest in and ownership of such books (and texts) outside the gentry, the trend should not be exaggerated. Undoubtedly the majority of sales were to the upper classes and publishers were aware of this in their attempts to allay the concerns of the supporters of reason and enlightenment. Arriving in Russia in the wake of the Enlightenment, fortune-telling books had had to gain acceptance in the teeth of hostility from these quarters. It was after all the literate and affluent in a supposed Age of Enlightenment who were expected to reject superstition. In their forewords publishers and editors, torn between rational scepticism and the profit motive, recognized the problem. In the introduction to his three-volume compendium, *Soothsay, do not Jest . . .* (1808), the editor Ivan Kurbatov argued in a clear case of wishful thinking that superstition in the enlightened nineteenth century was fading not merely among the educated but also among the simple folk. The purpose of his book, he declared, was to entertain. The unusually strong insistence on the essential frivolity of fortune-telling reflects Kurbatov's profession; as a teacher he was supposed to be in the vanguard of enlightenment. One can only assume that Mammon led him into publishing. The same sentiments appear in the introduction to the 1818 edition of *The Magic Mirror. . . .* Other editors could not decide whether to attract readers with promises of efficacy or pacify educated opinion, sometimes with ludicrous results. The introduction to the first dreambook (1768) declares that 'without doubt to believe in [the book's] predictions is a sign of utter superstitiousness', but, after adopting this enlightened stance, the editor then blots his copybook with the remark that from his own experience he knows the book 'very rarely makes an error in its predictions'! The conventional way of dealing with the problem was to assign books to the category of harmless entertainment.[31] On this level, they enjoyed widespread tolerance. Even the well-known and ostensibly sternly intellectual eighteenth-century writer Sumarokov turned his hand to a modest oraculum, *A Little Divinatory Book about Love,* compiled from couplets taken from his own verse tragedies. Expressly intended for fun, it supplied answers to the user's questions about her (or his) romantic prospects. Its success may be gauged from the four editions it enjoyed.

Disclaimers and justifications aimed at appeasing the censorious were occasionally omitted in the 1790s. They were probably redundant in cheap books, which, printed on rough paper with crude print and prose texts rather than verse couplets, were aimed at the less affluent and less well-educated reader. However, this omission also applies, though less frequently, to some of the more elegant books and expensive compendia: for example, a dreambook first published in 1799 not merely dispensed with a foreword full of excuses, but adopted a title boasting of its veracity: *A Dreambook, Telling Mother Truth.* The introductory quatrain assured the reader not only of value for money but also reliability:

> This Dreambook gives your dreams an honest explanation.
> Here's nothing but the truth, with no exaggeration.
> If you'll pay but fifteen farthings for it, why,
> This little book of dreams will serve you till you die.

It may be assumed that, in the case of cheap books, publishers felt they were unlikely to encounter serious objections from readers, while, in the case of the larger or finer editions, divinatory literature was becoming so accepted that apologies were no longer essential.

It does not follow that approval was universal. Far from it; superstition in its various manifestations is frequently condemned in eighteenth- and early nineteenth-century Russian letters, and fortune-telling books even in their guise as entertainment were not immune from mockery – witness the use of a dreambook as a symbol of ignorance by Izmailov. Officialdom disapproved of divination and magic, but as is clear from the Welfare Ordinance of 1782 (*Ustav blagochiniia*) instituting a government office concerned with public order and administration, professional dream diviners and fortune-tellers were the targets, rather than domestic fortune-telling activities. In the eighteenth century censorship never specifically targeted fortune-telling books, which suffered no more and no less than other books in times of exceptional official suspicion about the printed word. The sole instance of the banning of one of these books before 1840 occurred in 1828 when the censor I. I. Izmailov rejected *The Newest and Most Complete Interpreter of Dreams* on the grounds that 'such a book, even if presented as a jest without any pretensions, might perhaps have an impact on the weak, the uneducated and those of little faith'.[32] In other words, he was not convinced that such books were the harmless entertainment they had long pretended to be. The ban indicates how fortune-telling books were gradually losing the respect of the upper classes and sliding down the social scale; Izmailov would not have included noble readers among 'the weak and uneducated'. Nor was contempt for fortune-telling books the exclusive domain of the enlightened classes, though evidence of this is hard to come by. A semi-literate note penned by one Ery Kalkin on the end pages of a dreambook published in Kaluga in 1787 declares he had looked through the book 'only there weren't no truth in it' ('ia smotrel nytolko nechego neprav"da'). It is possible that he disapproved because the interpretations were not familiar oral ones, but more likely, his declaration is a rare example of an untutored sceptic's views. The gender attitudes that underlie it are examined in the next chapter.

Apart from the secular authorities, the Orthodox Church seems the obvious institution to wage warfare on fortune-telling books and beliefs in prediction. The presentation of fortune-telling books as harmless entertainment by their publishers could not have bamboozled them into ignoring the widespread ingrained attachment of Russians to various forms of divination. In fact, the Church seems to have taken virtually no interest in the eighteenth and early nineteenth centuries. Part of this was due, as already mentioned, to the appallingly low educational level among the lesser clergy; the village priest in Russia had long been the symbol of ignorance, drunkenness and avarice. The ecclesiastical hierarchy, drawn in the Orthodox Church from the monastic body, displayed a lack of vigour in the pursuit of good educational levels for the married white clergy. After a sluggish initial reaction to Westernization it had become too concerned by the end of the eighteenth century about the dangers of Western free-thinking to bother with superstition. Though fortune-telling books came to Russia along with Westernization and consequently might have been viewed as part of the dangerous flood of ideas and trends, their guise of harmless entertainment seems to have deflected unwelcome attention. Furthermore, as they were adopted by women, who were more devout than men as well as less educated and so, presumably, not so susceptible to dangerous ideas, they were even less likely to be seen as a threat.

The Church apart, by the 1820s hostility was more frequent and overt. The main complaint of detractors at this point concerned the negative effect fortune-telling books had on the market. The most vociferous critics were those with an interest in the promotion or publication of serious literature; for example, in 1824 Bulgarin deplored the public's preference for translated over native literature. If only, he lamented, they would buy Russian books rather than French. This would allow Russian books to go down in price, permitting booksellers to stop selling inferior products like dreambooks and songbooks.[33] Behind this comment on the book market lies a set of perceptions that were to become characteristic of the emergent intelligentsia. He is not simply making a plea for a larger market for Russian works including his own, but arguing from the position that the educated élite should defend cultural values, play the rôle of educator and foster a national literature. On the one hand Russian literature was squeezed by foreign literature, and on the other by popular trash. Pushkin, who loathed Bulgarin, shared his views in this instance, and they became commonplace among writers and thinkers. In the coming decades attitudes grew harsher and more entrenched. As the reading public expanded after 1830, and Romantic tolerance of 'superstition' was replaced by Slavophile respect for the supposedly purely national beliefs of the peasants, the climate for fortune-telling books, now regarded as products of a degraded urban culture, worsened markedly. In retrospect, the early period appears one of acceptance and tolerance.

After 1830 references to fortune-telling books disappear from literature with an upper-class setting, except as symbols of rural backwardness; in Nikolai Gogol''s story 'Ivan Fedorovich Shpon'ka and his auntie' (1832), the hopeless Shpon'ka reads nothing except his dreambook (which does not help him cope with his terrifying dreams of grotesque wives). Lavretskii's deceased aunt in Turgenev's *Home of the Gentry* (1859) owned only calendars and dreambooks, while the inhabitants of Dostoevskii's village of Stepanchikovo in the story of that name (1859) regularly read palms and cards. Memoirs reinforce this impression; at the end of the 1830s or in the early 1840s, N. S. Sokhanskaia, then a young woman stuck in a provincial backwater and desperate for some good reading, noted with dismay that even her family's miserable library was rich compared with the neighbours', who between them owned two books, a popular *lubok* chivalric tale and an *Oracle*.[34]

As readers from less affluent social groups took the place of aristocratic users of fortune-telling books, publishers responded by issuing shorter, cheaper books. Minor officials, shopkeepers, merchants, lower-middle-class urban dwellers and others discovered reading matter to fit their tastes and pockets. As the journal *The Reading Library* observed in 1843, 'books are being printed for servants, because there are more of them than there are masters'.[35] Just as *lubok* books had become the reading matter exclusively of the humblest readers in the course of the first few decades of the century, so now the market for printed books was fragmenting. It came as part of a general trend in which the cultural gulf between upper and lower classes was widening. Whereas, in the 1820s and 1830s, Tsar Nicholas I had paid visits to the fairground in the interests of *narodnost'* or national spirit, by the 1840s he and the élite classes as a whole had lost their taste for popular entertainments.[36] Publishers were increasingly catering for a socially segmented market. From 1860, as literacy spread among the urban poor and even touched the peasants, books reached these groups at prices far lower than could have been imagined in 1830.[37] By the Revolution peasants were buying more books than any other social group. Unfortunately, neither they nor urban lower- and middle-class readers were the sort to comment on their favourite reading or compile a catalogue of their libraries, and hence the social class of readers and their tastes mainly have to be deduced either from fortune-telling books themselves, their format, price, contents and presentation, or from comments, which, in the case of fortune-telling books, were overwhelmingly hostile.

As was discussed in chapter 1, the descent of fortune-telling books down the social scale resulted in the disappearance of expensive volumes as well as of omnibus editions before the 1890s. Instructions were reduced to a minimum, suggesting that readers were already familiar with the books' contents, and were not looking for novelty. Texts were often simple or abbreviated and, especially in the cheapest editions, lacked any introduction, unnecessary when purchasers were frequently barely literate and unlikely to struggle through a discussion of, say, the supposed scientific nature of dreams. Disclaimers, originally intended to ward off criticism, less from purchasers than from their family or friends, had by now ceased to be relevant or necessary. The rare instances of their retention are in books for the more affluent urban reader. Thus the editor of *The Most Complete Dreambook and*

Interpreter of Various Omens (1872, 1878 and 1891) informs the reader that he is publishing Tycho Brahe's table of lunar dreams 'more as a monument to the credulity of the mistrustful than as a guide to the conduct of life', while no doubt hoping that its inclusion would be a sales plus. The book is just as old-fashioned in its inclusion of a quatrain along the same lines as the comment above. In general, verse introductions are as rare as disclaimers, belonging exclusively to the more expensive volumes aimed at the urban middle-class reader. That 'expensive' no longer meant 'for the élite' is demonstrated by a comically inept verse in the introduction to *A Dreambook or Interpreter of Dreams. A Merry Tale-Teller for Old and Young*, 1858:

> Interpret your dreams if you will,
> But believe in them at your perĭl.

Only semi-educated readers with pretensions to refinement could have been impressed by such doggerel. The sentiments reflect the old presentation of fortune-telling as fun, which by then had virtually disappeared. In the thirties and early forties, a few titles such as *An Egyptian Oracle, or the General, Complete and Newest Divinatory Means, Providing People of Both Sexes with Innocent Amusement . . .* (Moscow, 1841) still emphasized this. However, since the title had been repeated verbatim from the first edition of 1796, what we have here is not an example of contemporary views of fortune-telling but evidence of the innate conservatism of publishers.

Though fortune-telling books ceased to be respectable among the upper classes, they were still treasured by some and familiar to everyone else, so much so that they were able to serve as a splendid vehicle for parody and satire. In 1857 N. F. Shcherbina, bucolic poet, critic and satirist, compiled a parodic *Dreambook of Contemporary Russian Literature Arranged in Alpabetical Order and Serving as an Essential Supplement to the Famous 'Dreambook of Martyn Zadeka'*, which declared itself 'the hundredth edition without changes, like everything else in God-preserved Russia'. The title page claimed the book had been printed in Suzdal′, one of the centres of *lubok* publishing, by the printers attached to the 'Committee for Popular Obscurantism', a distorted version of the name of the education ministry, the Committee for Popular Enlightenment.[38] Looking through the alphabetical list of literary figures, the reader could discover that dreams about censors meant incarceration in the madhouse, dreaming of the critic Bulgarin meant a beating and so on. The Slavophiles came off particularly badly. Here the satirical targets were not dreambooks, which functioned in their conventional rôle as symbols of backwardness, but the literary figures. What Shcherbina could count on was his readers' familiarity with, and amused contempt for, the satirical vehicle.

Similar attitudes underlie the comments made by the critic Vissarion Belinskii in a book review written in 1839.[39] The book was the latest edition of a volume that originally contained practically no divinatory component, but which, with time and a less well-educated publisher and public, had come to incorporate several fortune-telling texts; *The Newest and Most Complete Astronomical Telescope* . . . was an insult to the young intellectual critic with his passionate interest in art and its moral value. Having escaped the sort of background where fortune-telling was taken seriously, Belinskii was contemptuous of everything in the book, from its 'ungrammatical and vulgar title' to its crude style, its inclusion of two sections numbered seven, as well as the grotesque distortion of science in the astronomy section. For him it was a product typical of the urban lower-middle classes, and attractive only to the semi-educated. It was, in fact, a book for 'lackeys' as *The Reading Library* had scornfully termed lower-class urban readers. Though Belinskii's vehement contempt was fed by personal circumstances, it also epitomizes the growing distaste of the élite for popular culture. What is particularly interesting, however, is not so much his predictable scorn for a book which no intellectual would take seriously, but the very fact of a prominent critic (albeit an impoverished one) writing a review of it. Evidently, the book market had not fragmented to the point where books of this type would be ignored completely by journals, as happened later in the century.

Whereas Belinskii's main complaint is the sheer ignorance displayed by the editors of *The Astronomical Telescope*, later commentators were more concerned to deride readers and their tastes, and when fortune-telling manuals began reaching the peasantry, to worry about their moral impact. Ethnographers such as Tereshchenko particularly disliked them because they were not of the people like the folk belief he mainly wrote about. Their readers, he felt, should know better than to take them seriously.

Writing in 1848, he declared that many people turn to dreambooks and oracles to discover the meaning of their dreams, believing in them absolutely, and preferring them to any 'useful moral tome'. They 'are guided by these meaningless interpretations in any undertaking, preserving and guarding the book of dreams as though salvation of the soul lay within'.[40]

The ethnographer and folklorist, A. N. Afanas'ev, shared Tereshchenko's preference for oral over printed beliefs, but was less interested in castigating the morals of those who used fortune-telling guides. Instead he returned to an earlier focus of blame, the publishers. In the first chapter of his monumental work on Slav mythology and folk belief, *The Slavs' Poetic Views of Nature* (1865), Afanas'ev views dreams as a metaphorical language which the ancients had sought to decipher. Researchers, he urged, should seek vestiges of this antique skill 'in those out-of-the-way places, where literacy has not penetrated and where olden times are preserved intact'.[41] Such an approach was essential, Afanas'ev thought, because dreambooks with their utterly unreliable interpretations were in circulation among 'the poorly educated classes of society', and, horror of horrors, might reach the simple folk, where they would spread foolish ideas! Afanas'ev's hostility towards urban popular culture, together with the concept of the peasants as, on the one hand, children, but, on the other, bearers of a precious national tradition, are entirely conventional. They were standard among contemporary European folklorists, and shared by the Russian folklorists who succeeded him. In Russia they possessed additional resonances given the debate, then gathering force, about the economic and political need or otherwise of educating the peasantry. Afanas'ev goes on to criticize the publishers of dreambooks for not bothering to collect folk interpretations, which would have provided valuable scholarly material. Unfortunately, he remarked, 'the publication of dreambooks was always a business for speculators, who relied on the ignorance and simplicity of ordinary folk; in compiling their bulky volumes, they did not think of collecting what the folk really believe, but dreamt up their own interpretations and told lies . . .'.[42] Though this last comment fits the view of the degeneracy of popular printed culture, it is frankly disappointing coming from Afanas'ev, whose book on the Slavs' mythological views ranged well beyond Slav beliefs to encompass ancient Greek, Teutonic or Sanskrit myths.

The vast majority of the dreambooks which he dismisses so scathingly stem ultimately from ancient Greek or Assyrian tradition, and, as noted in chapter 1, may coincide with Russian folk interpretations. Nor can he be excused by suggesting that their origin was unknown. In 1861 M. S. Khotinskii had published a scholarly work on 'superstition', which, while condemning it as 'probably the most constant enemy of the human mind and happiness', noted the serious interest in dreams among the ancients and the popularity in Europe of dreambooks derived from their observations.[43] Afanas'ev, blinkered by his own belief in the myth of peasant purity and his fear of the contagion of popular printed culture, did not investigate the source of dreambooks. Even in the case of original Russian dreambooks, like the Kindly Old Man's which appeared two years before Afanas'ev's comments or O. Mil'chevskii's of 1869, the accusation of charlatanism is clearly without foundation. Both these compilers took their work very seriously.

By 1850 the idea that dreambooks and other fortune-telling books might be dangerous for the lower orders was gaining ground. The reason was not the folklorists' Romantic view that they supplanted or contaminated national folk beliefs, but that they counteracted efforts to lead the folk out of their state of superstitious ignorance. Tsar Nicholas I took a personal interest in censorship, especially after the revolutionary year of 1848. His channel of communication was the special Committee of 2 April 1848, which had been formed to oversee the work of all other censors. In 1850 the committee issued stern guidelines about the need for suitable books for the people. A new edition of *The Shop of All Delights . . .* was the first to fall foul of the rules. The committee turned to the Moscow censorship committee to find out why on earth the author should think that the stars influenced people's lives. The Moscow committee, which was better informed both about the book and the constant republication of fortune-telling texts, pointed out with irritation that this was the hundredth edition. It had no idea why the author held such views. Nicholas I, asked to adjudicate on the matter, replied that he saw 'no reason not to ban such books entirely from now on'.[44] The consequences of this dictum lasted close on a decade. Although the expensively produced *Eastern Planetary Oracle* appeared in Petersburg in 1851 and a new type of cartomantic guide similiarly designed for a urban clientèle in Moscow in 1852, presumably before the ban took complete effect, practically no fortune-telling books appeared until 1859, when, following the accession of Alexander II, the climate softened.[45] Given social attitudes of contempt or hostility, it is surprising that fortune-telling books did not run foul of the censors more often. Presumably, most censors regarded them as harmless, equating them with popular books, street shows and films which were little harassed by the censors before the Revolution.

As literacy and popular publishing expanded in the 1860s and 70s, fortune-telling books began to reach the peasants in ever increasing numbers. Educated observers lamented their popularity, noting that these standard items of the colporteur's box sold in their hundreds of thousands.[46] By the 1880s the readership of fortune-telling books was concentrated, though not exclusively, among the peasants and lower classes, where *Solomon* had long been known.[47] Certainly, by the Revolution fortune-telling guides, especially dreambooks and *Solomon*, had come to be seen as 'people's books', a term used to describe cheap literature held dear by the folk.

Educators argued that such books were popular because little had been achieved so far in the fight against superstition. In a popular work seeking to elucidate the true origins of dreams, N. Bukhalov noted that the untutored person always wanted to know what his dreams meant. Either he or she would turn to an old woman for advice or 'spend hard-earned pennies on a *Dreambook* (there are even books that interpret dreams!), and use that to work the answers out'. This solution was, in his view, even more lamentable. Despite the evidence of huge sales of fortune-telling books to newly literate peasants, he fell back on the mistaken nineteenth-century assumption that the mere existence of literacy would banish irrational beliefs, adding that 'the more outspoken literate person will declare dreams mere fantasy'.[48] One may add that his amazement that dreambooks existed indicates either a circle of acquaintances drawn almost entirely from the intelligentsia or a modest number of female friends, or both.

It was perhaps essential for those attempting to bring education to the peasants to subscribe to the view that they would abandon irrationality with the acquisition of literacy. Before them lay the example of the élite classes, whom education and social attitudes had gradually detached from their fortune-telling books. With the peasantry, many of whom needed persuading of the virtues of change, the process was going to be much slower. There was scant encouragement for those who considered the process under way in the last quarter of the century. Some writers of popular commercial fiction wrote stories debunking superstition, which would not have been published so frequently had they not found favour with the public.[49] On the other hand, how many of their readers took the point? Objectors from outside the intelligentsia seldom expressed their views. A rare exception to this was Roman B., an elderly peasant who told N. A. Rubakin, one of those who believed in the uplifting power of good books, that it was understandable why people valued such books. In his view, however, they were 'lies or more likely, a rip-off'.[50] Coming from a village not far from Petersburg, he may have been more sceptical than peasants from remote areas, though, on the other hand, as mentioned earlier, there had always been some sceptics, regardless of class.

Dreambooks and other divinatory texts had thus ceased to be a joke or harmless fun for the educated classes, and were increasingly viewed as an obstacle to progress. Particularly exercised were those involved in the movement to provide 'books for the people', that is, books combining entertainment and instruction for new readers. As the authors of a survey of books for popular reading in 1891–2 wrote, 'it is obvious how much books like this assist the development of superstitious attitudes among the folk'.[51] They were certainly exaggerating. The peasant magical world view permeated every aspect of life, and fortune-telling books simply replaced or added to the methods of tapping supernatural powers. The only senses in which they may have been right are, firstly, that, since print often carries the imprint of truth and authority, newly literate peasants accorded them considerable respect. Furthermore, long-standing perceptions of the connection between books and magic (the old Russian sorcerer was sometimes known as *chernoknizhnik*, one with a black book) probably also served to give fortune-telling books a degree of authority with some peasants.[52] If so, then the educators' concern was partly justified. Writing a few years later in 1899, V. P. Vakhterov lamented the lack of practical guides for the peasantry, who currently sought knowledge in the most futile places: 'from folk healers . . . sorcerers, wanderers, sectarians, in *lubok* books, oracles and dreambooks, in pagan traditions and beliefs'.[53] Rather than directing their anger against readers they thought had been duped, commentators preferred to point the finger at those publishers of whom more might be expected. E. Nekrasova found it particularly galling that Ivan Sytin still continued to put out rubbish about dream interpretation, cartomancy and love charms, despite his foray into publishing 'books for the people' with a discernible educational content.[54] In 1889 Kh. D. Alchevskaia condemned a book put out by the journal *The Soldier's Library*, which recounted the true story of a fortune-teller's accurate prediction. 'Don't the people already believe in all manner of happenings and predictions without this', she remarked with obvious revulsion.[55] It is noticeable that comment almost exclusively refers to the impact on the peasantry. The other groups who valued fortune-telling books were evidently believed beyond redemption.

In contrast to the fulminations of the intelligentsia, the Orthodox Church continued to ignore widespread divinatory beliefs and practices, though one of the problems facing the fight against superstition had ameliorated by the mid-nineteenth century. The education of priests had been formalized and improved, though some doubt on its effectiveness is cast by the writer Pomialovskii's horrifying picture of educational levels at the St Petersburg seminary where he had studied in the 1850s. Among other criticisms, he commented that the authorities did not combat superstition because they were not free of it themselves.[56] The chief enemies as far as the Church in the nineteenth century was concerned remained ideas that challenged faith and dogma: atheism, materialist philosophy and science on the one hand and Catholicism, Protestantism and the Old Believers on the other. The battle left no time for a struggle against peasant superstition. The peasants were not only resistant to change but also widely regarded as the most pious and true Orthodox believers. Even in the late nineteenth century the various popular journals put out by the Church made no mention of fortune-telling. It was left to the monastic community on Mount Athos to attempt to combat the widespread belief in dreams in a pamphlet that appeared in 1896.[57] Following ancient practice and dividing dreams into three types, those sent by God, by the Devil and ordinary natural dreams, the pamphlet pointed out the distinguishing features of the first two, and dismissed the others with the argument that dreams received differing interpretations from various specialists, and that often none of them turned out to be correct. Were they truly prophetic, interpretations would, it suggested, be both standard and reliable. Sensible though this advice was, it probably had little impact, like the pamphleteer's suggestion that, rather than visiting the folk healer or dream interpreter, the people should have recourse to a spiritual adviser or priest (since, as mentioned in chapter 2, the uneducated often viewed priests as seers and healers in any case).[58]

Thus by the time of the Revolution, fortune-telling books were objects of contempt. Since, as Jeffrey Brooks observes, 'many educated Russians were committed to a conception of cultural order according to which the lower classes would share in a culture common to all Russians',[59] fortune-telling books represented the worst of both worlds, seen by them as pandering to the primitive superstitiousness of the peasants, and doing so through the medium of enlightenment – print. Whereas Europe was developing cultural diversity, Russian educators and intellectuals were trying to reverse the trend, and restore the cultural unity lost with Westernization and Peter. Ironically they sought to replace a popular combination of Russian folk belief and commercial literature of Western origin with an élite culture which itself originated in the West (despite development on Russian soil). The new post-Revolutionary order simply continued the propensity of the Russian intelligentsia to patronize the lower orders.

The social history of attitudes to fortune-telling guides in Russia reveals a process of gradual descent down the social scale. Whereas in Western Europe simple fortune-telling texts had gradually lost prestige among the intellectual élite, becoming the property of a variety of other literate and semi-literate social groups by the late seventeenth century, in Russia the process replicates the West European experience, but compresses it into little more than a century. The attitudes of the educated classes in the eighteenth century began with general acceptance of the rôle of fortune-telling books in leisure activities. At the same time, the enormous popularity of texts suggests that they also performed a more important rôle in the lives of some. Widespread social acceptance helped avoid problems with the censors. By the 1820s, despite a flurry of interest from the Romantics, fortune-telling books were beginning to be attacked for distorting the book market. In the following decade they lost all respectability with the upper classes except in rural backwaters. Instead, they became the property of 'middle readers' and later also of the most modest urban readers, all without much comment from moralists and educators, who held urban popular culture in contempt, and ignored it like the censors. It would be simplistic, however, to suggest that pockets of support for fortune-telling did not remain in all classes. It was not just 'the people' who held store by dream and other divinatory beliefs. Despite the nineteenth-century emphasis on scientific method and rational explanation of events, all manner of divinatory practices flourished among those who might be presumed to have been educated away from them. Just as in the eighteenth century esoteric pseudo-sciences achieved social acceptability in élite circles, so from the 1850s those who craved new paths of revelation turned to spiritualism, and at the turn of the century to the occult. Those who preferred the familiar continued with their fortune-telling books.

As literacy levels rose and distribution networks strengthened, books filtered down to the peasants, the overwhelming majority of the population. Their attachment to divination ensured that they, like other groups before them, found the books both accessible and attractive. This development found virtually no response in the Orthodox Church or among censors. Educators, populists and others were outraged, but efforts to combat the supposedly pernicious influence of fortune-telling books undoubtedly had a limited effect before the Revolution. There had always been a few sceptics in the countryside, and, as social changes occurring in urban society filtered down to the countryside, these people found their position reinforced. The advent of the Revolution meant their victory and the demise of fortune-telling books, at least until 1987. It would be mere hypothesis to suggest that the shifts in attitude towards fortune-telling books would have been identical to those among the upper classes and then other literate groups. What can be confidently asserted, however, is that, whatever educators thought, universal literacy would not have banished fortune-telling books, had the Revolution not intervened. Divination in a modern society forms a sub-culture, little discussed but maintained by true believers with the half-hearted support of others who may dabble in fortune-telling for fun, or maintain a sneaking belief in its efficacy. The fate of fortune-telling in Russia since the Revolution, reviewed in chapter 8, shows this to be the case for Russia as well.

CHAPTER 4

Printers and publishers

In seventeenth-century England both Oxford and Cambridge University presses struggled to gain permission from the Crown to enter the lucrative market for almanacs in the hope of acquiring 'a dependable foundation on which to launch more ambitious and academic projects'.[1] With astrology, alchemy and some forms of divination still respectable, reputable publishers and readers with intellectual pretensions produced or consulted books on these subjects, though simplified versions were already being printed for the less sophisticated and affluent reader. By the eighteenth century the divinatory market had largely been taken over by numerous specialist popular publishers. In eighteenth-century Russia, by contrast, the situation could hardly have been more different. Publishing before 1755 was a monopoly of State, Church and Academy of Sciences and it was not until the 1750s and 1760s that Moscow University and the various cadet corps based in St Petersburg were permitted to open their own presses.[2] New publishing opportunities arose; between 1755 and 1775 'students, teachers and recent graduates simply took over most of the institutional publishing houses, and used them as staging grounds from which they could construct a congenial intellectual life for themselves'.[3] Even later, in 1783, Catherine the Great issued an edict at last permitting private individuals to own and operate printing presses. This measure resulted in a huge rise in the number of titles, though some sense of proportion is required here, since, as Max Okenfuss observes, 'when Russian publishers numbered at most a few dozen in the entire eighteenth century, Germany boasted hundreds at any one moment . . . In the last quarter of the century, in any three year period, as many titles appeared in Germany as in Russia in the entire century.'[4] The reading public remained tiny and the climate for publishing fluctuated. Nonetheless, albeit belatedly, a commercial publishing industry did emerge in Russia at the end of the eighteenth century, expanding through the nineteenth century as Russia began to overcome its cultural lag. Publishing was generally a chancy business, and publishers often welcomed the opportunity to make money from sure sellers like fortune-telling books. This chapter documents the history of this area of publishing while attempting answers to various questions. To what extent did Russian publishing houses use fortune-telling books as a way of subsidizing other publications and, if so, was this characteristic only of the early years when, as shown already, they attracted some interest from the relatively well-educated, or a consistent phenomenon? How was a changing readership reflected in the range of publishers and their wares, and how soon did specialist publishers of divinatory literature appear? Is the usual assumption that Moscow became the centre of cheap print only in the nineteenth century borne out by the evidence?

In the first half of the eighteenth century, of the three publishers only the Academy had any interest in indulging readers' tastes, and might possibly have thought of subsidizing other publications this way, as Oxford and Cambridge University presses had done earlier. Its situation dictated otherwise; the Academy was not only a fledgling institution, jealous of its intellectual prestige, but was until later in the century dominated by foreign, mainly German, scholars, in whose home environment fortune-telling books were no longer respectable. It is true that the Academy held a monopoly on the highly profitable business of publishing calendars, which might, because of the inclusion of some astrological elements, appear a concession to frivolity and commercialism, but in fact calendars were regarded as, and indeed largely were, serious publications and useful practical guides rather than divinatory items. Despite the success of their calendars, the Academy suffered constant financial problems, and once other institutions and individuals had begin publishing fortune-telling books, the Academy did occasionally swallow its intellectual pride. In 1774 it issued *The Oracles for the Current and Following Year.* Tucked away at the end was a calendar for 1774, which may have been as much an embarrassed attempt to supply something useful in an essentially frivolous book as a decision to assist sales by including an item of guaranteed popularity. Then in 1787 it brought out *A New and*

Most Reliable Means of Fortune-Telling, or The Prophet at New Year, deciding to produce it on writing paper because better quality books sold well. This assumption, however, proved wrong; after one year the book had to be discounted by twenty per cent and after another, by fifty per cent, with unsold stocks still remaining in 1791. Since fortune-telling books underwent multiple editions elsewhere, the reasons for this failure must lie in the distribution problems consistently facing the Academy throughout the eighteenth century. Not surprisingly, the experiment was not repeated.

It seems unlikely that in the 1760s and 1770s the university press in Moscow would be more interested in a book with an obvious popular appeal than the cadet presses in Petersburg. The latter published lighter reading; they were never at the forefront of intellectual activity, publishing books chosen and (usually) financed by the cadets themselves.[5] Despite this, their interests did not run to divination. Though a number of fortune-telling texts were printed at the presses of the Artillery, the Naval and the Infantry Corps, most of these appeared in the 1780s when private individuals had taken over institutional presses. Two possible reasons for the cadets' lack of interest in divinatory books spring to mind. Firstly, the climate in the official city of St Petersburg reflected Catherine the Great's interest in the development of serious reading matter in Russian, notably through the Society Striving for the Translation of Foreign Books into Russian, which she formed in 1768, as well as her distaste for superstition and divination which led to her making dream interpretation and a variety of magical practices criminal offences. Secondly, the young cadets may have regarded divination with contempt as, on the one hand, part of the old outmoded Russian way of life, and, on the other, a gendered activity, belonging to women's sphere (see chapter 5). Since they financed their own publications, they can have had little regard for or need to make a profit.

Far from spurning fortune-telling literature, between 1765 and 1779 Moscow University Press issued all ten of the earliest Russian fortune-telling books.[6] It might seem curious that Moscow University, which tended to publish more books of a serious nature than the cadet presses in Petersburg, should be the first to put its imprimatur on fortune-telling guides, which no supporter of the Enlightenment could defend. While they might have assisted in the creation of a pleasant social environment, they could hardly be said to contribute to a 'congenial intellectual life'. However, the decision should be placed in context. At this period, as indeed in the first half of the nineteenth century, Moscow University Press published more books than any other press in Russia apart from the Academy. Perhaps the Press would have equalled the Academy, had it not undergone a decline, lasting most of the 1770s, after the leading literati around Kheraskov departed to Petersburg, and then the city and all commercial life was devastated by an attack of the plague.[7] With a policy of publishing serious works and a large range of titles in the context of small numbers of readers, the University Press, like the Academy, found it hard to make ends meet, and the introduction of printed divinatory literature to Russia reflects economic demands coupled to a recognition of the potential popularity of such material. What prompted the choice of particular texts, the editor's personal inclination or simply the availability of a foreign edition or a manuscript version, cannot be determined, but the espousal of the genre was a clear attempt to introduce variety and with it greater sales. Thus the commercial strategy of an eighteenth-century Russian university press unwittingly mirrored that of its English counterparts more than a century before, leading to a situation where fortune-telling books published before 1783 almost all appeared in Moscow rather than Petersburg.

After private presses were licensed, the output of fortune-telling texts increased – to about four per year in the years 1785–96. Though official presses still issued the odd text, such as the 1787 guide mentioned above, it was mainly the burgeoning private printers who recognized a good commercial proposition when they saw one. Though some, like the Dutch printer Friedrich Hippius at the Moscow Senate Press (which issued an edition of the popular physiognomy/chiromancy text, *A Curious and Brief Elucidation of the Worthwhile Sciences of Physiognomy and Chiromancy* in 1781), or Okurokov (two at Moscow University Press (1791, 1793) and one at the Moscow Senate Press (1791)),[8] still leased institutional presses, most were private publishers using their own presses. Thus Hippius moved to his own press in 1783, where, in 1786, he put out another edition of the same book he had published in 1781, as well as a further text.[9] As Gary Marker observes of the private publishers: 'collectively they published over two-thirds of all Russian books in the last quarter of the century and nearly four-fifths of them between the proclamation of 1783 and the onset of censorship in 1795'.[10] Unsurprisingly, some disdained fortune-telling books; the writer Nikolai Novikov saw to it that after he took over at Moscow University Press no more appeared under its imprint. Similarly, the publishers I. V. Popov and P. P. Beketov both had strong literary leanings and made no pretence of being commercial publishers.[11] Nonetheless, just like Moscow University Press in the previous two decades, some serious publishers had no such scruples; Bogdanovich in Petersburg, for example, issued an elegant little oracle in 1791.[12] Indeed, the majority of publishers, whether foreigners or native Russians, serious or more commercially minded, brought out what was by now a popular and profitable category of book: Claudia (1788 and possibly 1789),[13] Rüdiger and Claudia (1795, 1796, 1798),[14] Schnorr (1795),[15] Henning (1784, 1785),[16] and Zederban (1793)[17] as well as Ovchinnikov (1786),[18] Zelennikov (two in 1794 on commission),[19] the Ponomarev brothers (1788),[20] Baturin in Kaluga (1787),[21] Okurokov (1791, 1793),[22] Selivanovskii (but not before 1811), the Glazunovs and Reshetnikov.

The same situation obtained right through to 1830, with only determinedly intellectual publishers resisting entirely the profitable blandishments of fortune-telling literature. The practice of leasing was to continue well into the nineteenth century; it is to be assumed, for example, that this explains the half-dozen fortune-telling guides published by the First Cadet Corps between 1805 and 1822. However, some less high-minded publishers also spurned divinatory books, though in many instances they were in business for such a short period of time that no conclusions about possible principled objections on their part can be drawn. Similarly, when the proportion of fortune-telling books in a publisher's output is very low, nothing can be stated with certainty about his attitudes; after all, though the Ponomarevs in Moscow produced one such book out of the 141 they published in the eighteenth century, it does not necessarily follow that they approved of fortune-telling books more than those who did not publish them at all. Nor does it indicate that the Ponomarevs can be regarded as more high-minded than, say, Bogdanovich (a mere couple of divinatory books out of a total of 123), especially when he, like many others, printed some books on order for other people. Only when figures represent sizeable proportions of the total number of books published can conclusions be drawn. On this basis, it can be said that most publishers put out some fortune-telling books before 1825, but equally that a degree of specialization was emerging, with three having the strongest commercial interest in this area: Sytin in Petersburg, the Glazunov firm in both Petersburg and Moscow, and Reshetnikov in Moscow.

Ivan Iakovlevich Sytin, no relation to the famous late nineteenth-century Muscovite publisher, Ivan Dmitrievich Sytin, published five fortune-telling books out of a total of fifty-nine books in the years 1791–96, and three more in 1801–2 on the press of the Smolensk Provincial Administration. The Glazunov family, who operated bookshops and printing presses in Moscow and Petersburg, survived as a firm up until the Revolution. In the first quarter of the nineteenth century they were second only to Reshetnikov in the production of fortune-telling books, including the popular omnibus editions which cost anything from two and a half to six rubles, a sizeable sum in those days.[23] The Moscow branch issued one in 1807, as well as commissioning others from other publishers in the 1790s and early years of the nineteenth century. Between 1817 and 1823 they published at least another eight, mainly in Petersburg .

Reshetnikov had begun his career in Moscow trimming the edges of fortune-telling cards.[24] In 1789 he opened his own press, only to have it closed in 1797. For a number of years between 1798 and 1816, he published books on the press of the Moscow Provincial Administration, but, following the lifting of the 1796 ban on private presses, in 1808 he also began operating his own. Closed in 1843, it restarted operations shortly afterwards under the management of his son. Out of a total of 220 books published by Reshetnikov between 1788 and 1797, eight were fortune-telling manuals,[25] to which may be added another twenty produced between 1799 and 1821 on one or other of his presses. Total figures of books published by Reshetnikov in this last period are not available, but, since the number he published from 1801 to 1843 was only 475, it must be assumed that fortune-telling books were more than a mere sideline. Some were certainly printed to order (both the 1799 and 1818 versions of *The Magic Mirror . . .* were for one of the Glazunov brothers), but it seems unlikely that all these would have been commissions; Reshetnikov very probably set out to supply the market and knew full well that he did not need commissions to be sure of covering his costs. As a consequence, he was the main publisher of the popular large – and hence relatively expensive – fortune-telling compendia in the first two decades of the century. When the figure of twenty-eight books published 1788–1821 is compared with the two published by René-Semen who was in business 1820–46 (one of which was an order from Matvei Glazunov), or three by another major publisher Selivanovskii (1811 and two in 1829), it is clear that Reshetnikov was the first publisher to specialize in divinatory literature, even though most of his business was with primers, textbooks and popular books on history.[26] Why he ceased to produce them after 1821 is a mystery, though one may hazard a guess that his son, who was better educated than he was, may have disapproved. Overall, partly as a result of this single firm's output, Moscow was even in the first decades of the nineteenth century on its way to becoming the centre for fortune-telling books.

In 1826 a harsh new censorship code was promulgated, which, though revised in 1828, caused a decline in the production of all books, divinatory literature included.[27] When the situation ameliorated in 1829–30, changes were evident, above all in the numbers of readers; the journalist Senkovskii estimated that the number had quadrupled in the decade from 1824.[28] Inevitably, new social groups had been drawn into the circle of book buyers. At the same time, as already noted, the social prestige of fortune-telling books was declining. The development coincided with a decisive shift towards Moscow as the centre of production, a position of pre-eminence it was not to lose before 1917.

Moscow had only Petersburg as a rival. Printing in the provinces was a rarity before the end of the nineteenth century. For example, taking the period 1826–60 for which figures are available, a mere 381 books of all kinds were published outside the two main cities and the university town of Kazan′.[29] Fortune-telling books conformed to this trend, with almost the only provincial publications a few from Smolensk in 1801–2 when private publishers were forced to find alternative ways of continuing their trade.[30]

In the eighteenth century Petersburg printed more books of any kind than Moscow, whereas in the first half of the nineteenth century, numbers were roughly equal even though there were more printing presses in Petersburg. It is usually assumed that Moscow became the centre for popular commercial publishing only in the second half of the nineteenth century. Comparisons between Moscow and Petersburg as centres for the publication of fortune-telling books reveals that, contrary to the evidence provided by overall totals for book production and common assumptions, Moscow was always more active in this area. Thanks largely to the sizeable number put out by Moscow University Press in the early years, the total number of fortune-telling books printed in Moscow in the eighteenth century outnumbers those produced in St Petersburg, just as the range of publishers who issued them was wider. As a city Moscow bore less of an official character, had fewer pretensions to sophistication and its booksellers and publishers, even at this period, possessed better rural distribution networks through colporteurs who carried cheap woodcut books and prints to country dwellers. What is more, a clear distinction in tastes, or more likely, what publishers thought the public in their city would buy is evident even in the eighteenth century; Petersburg publishers preferred books which were not strictly divinatory, such as conjuring tricks, trick arithmetic or weather predictions, which, when based on observation of natural phenomena, had greater claim to be termed scientific. In the first three decades of the nineteenth century, thanks largely to Reshetnikov, Moscow publishers put out about two and a half times more fortune-telling literature than Petersburg publishers.

In the following two decades (1830–50), six times as many emerged from Moscow presses. In Petersburg the best known publishers, Smirdin, Pliushar′, I. I. Glazunov, Isakov and Bazunov shunned this type of book, and no publisher specialized in this area. A considerable number, including Krai, Vingeber, Bocharov, Feiershtein and Zhernakov, published the occasional text. At least two were not simple reprints of old texts, but new editions with copious illustrations and assurances of their Parisian origin.[31] They, together with *The Book of Fate or The Fortune-Teller of the Drawing Room* (1843), suggest that Petersburg publishers continued to target a more genteel and almost entirely urban market, compared with their Muscovite counterparts, who went for multiple editions, reasonable prices and large sales to town and country. Thus the trends of 1765–1830, whereby Moscow produced more fortune-telling literature than Petersburg, were intensified between 1830 and 1850.[32]

Overall, about thirty different private presses operated in

Moscow in the first half of the nineteenth century, though not all at the same time of course, and some for relatively short periods. Two thirds, a higher proportion than in the eighteenth century, did not publish fortune-telling books at all. Since we already know that up to 1825 most did publish at least one fortune-telling book, these figures indicate how rapid was the move towards specialized markets after 1830 among private publishers.[33] The practice of printing to order continued. For example, a figure much involved in commissioning fortune-telling and other popular books in the second quarter of the nineteenth century was the bookseller V. V. Loginov, who ran stores in Kharkov and at six major fairs round the country.[34] He did not use his own press, and the extent to which he placed orders with institutional presses or with private publishers is unclear. The system of commissions or of leasing sometimes resulted in grotesqueries; in 1850 a chiromantic text was printed on the press belonging to the Moscow Police, and, even more ironically, in 1833, an edition of *Solomon* was printed on the press belonging to the Ministry of Education![35]

In general institutional presses printed fewer divinatory books after 1830, since the problems over the right to own private presses encountered before 1783, and briefly after 1796, no longer existed. Furthermore, the book trade was increasingly professionalized; printers knew their markets better, and the wealthy gentlemen-publishers, who in previous decades had leased presses as a way of contributing to the spread of enlightenment, but who sometimes needed a money-spinner, had turned their attentions elsewhere.[36] Some leasing continued; for example in the 1830s the Theatre Press in Moscow continued to be leased to I. I. Smirnov, a foremost publisher of fortune-telling books, who also operated his own press from 1835. Moscow University Press also reprinted two cheap cartomantic guides and a fortune-telling compendium in the 1830s. Since the press, the most prolific in Russia in the first half of the nineteenth century, was not leased out, it must be concluded that it took commissions and was not too fussy what they were.[37] The Academy of Sciences preserved its principles and its independence; only one book resembling a fortune-telling text appeared under its aegis, *The Characteristics of Man or the Simplest Means of Determining Character* (1839), and this was in fact a scientific treatment of physiognomy, evidently put out as a counterweight to popular books on the subject.

Much more surprising is the active rôle played by another institutional press – that belonging to the Lazarev Institute of Oriental Languages, the Armenian institute of higher education in Moscow. Its press opened in 1829 with the aim of producing books in Armenian. Initially supported by the Institute, it was soon obliged to cover its costs. This led to it being leased between 1846 and 1850 to V. K. Lukin, a man of decidedly popular tastes. One might expect the dozen fortune-telling books with the imprimatur of the Lazarev Institute to come from these four years, but this is not the case. Since the Institute, apart from books in Armenian, published large numbers of textbooks as well as literature, foreign language material and treatises on agriculture, the inclusion of fortune-telling literature is startling and can only be explained by the Institute's willingness to accept commissions that would help keep it afloat.[38]

There were twelve major private publishers in Moscow in the 1830s and 1840s: Selivanovskii, Reshetnikov, René-Semen, Ponomarev, Kol'chugin, Shiriaev, the Salaev brothers, the Kuznetsov brothers, the Evreinov brothers, the Stepanovs, Kirillov and Smirnov. As fortune-telling descended the social scale, the first four, who had all published such books in the 1820s or earlier, stopped doing so. The next three, Kol'chugin, Shiriaev and the Salaevs, were interested in serious literature and more expensive editions, and did not in any case publish huge quantities of books. The Kuznetsov brothers, whose press operated from 1820 to 1833, also specialized in literature though they did publish one dream-book in 1831.[39]

The remaining four effectively cornered the market. Their humble social backgrounds naturally pushed them in that direction, as it had Glazunov and Reshetnikov in the first quarter of the nineteenth century, that is until they moved up in the world. The critic Vissarion Belinskii sneered at the compilers of such books, in many instances the publishers themselves, in his review of *The Newest and Most Complete Astronomical Telescope* (1839).[40] In comments which indicate the low status of those associated with the production of fortune-telling books by then, he describes the style and language of the book as a ludicrous example of *frizovii* language, which he explains as deriving from the word 'frieze', referring to the cheap woollen cloth from which their overcoats were made. Such people, he added contemptuously, only wash and shave on Sundays, and like taking snuff.

Whatever their common bathing habits, these publishers did

not occupy indentical niches in the market. From the moment they set up in 1836 Aleksei and Sergei Evreinov declared that they were publishing 'entertaining literature for the bored landowner on his estate'.[41] They simultaneously, however, printed very cheap books and *lubok* pictures for sale to the poorest urban readers (tradesmen, house serfs, for example) and some peasants, and their dreambooks and other fortune-telling books were probably designed as much for this group as the provincial gentry. In particular, their *Solomon,* which cost only fifty or sixty kopecks a copy, was the first to rival the appeal and low cost of the woodcut *Solomon.*

The Evreinovs were not the most prolific publishers of divinatory literature at this time. Stepanov's press, which began printing in 1827, was altogether a larger operation, issuing 800 books by 1850 as well as Nadezhdin's journal *The Telescope.* It published good quality literature as well as primers, medical books and housekeeping guides.[42] Nonetheless, between 1829 and 1845, T. N. Stepanov and his son Nikolai produced around twenty fortune-telling books. Whether the volume so despised by Belinskii, which came out under Nikolai Stepanov's name, was printed on the main Stepanov press is unclear, but it is likely that father and son enjoyed a period of cooperation. Some of the Stepanovs' books were cheap editions of *Solomon,* but if the edition of 1844 is anything to judge by, at a ruble a copy, these were better produced books and even less likely to be sold to peasants and the poorest townsfolk than the Evreinovs' versions. This would seem to be confirmed when it is noted that most of Stepanov's books cost one ruble, with the exception of a bulky fortune-telling compendium which ran to three editions and cost two rubles.[43] A number were reprints of books originally published in the late eighteenth or early nineteenth centuries. It seems likely that while the Evreinovs were more interested in the rural market at various levels, Stepanov and son catered for the urban market apart from the poorest readers.

Kirillov's press opened in 1836, and by 1850 had published around four hundred books.[44] It openly specialized in books for the less sophisticated reader, such as practical guides to mushroom identification or gardening, folk tales, popular fiction and the works of certain Russian writers. At least thirteen fortune-telling books were produced, including a number of editions of *Solomon,* and a version of *The Shop of All Delights.* Though some books, priced at one ruble, were aimed at the urban middle-class reader, one written by Fedor Kuzmichev, a writer of cheap literature, and entitled *The Miraculous Diviner Reveals Your Thoughts,* sold for a mere thirty kopecks.[45]

The last significant publisher of fortune-telling books, Smirnov, began, as already mentioned, at the Theatre Press but opened his own in 1836, printing around 340 books from 1836 to 1850, including at least a dozen fortune-telling books, mainly dreambooks. What information is available about the prices of his books suggests that they cost one or one and a half rubles, and did not include *Solomon.* He therefore, like the Stepanov firm, catered for the urban middle-class market.

Of the many minor publishers, only one, the little-known publishing house of Khavskii, attempted fortune-telling literature, issuing a dreambook in the late 1830s. Perhaps more might have prospered had they done so.

Although there is no evidence that books became cheaper over the period 1830–50, the new readership clearly favoured books at affordable prices. Expensive items like the set of divinatory cards produced in Petersburg in 1830, *The Complete Fortune-Telling Cards or A New Revelation of the Secrets of Cartomancy,* which cost a staggering twenty-five rubles a set, were the last of their kind. Nonetheless, as has been seen, relatively few of the publishers of the period 1830–50 attempted to cater for the poorest market of urban workers and peasants, doubtless because production costs, and hence prices, were generally too high and literacy levels too low. Furthermore, producers of *lubok* pictures and books may well have dominated the modest colporteur system.

After the ban on fortune-telling books following the tsar's comments in 1850 (see chapter 3), few fortune-telling books saw light of day until the very end of the decade. Those that did tended to be produced in Petersburg, where the censors were, evidently, less vigilant. By contrast, after 1860 the quantity of fortune-telling literature increased dramatically, a development in line with changes in popular publishing as a whole. The rapid development of the system of colporteurs, technical advances in printing, and the growth of literacy in the countryside following the emancipation of the serfs in 1861, all led to expansion. Over the next four decades, more than a hundred publishers vigorously competed to supply this market.[46] Dostoevskii's journal *Time* noted that 1861 saw the appearance of a huge number of fortune-telling books, cards, dreambooks, horoscopes and chiromantic guides in brightly coloured wrappers and with enticing titles.[47] In 1894 alone, seventy-two cheap books of a practical nature (calendars, writing guides and fortune-telling books) were published in a total of 859,560 copies. They constituted ten per cent of the total number of cheap books, of which a further third were books with a religious or moral content.[48]

After 1860, numerous publishers catered exclusively for the expanding peasant readership. It is usual to divide them into those who published the traditional material of cheap commercial publishers, the chivalric tales and the adventures of the bandit, Van'ka Kain, and those who preferred newer forms of fiction that more closely reflected current concerns of the newly literate reader.[49] Such a distinction has little validity in the case of fortune-telling books. Both types published the well-known types of text (see chapter 1), indicating that in this respect the publishers who brought in new types of fiction were totally traditional. As Blium observes: 'every *lubok* publisher, along with didactic-religious books and fiction considered it his duty to publish a variety of guides and handbooks essential in everyday life'. Such essentials included fortune-telling books.[50] On the other hand, the alternative division of publishers into those who provided for the cheap urban market and those who concentrated on the countryside is more useful. While publishers for the rural market stuck to tried and tested material, as shown in chapter 1, a few of those who targeted the urban popular market above the cheapest level brought out innovatory texts.

In the second half of the century, the publishing trends of the 1830s and 1840s in Moscow and Petersburg considerably intensified; St Petersburg supplied the middle- and lower-class city dweller, and made little use of the colporteur system. In 1893 a survey by the Literacy Committee of the Imperial Agricultural Society in Moscow observed that 'comparing the activities of Moscow and Petersburg popular publishers, we may observe that the Petersburg publishers adhere to the old traditions of the *lubok* market less firmly. We find neither chivalric tales, nor dreambooks and writing guides, nor the tales of Bova and Eruslan.'[51] Most cheap books had to be brought in from Moscow, giving rise to the term 'Moscow wares' for the contents of two shops in the Apraksin Market.[52] Despite this comment, a few publishers of cheap literature, such as Kholmushin, were based in Petersburg. After a modest beginning, trading on a mat laid out at Apraksin Market, Kholmushin prospered and by the 1850s he had a sizeable shop, in which he sold cheap books from Moscow. He left his shop to a relative, Shataev, whom he had encouraged to go into publishing.[53] Shataev, evidently determined to rival Moscow, printed several editions of a misleadingly entitled little book, *The Most Complete Dreambook and Interpreter of Various Portents.* At twenty kopecks it was obviously designed for the poorest end of the market, though without a developed colporteur system, sales were bound to be limited to peasants from nearby villages and poor workers. When Shataev died, the business was inherited by another Kholmushin, who seems to have recognized the futility of trying to compete with Moscow publishers at the bottom end of the market. The family firm continued into the second decade of the twentieth century, targeting the urban reader with a few more kopecks to spare. Its range included multiple editions of fortune-telling books as well as a reprint of a lengthy dreambook popular in the first two decades of the nineteenth century. At 320 pages, this was beyond the reach of many pockets.[54]

Despite ignoring the growing peasant market, a considerable number of publishers in Petersburg did issue fortune-telling books in the second half of the nineteenth century. Recognizing the need to make books attractive to more affluent and educated urban readers, they adopted the strategy of promoting either new types of book, or attractive editions or both. Thus Ia. Trei's *Eastern Oracle of the Planets* (1851) had twenty-one lithograph engravings and was a new type of book, claiming to be a translation of a Persian manuscript. Iu. Strauf, who put out the dream interpretations of the Kindly Old Man from Duck Street, doubtless had similar aims.[55] Urban readers and users of fortune-telling books were, as argued in chapter 1, less conservative than the country dwellers who would buy the cheapest books from a colporteur from Moscow. Change was likely to attract rather than repel them – hence the considerable variety in the types of text published in Petersburg. Thus in 1883 Mikheev printed 6,000 copies of a book on card tricks, to which he appended a section on spiritualism. As occultism came into vogue in the late nineteenth century,

Petersburg publishers responded quickly; Demakov on behalf of the journal *Rebus* published a couple of books about the rebus (1883, 1885), while D. A. Naumov and the Literary Bookstore (Literaturnaia knizhnaia lavka) put out books on tarot in 1912 and 1917 respectively. Prices were also fixed in a way that showed sensitivity to the market: in the 1880s, when fortune-telling books from Moscow cost from five to twenty kopecks, the books produced by Petersburg publishers like Transhel′, Shaikevich, Pozdniakov and Rumsh cost between fifty kopecks and one ruble. When it is also borne in mind that print runs in St Petersburg (averaging 3,000–5,000) were considerably lower than in Moscow, where the reissuing of popular texts was an almost annual affair, it is clear that the customers who purchased Petersburg publications were not only more affluent, but fewer in number, and that publishers were sensitive to this.

In Moscow, where cheap publishing was centred on the Nikolskaia Street, particularly around Vladimir Proezd, near the Vladimir Church and the Trinity Fields, there were, as in Petersburg, publishers, such as Presnov, Leukhin, Manukhin and Zemskii, catering for the urban market. Only two, Leukhin and Zemskii, neither of whom produced much fortune-telling material, showed the slightest interest in innovation. They published for the semi-educated, gullible reader, who was less well-off than those targeted by their Petersburg counterparts. They were not averse to a few sharp marketing tricks. Leukhin employed cunning ruses to sell to the naive, for example putting out works by total unknowns, who happened to have famous names like Pushkin, while Zemskii saw no problem in including his own poems in a collection of Pushkin, Lermontov and Kol′tsov.[56] His attitude to his customers is epitomized in the following anecdote: his earliest publication was a volume, enticingly entitled *The Domestic Magic Book of Akhnazarus Tovius of Moldavia*, which promised to help the reader transform his or her home into an enchanted castle.[57] When, in 1917, readers complained to a newspaper that it did not work, Zemskii cheekily replied that the book had helped him at least acquire a nice big house![58] D. I. Presnov, whose career, like Kholmushin's, began with selling books in the 1840s, preferred to make exaggerated claims for his books; *The Seer and Prophet in Your Drawing Room* (1874), for example, informed the potential purchaser that it included more than one thousand illustrations, and an 1891 dreambook that it contained interpretations of one million, two hundred thousand dreams. Both estimates were considerably inflated. Despite this, Presnov was, perhaps, from an older, more scrupulous generation than Leukhin and Zemskii – exaggeration, if not of the numerical kind, had, after all, been found in titles of fortune-telling books from the eighteenth century on. And, just as Presnov indulged in exaggeration of a traditional kind, so his range of fortune-telling books was designed for the conservative reader. Thus, in the 1870s Presnov put out a throwback to the early years of the nineteenth century, a Bruce calendar and guide to physiognomy and chiromancy. This had a print run of 12,000 and cost a ruble. It indicates that there was a substantial market for a more expensive but familiar type of book. Manukhin, another popular publisher about whom little is known, published a similar range of familiar material in multiple editions: a book on Yuletide divination and chiromancy and *An Interpretive Dreambook* (or *A New Interpretive Dreambook*), *a Collection of Interpretations of Various Dreams from the Experience of my Hundred-Year-Old Relatives.* In 1882, its third edition had sixty-four pages, cost thirty kopecks and had a print run of 10,000.

Apart from supplying customers with a little more money to spare, Manukhin and Presnov also produced books at rock-bottom prices. The introduction of rotary presses in the 1870s and the rapid development of the colporteur system which now reached all except the deepest backwaters of Russia allowed a number of firms to prosper selling really cheap books, which always included fortune-telling guides. Of those operating in the 1870s only one, Smirnov, had been in business before 1850, publishing the prototype of the small Martyn Zadeka dreambook in 1848 (8th edition 1877),[59] as well as several editions of a book on Yuletide divination in the 1860s.[60] Every publisher produced at least one multi-edition cheap dreambook, which by this time had become the most popular type of divinatory literature, happily pirated from a competitor: for example, through the seventies, eighties and nineties, Ioganson and Manukhin published the same dreambook, while the Filatov firm took over the title favoured by Abramov and was still publishing it in 1915. By the 1890s prices had fallen to one and a half kopecks for a small book. The more successful firms at the end of the nineteenth century produced not only these short, cheap texts but also those of varying lengths for the more affluent, with, from about 1890, increasing numbers of fortune-telling compendia with a couple of hundred pages or more. For example, Konovalov, and later his widow, sold just such a range so effectively that the firm became the chief rival to Sytin in the first decade of the twentieth century, that is, until 1913 when Konovalova was forced to sell out to him.[61] The success of some publishers may be gauged by noting that Abramov's turnover in the 1880s was 200,000 rubles.[62]

The activities of these late nineteenth-century publishers have been relatively little studied because of the enduring contempt in Russia for popular commercial publishing, especially from the last years of the Russian Empire, but something is known of a few. Most were poor peasants made good. One of those who can be classified as the conservative type of publisher is I. A. Morozov, who came to Moscow from Tver′ as an illiterate peasant. From peddling various goods on the streets of the city he moved to pictures, and after the Crimean war into *lubok* prints and traditional people's books – saints' lives, tales and fortune-telling books. By the 1870s, still semi-literate, he had acquired the goods and trappings of a Moscow merchant.[63] E. A. Gubanov, on the other hand, was the type of popular publisher willing to take chances with new material, especially fiction. Originally from Tver′, he began as a horse doctor before becoming a colporteur, then a bookseller in Moscow and finally a publisher of prints and cheap commercial literature in both Moscow and Kiev.[64] The Kiev branch lasted until the Revolution. Whatever the novelty or conservatism of the fictional material they published, both put out traditional fortune-telling texts, such as the Bruce calendar (both had editions in 1883) and dreambooks large and small. In the 1880s, Gubanov was as successful as the most famous of the popular publishers, Sytin.

No discussion of popular publishers is complete without a consideration of the career of Ivan Dmitrievich Sytin.[65] Like Morozov and Gubanov he was of peasant stock, but, unlike them, came from a literate family and had received some schooling. Young Ivan went to Moscow to work for one of the conservative publishers, P. N. Sharapov, who, apart from the usual religious texts and chivalric romances, published, or more frequently, republished, fortune-telling texts like the *Newest Complete Oracle, Divining and Predicting with Clear Answers the Fate of Young Lads and Lassies . . .*, 156 pages, 1875, an exact copy of the fortune-telling handbook regularly issued by the firm of Smirnov. Conservative though he may have been in terms of choice of material, Sharapov was clearly attuned to the developing peasant market, since in 1877 he produced two more editions of the above title, heavily abbreviated to one printer's sheet or thirty-two pages. He also regularly published dreambooks, varying in length from thirty-five to forty-eight or seventy-two pages. His success with the distribution system of colporteurs may be measured by the number with whom he had contact – up to five hundred.[66] Sytin's energy and enterprise soon won over Sharapov. In 1882 he opened a shop on his own by the Il'inskii gates, near the one in which he had worked as an apprentice. Rapid expansion followed; turnover was 200,000 rubles in 1883, 585,000 ten years later and 8 million in 1913. Efficient production and marketing, including the further development of Sharapov's network of pedlars, allowed Sytin to undercut his rivals' prices and ultimately to drive them out of business.

Sytin's claim to fame, however, rests on his unique achievement among publishers of cheap literature (people's books) in breaking into the world of respectability through his involvement with the publication of edifying texts for the peasants (books for the people), as well as school textbooks and newspapers. Was his promotion of good books for peasants, which he financed through his commercial publishing activities, merely a cynical ploy designed to ensure his acceptance by intelligentsia and establishment? Or was it the result of a genuine desire to bring education to the peasants, even though he himself was the prime supplier of those fortune-telling and other cheap books that, in the educators' views, undermined their efforts?[67] Commentators have disagreed. In his biography of Sytin, Charles Ruud is inclined to give him the benefit of the doubt, but in so doing tends to overlook just how much cheap literature Sytin continued to print and sell in the twenty years before the Revolution. By 1916 he held a virtual monopoly on the trade, such that at the 1915 fair at Nizhnii Novgorod only one other publisher displayed printed material.[68] There were others like Bel'tsov, Starye zavety and Filatov still in business, but on a much more modest level. Sytin never gave up what was the backbone of his business, fortune-telling books and cheap fiction.

It seems likely that Sytin himself felt extremely uneasy about the bedrock of his publishing success, for in his catalogue for 1900 he fails to mention 'people's books' (*narodnye knizhki*) at all.[69] By 1910, when a survey of the publishing activities of Sytin and Co. was published, he could not avoid including a section on 'people's literature', but he took care to tuck it away at the back.[70] Improving moral and religious reading came first, followed by a section on 'belles lettres', emphasizing good literature both Russian and foreign. Next came a brief discussion of the popular chivalric tales, which were defended on the grounds that they were better than current pulp detective fiction. At the end came the following comment: 'It is impossible not to note such relatively important activities as the publication of oracles, dreambooks, manuals of letter writing and songbooks.' While the last two, it declares, can be defended on the grounds that they introduce serious material and good poetry as song lyrics, the former are produced in order to satisfy what is still a very buoyant demand from the people. Sytin had stopped pretending the business of printing fortune-telling books did not exist, but could not find any justification other than the satisfaction of the market, not a defence likely to appeal to the Tolstoians or other intellectuals and educators.

The demand to which Sytin refers must, however, have been considerable, since the catalogue for 1914 lists no less than fifteen fortune-telling books.[71] For the better-off reader there were five different compendia, either called an oracle of some kind or a dreambook with other sections appended (cartomancy, chiromancy, physiognomy, coffee grounds or bean divination) as well as two lengthy detailed dreambooks.The longest at 716 pages cost one and a half rubles in hardback, those between two and three hundred pages cost thirty or fifty kopecks, and those between one and two hundred pages ten or fifteen kopecks. For the cheap end of the market there were three ninety-six-page books (an *Astrologer*, a *Dreambook* and an *Oracle*) at five kopecks each, a sixty-four-page dreambook at three kopecks, and an oracle and a dreambook of thirty-two pages each at one kopeck. Apart from this, Sytin was selling copies of the famous Bruce calendar at fifteen kopecks and *Solomon* in broadsheet form costing forty-five kopecks per hundred copies wholesale. It will be remembered that this last item cost between fifty kopecks and one ruble in the 1830s, a measure of how technology and a mass market had driven down prices. With this range of books Sytin could cover the demands of a voracious public, whether urban dwellers or by now mainly rural folk. If they could afford books, they could afford his. He knew his market, knew its innate conservatism and made no attempt to produce any fortune-telling text whose popularity was not tried and tested. There is little doubt that they were money-spinners – Sytin's term 'relatively important' is more than a little disingenuous. Doubtless, with his social pretensions, he would have given them up if he thought he could have afforded to, but the businessman in him knew he could not.

Thus the period from 1860 saw extraordinary expansion in the market for cheap commercial literature in general and for fortune-telling books for urban and rural readers in particular. This resulted in reduced prices, larger print runs, a more varied range of books as well as the concentration of activities in Moscow. At the same time it saw the development of some printing of fortune-telling literature in the provinces. Apart from Gubanov, there was also Barskii in Kiev in the 1880s and 1890s (cartomancy guides), Iakobson in Riga (a cartomancy guide in 1886 at twenty-five kopecks in a print run of 3,000), Sh. Neiman in Pskov (*Morpheus – Interpreter of Dreams in Alphabetical Order*, 1876), and at the opposite end of the market, a couple of Muslim dreambooks, published by Kazan′ University Press in 1901–2. In the 1860s and 1870s before advances in printing made engraved books uneconomic, multiple editions of an eight-page lithographed *lubok* booklet *Dreambook with 215 Dreams* were produced in Mstera. The town was famed for the production of icons and *lubok* prints, and the area was home to thousands of colporteurs. Mstera productions thus had a ready-made distribution system, which would not have been the case for other towns, though Kiev must have developed one. How well provincial editions sold is not known.[72]

There were more than a hundred publishers of cheap literature in Russia in the last four decades of the nineteenth century, though many operated mainly as booksellers. Blium's declaration that they all produced fortune-telling literature cannot be verified, firstly because few books survive, in some instances, perhaps, because they were treated with scorn, in others because they were used to destruction. Furthermore, the books produced by many small and even larger publishers did not get placed on deposit in libraries, as the law demanded, or have not survived once there. Certainly well over fifty publishers of dreambooks, oracles and the like were active in this period, and even newspapers like the

Petersburg *Russian Reading* or *Sport and Science* in Odessa published dreambooks.

The popularity of fortune-telling books was phenomenal. Granted Russia was huge, but with literacy in the country still so low by the time of the Revolution, the torrent produced suggests that a high proportion of the literate or semi-literate owned one. Overall, the numbers produced do not rival the figures for cheap fiction, but it must be borne in mind that fiction was much more varied, and a reader who had enjoyed one story might well be tempted into buying another. Fortune-telling books, by contrast, satisfied a long-term demand. A reader might buy a replacement when a much used guide was worn out, or opt to put an *Oracle* on the shelf along with her (or his) dreambook, but was unlikely to make many purchases of variant texts.

It may be concluded that the practice of subsidizing serious publications through fortune-telling literature was even more characteristic of Sytin than of the early publishers operating in a largely socially undifferentiated market before 1830. Sytin was, however, the exception in his day. As the market expanded during the course of the nineteenth century, specialist publishers appeared in Moscow, who concentrated on the cheap market and had no interest in publishing good books. Almost all of them published fortune-telling material regardless of how conservative their publishing policy was in other areas. Texts were tried and tested, and demand from a conservative public constantly grew. Many publishers also produced longer and more detailed books for urban and rural dwellers who had more kopecks in their purses. The publishing of fortune-telling books was a thriving business by the Revolution, but one which could not survive in the new climate.

CHAPTER 5

Women, men and domestic fortune-telling

Today, as in the eighteenth and nineteenth centuries, the devotees of fortune-telling books are assumed to be mainly women. Such an assumption needs testing for Russia before gender and fortune-telling can be considered. In seeking to do so, the problem of sources becomes acute. As I remarked in the introduction, the study of fortune-telling is itself fraught with difficulties, but where it relates to women, these are multiplied. The factors that consigned fortune-telling to virtual scholarly oblivion were compounded in this instance by the entrenched view of men as logical creatures and women as vessels of the irrational. Such attitudes further marginalized fortune-telling by assigning it to the negative female side of the human personality. They led, firstly, to a paucity of comment on fortune-telling as a women's skill and, secondly, to jaundiced observation. What published material does exist is almost entirely male-authored, and as such, presented with deprecating or even hostile comment. Most commentators, even when they turned their attention to fortune-telling, did not overtly refer to the gender of its practitioners or votaries, which must therefore be deduced from throwaway remarks or insinuations.

Nor did women commentators pay any greater or more sympathetic attention to fortune-telling. All over Europe, educated women shared the views of men; in 1792, Mary Wollstonecraft had cited a belief in divination as an instance 'of the folly which the ignorance of women generates'.[1] In Russia, the well-meaning women attempting to bring education to the peasants in the last decades of the nineteenth century took the same line as their male colleagues in considering fortune-telling books worthless. Such comments are rare in themselves, for when women ethnographers emerged in the late nineteenth century, they largely ignored the subject. The absence of references to fortune-telling in their writings, as well as its virtual disregard in women's memoirs and fiction, stem from educated women's desire to escape female stereotypes, and demonstrate the benefits of a rigorous education for the gentler sex. Catriona Kelly has argued that the general understanding of street and courtyard culture as vulgar precluded its appearance in the writing of women 'which had, since the late eighteenth century at the latest, been associated with refinement and gentility'.[2] The neglect of fortune-telling by women writers came about, I would suggest, for different reasons. Far from being seen as vulgar, fortune-telling, which was often conducted in drawing rooms by genteel ladies, was neglected because of its perceived connections with stereotypes of women as frivolous and irrational. Women writers were keen to escape any such associations. They would naturally have tended to be, if anything, more hostile to irrational superstition than their male counterparts, simply because they felt threatened by potential accusations of ignorance and irrationality. Sokhanskaia's disgust at discovering, in the late 1830s or early 1840s, that her provincial neighbours owned two books between them, one a fortune-telling manual, exemplifies this attitude.[3] Apart from Sokhanskaia's derogatory observation and a casual comment in Mariia Tsebrikova's story 'Which one is better?', women writers in the eighteenth and nineteenth centuries paid no attention to fortune-telling in an urban and literate environment. Far more challenging and interesting intellectual topics existed for those escaping stereotyping.[4]

In trying to establish the validity of the claim that fortune-telling was part of women's sphere, it may be argued that, in view of the gender-specific social factors surrounding fortune-telling, the absence of comment by women ethnographers and writers, paradoxically, reinforces the suggestion that the phenomenon was indeed a despised part of women's culture. Demonstrating this leads to consideration of the extent of male interest and involvement in domestic fortune-telling at various stages from 1760 to 1917. Since the books replaced rural tradition, it may be asked whether male and female participation mirrored traditional practice, or whether the function of fortune-telling books in an urban/literate social context changed. What were the strategies adopted in the transferral of divination to an urban environment? Does women's continuing attachment to fortune-telling merely indicate cultural backwardness and a passive approach to life? Such questions follow inevitably from the examination of gender involvement in fortune-telling. Gender issues as they relate to professional fortune-tellers are discussed in chapter 6. Here the focus is on fortune-telling books and domestic practice based on them.

Perhaps the first step in presenting the case for fortune-telling as a primarily female preoccupation and skill is to place it in its wider context. General as well as historical factors support the contention that fortune-telling was associated with women's culture. Part of the argument has already been rehearsed in chapter 2, and may be summarized here. Traditionally, women have been accorded the home as their sphere of influence. This involves what has been called kin-work, the maintenance of family and community structures and concern for their welfare. In traditional society the functions of divination were closely connected to family and community wellbeing, with important times in the individual's life accompanied by prognostication.

Gender participation in divination in traditional Russian society corresponds closely to this general situation. As was seen in chapter 2, divination formed an integral part of the peasants' belief system. Both sexes were involved in everyday as well as specialist divination; women's area was personal and household divination. On a regular day-to-day basis, they interpreted the meaning of domestic omens, elucidated family members' dreams and participated in divinatory rituals at festivities and on other occasions. Both male and female magic specialists made predictions about the fate of individuals, though women predominated where the curing/caring rôle was involved (as folk healers, midwives).[5] Divination may be categorized as part of the problem-solving activities in village life, and possessed, as was seen in chapter 2, functions ranging from the provision of merriment to group, family or community bonding, a sense of control over life as well as individual emotional relief and consolation. For this it was valued, though it did not, of course, prevent men making deprecating remarks about women's activities and perceived attributes, just as village women did about their men.[6] Thus in Russian peasant society every adult was both the recipient of predictions and prognosticator, though many men probably restricted themselves to the interpretation of omens and signs of various kinds.

For women, by contrast, divination, in which they were actively involved, was an integral part of their lives.

Upon their removal to towns or transfer to the realm of the literate, both men and women were gradually cut off from divinatory beliefs, but this loss was greater for women, whose rôle in the community depended more on this than did men's. Pressure to reject superstition, it has already been argued, went hand in hand in the eighteenth century with a belief that man could, through education and rational thinking, 'recognize his own nature and destiny, and, in so doing, possess the key to public and private happiness'.[7] In the nineteenth century, divinatory beliefs clashed with the concept of a materialist society proceeding towards the triumph of rationality, which rested on the view that man was not essentially irrational. All over Europe, magic and divination came under increasing attack. On account of their attachment to 'superstitious' beliefs and supposed inherent irrationality, women were a particular target of derision.[8] Whereas in village society they had enjoyed a degree of respect for placing their divinatory skills at the service of family and community, in nineteenth-century urban and 'literate' society their position grew altogether more precarious.

Divination continued to be regarded as part of women's sphere in the new environment. In 1796, N. P. Osipov remarked in the foreword of a book he had translated that '. . . fortune-telling for the most part belongs to women'.[9] Publishers of some fortune-telling manuals were recognizing a female market when they included instructions for Yuletide divinatory rituals, or texts enabling the user to discover the name of 'her' future beau rather than 'his' sweetheart. Some brought out titles expressly aimed at women, such as *A Lady's Album, or A Fortune-Telling Book for Entertainment and Pleasure* (1816 and 1820), while others added men as an afterthought: *A Girlish Trinket, With Which Men Too May be Diverted . . .* (1791). Apart from titles, some forewords informed readers that the contents would enliven a lady's leisure hours. Some women obviously valued their books more highly than that, as the inscriptions in a copy of the *Lady's Album*, made by the book's female owner between 1824 and 1856, reveal. Evidently regarding the book as a treasured personal possession, she used the blank pages at the end to record the major events in her family's history.[10]

Fortune-telling books or sections of books were never designated solely for men. At first sight, this would appear to demonstrate conclusively that fortune-telling books followed traditional practice in being predominantly part of women's culture. While this may hold generally, it is, at least for the period 1760–1830, a simplistic view. There was no need to declare such books were intended for men, since books were still a predominantly male preserve.[11] Did men therefore simply produce fortune-telling books for women or did they also use them themselves?

For the eighteenth and early nineteenth centuries at least, the latter seems closer to the truth. The spread of literacy to the lesser rural nobility in the 1760s and 1770s was primarily a male phenomenon; sons, not daughters, went into state service. Older women tended to cling to old ways, while younger ones were granted fewer educational opportunities than their brothers.[12] In eighteenth-century Russia book-buying, and to a great extent reading, seem to have been largely male occupations. With the exceptions of atypical figures like the Empress Catherine and Princess Dashkova, private libraries belonged to men; as late as the second decade of the nineteenth century, the womenfolk in backward rural gentry families, like the Oblomovs in Goncharov's novel, did not read books, preferring to rely on oral divinatory tradition for predicting the future. A picture of Smirdin's bookshop from 1834, which features eight male customers and only one woman,[13] suggests that women still did not go to bookshops in the 1830s, but this may mislead. The conclusion to be drawn is not that women were indifferent to books, but rather that their access to reading matter was limited and indirect. Before women learnt to read, men probably shared their books by reading them aloud to the rest of the family. As women became literate, they would order books through their husbands or, like Pushkin's Tat'iana, swap books belonging to a male member of the family for a dream-book out of a colporteur's box. Even though women from more sophisticated groups had begun in the 1790s to find an increasing number of books and journals designed especially for them, many probably passed their orders through husbands or fathers. Some participated more actively in the book market by joining subscription lists, though it is possible that this occurred mostly when there was some kind of connection with the book's author.[14] Men's access to books and higher educational levels ensured that they formed the majority of purchasers and readers at this period.

Fortune-telling books were no different. Men bought most of those sold in the eighteenth and early nineteenth centuries, though the proportion who bought them on request from their womenfolk remains unknown. Inscriptions in fortune-telling books from the first two decades of the nineteenth century almost all indicate male ownership. However, after a flurry of interest in the 1820s and 1830s among educated young men influenced by Romanticism, fortune-telling books were left to women and the lower classes.

Apart from low literacy levels among women and their restricted access to books, a further reason for male ownership and use of fortune-telling texts prior to this date may lie in the novelty of book-buying for many men. New readers of books in the eighteenth century were not sophisticated, naturally preferring books that were lively, entertaining and readily comprehensible, in particular belles-lettres and 'general-interest non-fiction that presented easy and concrete examples or guides to personal behavior and fulfillment'.[15] Fortune-telling books fell into that category; for example, many translated dreambooks came complete with disquisitions of a pseudo-scientific character. They satisfied the desire to interpret the future while not offending the unsophisticated reader's feeble grasp of the rational and scientific approach to life.

Whereas within a short space of time the vast majority of men lost interest, a 'household' variant of such pursuits became an essential part of women's abiding interest in divination. Its vitality was maintained not only by books but also by lore passed from one family member to another, creating an interesting mélange of printed and oral traditions. Educated men deserted fortune-telling books, and as more women acquired an education which was antagonistic to all forms of irrationality, the less educated and poorer Russian women became the main support for both books and practice. Fictional references to domestic fortune-telling in noble houses after 1840 locate it among old-fashioned country women, such as Lavretskii's aunt in Turgenev's *Home of the Gentry* (1859) and Mar'ia Petrovna in Grigorovich's 'Landless peasant' (1848), or to semi-educated merchant women like the would-be bride in Gogol''s play 'Marriage' (1841) or provincial widow, Chebotarikha, in Zamiatin's 'Provincial tale' (1913). At first sight, Gogol''s Ivan Fedorovich Shpon'ka, who is deeply attached to his dreambook, looks like the exception to the rule, but in fact the unfortunate Shpon'ka is a misfit in the male world of the army, joining in none of the normal pursuits of an officer. A military failure, he retires to his estate where his fearsome Amazon of an aunt takes over his life. All is well until she begins organizing a bride for him, something the poor Shpon'ka cannot cope with. While the aunt is startlingly masculine, Shpon'ka's character represents an inversion of male characteristics, and his attachment to his dreambook expresses one aspect of the author's own negative perceptions of women.

Once upper-class indulgence was withdrawn, fortune-telling books lost any pretence of respectability. The paucity of sources on fortune-telling books in the period after 1840 from any social sphere indicates not only educated male scorn, but also, no doubt, women's own attempts to keep their interest in fortune-telling away from hostile eyes. Fictional references suggest that this was an interest and skill shared only with others of like mind, mostly other women. The general's wife in Dostoevskii's *Village of Stepanchikovo* (1859), or Mar'ia Petrovna in Grigorovich's story, 'Landless peasant' (1847), practise cartomancy only with other women.

The process whereby women only gradually gained access to the book market, making their own book selection and purchases, would appear to have been repeated as literacy descended the social scale. Since literacy among male peasants and urban dwellers was much higher than among female,[16] they would have been the first to purchase books. The consistent presence of *Solomon* among the array of *lubok* literature on sale to a predominantly peasant market from the early 1800s implies that men bought divinatory books.[17] Unfortunately, evidence for this process is extremely hard to come by. Nonetheless, as Sakharov remarked at the same period, belief in dreams was as prevalent among women in towns as in villages, a view reiterated at the end of the century.[18] It may be assumed that as women became literate and, no less important, had a few kopecks of their own, they began to buy fortune-telling books. Certainly among Russians today, interest in divination is much more developed among women than men (folklorists apart).[19]

In making the transition from folk to 'literate' cultures, Russian women, therefore, had to cope with the antagonistic attitudes to activities involving illogical processes that characterized a modernizing culture. This world derided domestic fortune-telling.

Since the system of book production (and, in the eighteenth and early nineteenth centuries, consumption) was then part of the male sphere, women had no direct say in publishing decisions. Only gradually did women make their tastes felt through their selections as purchasers. These factors made fortune-telling's struggle for respectability well-nigh hopeless. But while men dismissed fortune-telling as 'feminine' intuition and irrationality, they were, as will be seen in chapters 6 and 7, not averse to co-opting aspects in which authority resided.

The period of relative tolerance enjoyed by domestic fortune-telling in the late eighteenth and early nineteenth centuries should not be attributed solely to the novelty of reading for unsophisticated people. It is much more the consequence of a shift of emphasis in the function of divination, a necessary strategy in the new literate Europeanized society, and one already adopted in Western Europe. The forcible wrenching of the upper classes from traditional culture during the eighteenth century shifted the emphasis towards entertainment. Although, as members of the wealthy classes, they had been less bound by the agricultural calendar than the peasants, whose leisure combined merriment with important rituals, they still observed many of the traditional ways of structuring and passing the time. Peter the Great's Europeanization loosened their ties with the past, in particular by bringing upper-class men and women together socially in a previously unknown manner. Since many traditional activities (notably those associated with calendar festivities) were now designated crude and inappropriate, something was required to fill the hours of leisure.[20] The need arose for pastimes appropriate for both mixed and single-sex social occasions. With gathering impetus towards the end of the century, leisure time was 'feminized' – women were perceived as mistresses of the art of conversation, reflected in changes in the literary language designed to embody the supposed tender sensibilities of women, their elegance and flirtatiousness. Cultural emphasis shifted to the more intimate sphere of the boudoir or domestic setting.[21] Fortune-telling books, like *A Newly Appeared Wizard Recounting the Divinations of the Spirits. An Innocent Distraction in Hours of Boredom for Those Not Wishing to Engage upon Anything Better* (1795), were part of this change. The addition of non-divinatory sections on conjuring tricks or 'mind-reading' to fortune-telling compendia underlines the trivialization of fortune-telling. It was thus equated with activities only ever intended for temporary mystification and light-hearted amusement, such as ways of finding out a secret number or the name of the person for whom someone sighed in secret. Less commonly, titles also emphasized the intended rôle of the book in mixed society; one such is *The Egyptian Oracle, or a General Complete and Novel Means of Telling Fortunes, Serving as Innocent Entertainment for Persons of Both Sexes,* Moscow, 1796, reprinted 1841. However, in recognition both of women's traditional attachment to divination and their new task of diverting society, publishers and editors more frequently oriented their fortune-telling books specifically towards them. Ivan Kurbatov was expressing a view common among editors when he hoped that his portmanteau collection of fortune-telling texts, published in 1808, would commend itself to the fair sex, the guardians of the gentle art of conversation. The eighteenth-century poet Sumarokov's *Little Divinatory Book about Love,* elucidating romantic prospects, was intended by its author not to pander to superstition, but provide entertainment for the fair sex. The number of titles and editions available in this period suggest that many enjoyed working out the name of their intended or wielding a pack of cards for fortune-telling.

By the beginning of the nineteenth century, leisure activities were not only well established, but also, even in mixed company, differentiated according to gender. In his poem 'Winter. What is there to do in the country?' (1829), Pushkin evokes the tedium of a winter's evening on his friend P. I. Wul'f's estate:

> I cease to quarrel with my lyre. Tired and vexed,
> I try the drawing-room. They're talking of the next
> Elections or the sugar-mill or both together.
> The mistress of the house frowns, gloomy as the weather,
> Steel needles swiftly flickering, or else she starts
> To read the cards, tell fortunes from the King of Hearts.

Here the mistress of the house either knits or tells fortunes on her own, though she may have persuaded her guests to let her divine their future. The men discuss politics or, as later in the poem, play draughts. The division of leisure according to gender thus placed fortune-telling firmly in the female sphere.

Though geomancy, physiognomy and chiromancy were all popular drawing-room and domestic activities in the late eighteenth and early nineteenth centuries, it is card-laying that best illustrates gender-specific pastimes as well as the downgrading of fortune-telling to mere entertainment. Whereas physiognomy and chiromancy, as pseudo-sciences, had many influential male devotees,[22] cartomancy seems always to have been a female occupation. Not only Pushkin's poem but also his *Captain's Daughter* presents cartomancy as a female pastime; in chapter 4 of the novel, Vasilisa Egorovna lays out the cards on her own while the men discuss the military situation. Tat'iana also takes cartomancy seriously (*Eugene Onegin*, v, 5).[23] The widespread popularity of cartomancy among women is attested by the introduction to the relevant section in *The Book of Fate. The Pages of Sambeta, the Persian Sibyl*, published in 1838. The anonymous editor declares that cartomancy 'is almost exclusively a female occupation. Rare is the house where no one knows how to do it, and rare the girl who cannot lay out the cards and interpret their meaning for herself.' Evidence that cartomancy continued to be a women's skill later in the century may be gleaned from the 1860 edition of *The Magic Indicator* . . ., which announces on the front cover that it has been 'compiled for the fairest sex'.[24]

Cartomancy may be regarded as the female counterpart to card gaming, a predominantly male use of cards. In the course of the eighteenth century, card-playing had become one of the most popular leisure-time activities as it had in Western Europe. Card-games were conventionally divided into two types, those suitable for mixed company or a domestic setting, and 'games of hazard'. The first type, which employed skill as much as chance, was regarded as a pleasant pastime, even when, as often happened, players gambled small sums of money. The official court diaries detailing Catherine II's daily activities in the 1760s show, for example, that she played cards on an almost daily basis.[25] Not until the nineteenth century, and then only when social card-playing bordered on obsession, might it attract criticism.[26] Games of hazard, on the other hand, were played almost exclusively by men, and, far from being regarded as 'innocent entertainment', were seen in aristocratic society as a dangerous duel with chance, which young men took up as a challenge to their manhood.[27] Scenes of ruinous gambling abound in Russian literature, where Vasilii Maikov's 'The ombre player' (1763), Zhukova's 'Baron Reikhman' (1837), Gogol''s 'The carriage' (1836) and Pushkin's 'Queen of Spades' (1833) and 'The shot' (1830) all depict gambling among army officers and wealthy young men. Gogol′'s 'The gamblers' (1841) portrays gambling in taverns, and the 'Order of Vladimir' (1832–41) a passion for whist. Dostoevskii's own ruinous passion for the gaming table is well known. There was no clear dividing line between the two types of card-games, for the possibility of winning even modest sums of money drew men to the card-table more than women, as the literature of the period attests; in the introduction to his *Yuletide Gift*, D. Kniazhevich reports the views of the Countess T., who, lamenting the decline in St Petersburg's social life over the New Year period, complains that at balls the men play cards and the girls simply gossip. Gogol′'s *Dead Souls* best evokes the social role of card-playing among the provincial gentry and officials; in part I, chapter 1, fashionably dressed thin men dance attendance on the ladies, while the fat men, senior government officials, and solid respectable landowners play whist. The confidence trickster, Chichikov joins the second group. Not only did social card-playing require no apologies, but even gambling with its often desperate consequences for individuals and families was such a widely accepted part of male society that it attracted neither widespread condemnation, nor serious official efforts at suppression. The contrast with social attitudes to cartomancy, which had to be defended as 'innocent entertainment', is striking.

Whereas the exclusively male use of cards was connected to gambling, when women took up a pack of cards it was as frequently to tell fortunes as to play social card-games. Given that most of the cards did not differ from conventional ones used in drawing-room games, the production of special packs was evidently a commercial ploy, and many women undoubtedly used ordinary household cards, a standard component of male leisure, for fortune-telling.

Women wasted little time in adopting cartomancy as part of their culture. Since there was no comparable tradition of fortune-telling in Russian folk culture, the speed with which the process occurred should be attributed to the accessibility of the equipment. Perhaps because this form of fortune-telling had no exact parallel in oral tradition and, more importantly, did not pretend to be a 'science', it was never taken up by men. Left to women, it never lost its associations in polite society with amusement and entertainment, much vaunted by the first publishers of fortune-telling books. As late as 1860, the *lubok* guide mentioned above was declaring not only that it was directed towards women, but, expressing itself in elegant eighteenth-century style (undermined by appalling spelling), that it served 'as innosent entertainment and a pleasant passtime. Replacing all orikles, caballisticks and other divination.'[28] Thus the price of admission to drawing rooms was the designation of cartomancy as light entertainment, associations which it failed to shake off entirely even when laying out the cards became so popular among those without drawing rooms.

Originally justified as innocent entertainment, with time cartomancy came to be viewed negatively as 'frivolous' and then 'emptyheaded'. It is almost without exception denigrated as a sign of passing or constant foolishness. Country women, who learnt cartomancy from their house serfs before passing it on by word of mouth, did not take it as seriously as other forms of divination.[29] Catherine II, who, as mentioned, loved playing cards, did so usually with men or sometimes in mixed groups, but, just as she despised anything that smacked of superstition or the occult, she was contemptuous of women's enthusiasm for cartomancy. In the satirical diary of a young girl published in *Facts and Fables*, the girl's foolish elderly aunt tells fortunes in the cards and has had to buy a new pack because the diamonds (the most auspicious suit) were quite worn away.[30] When Agaf'ia in Gogol''s play 'Marriage' (1841) cannot choose between her motley assortment of suitors, she decides, absurdly, to seek the answer in the cards. Mar'ia Lebiadkina, the half-witted wife of Stavrogin in Dostoevskii's *The Devils* (1871–2), is a further striking example. One of the negative facets of a female landowner in D. Grigorovich's 'Landless peasant' (1847) is her adherence to cartomancy, while the foolishness of the women in A. N. Ostrovskii's play of 1868 *Too Clever by Half* lies in their fascination with spiritualism and cards. Ostrovskii was probably unaware that women of the royal house and their circle had tried table turning and other occult activities in 1855.[31] Finally, in what is a neat demonstration of the gender use of cards, the general's ignorant wife and her cronies in Dostoevskii's *Village of Stepanchikovo* (1859) turn to cartomancy whenever the general flies into one of his violent rages on losing at cards with his male friends. Thus, in Russia, away from the neutral ground of social card-playing, the semiotics of cards varied according to the gender of the user, with negative value attached almost entirely to women's practice.

Whereas cartomancy best illustrates the trivializing of fortune-telling in polite society, oneiromancy, by contrast, demonstrates women's ability to maintain their reputation for prediction, albeit in strictly defined circumstances. In the rural environment dream divination fitted into a range of predictive, propitiatory and prophylactic rituals designed to affect a world largely beyond the control of human beings. As the urban and literate dweller learnt better to understand and control her or his environment, the need for such rituals diminished. Not so with dream divination. Vivid or distressing dreams plague men and women wherever they live, daily revealing how little we know ourselves. Little wonder that oneiromancy continued to be regarded with seriousness. That dreams should be thought to reveal the future rather than mundane happenings or the workings of the psyche simply brings together the most enigmatic aspect of human consciousness and the natural desire to exert more control over life by at least knowing what may happen. In pre-Revolutionary urban Russia older women retained their authority, presiding over breakfast sessions of dream interpretation, as the title of the 1791 dreambook, *A Morning Pastime over Tea*, indicates.[32] Dreams might also be discussed with other women outside the household just as dreambooks could be consulted on one's own. As urbanization and the disincentive factor of education gradually eliminated people's knowledge of comparable oral traditions, dreambooks became sought-after items.

The phenomenal popularity of dreambooks meant that, by the Revolution, there can have been few Russians who had neither encountered nor heard of them. High literary sources contain far fewer references to the use of dreambooks than to cartomancy. Oneiromancy as a serious morning activity conducted within the domestic circle did not adapt easily to light entertainment for mixed or female gatherings in the afternoons or evenings. After all, the dreamer may not wish to offer her or his dream up for bantering comment or public analysis. Furthermore, fictional sources, male and female-authored, tend to play down those domestic scenes that represent the female sphere of influence in favour of social gatherings of both sexes later in the day. Nonetheless, Pushkin's Tat'iana in *Eugene Onegin* is not alone in cherishing her dreambook. In Ivan Turgenev's *Home of the Gentry*, Lavretskii's deceased aunt was typical of poorly educated women landowners of the time in owning only calendars and dreambooks, while in Zamiatin's story 'A provincial tale' the gross widow Chebotarikha and her 'toy-boy' Baryba sit over breakfast having conversations that aid the digestion, 'about dreams, the dreambook, Martyn Zadeka, portents and various love spells'. Although references to the use of dreambooks are relatively rare after 1840, the numbers of editions and size of print runs, together with comments about widespread beliefs in dreams among women, certainly reveal the importance of dreambooks in women's culture. Sakharov's supposition of the 1830s that it was impossible to find a woman or girl who did not believe in dreams was echoed at the end of the century in a pamphlet put out by the Russian Monastery of St Elijah on Mount Athos, which regretted that 'many people, especially women, firmly believe that every dream . . . must mean something'.[33]

It was argued in chapter 2 that the belief that the dream had a significance for the dreamer points to the therapeutic function of dream divination. This function changed very little in an urban and literate environment, remaining part of women's sphere. Since women presided over breakfast, doubters, mainly male, presumably accepted this as part of daily routine. Thus Aksakov notes that his grandmother always asked his grandfather at breakfast whether he had had any dreams. Despite being an old-style patriarchal figure, the old man tolerated the questions while refusing to offer any dream material for discussion. Presumably, though Aksakov does not say this, the same question was addressed to other family members, perhaps with a more positive response. Dream divination was thus the only domestic divinatory activity which men could take seriously if and when it suited them, by joining in breakfast discussions and without endangering their reputation for rationality in the world at large. Very likely some did so with greater or lesser degrees of scepticism. This is not to suggest that fun was alien to dream divination. So long as a dream was bizarre or comic, rather than frightening, deciphering it could be a highly entertaining activity for everyone.

Publishers played on this even when marketing a divinatory skill like oneiromancy which had more prestige with men. Of course, the designation of fortune-telling books as, at best, 'innocent amusement' and, at worst, superstitious nonsense did not prevent their owners from taking the books seriously, and continuing fortune-telling at home. Some editors and publishers (for example the editor of the first dreambook), while attempting to placate high-minded (mainly male) book purchasers, did so with assurances that the book would certainly work. Others were perhaps more confident of a trusting female audience; the introduction to *A Morning Pastime over Tea* (1791) did not guarantee absolute reliability, but thought the contents generally accurate. Such strategies reveal publishers' desire to avoid the contempt of the educated while maximizing the book's appeal to a largely female group, some of whom welcomed fortune-telling as entertainment, while others turned to it for genuine guidance.

The distinction drawn beween the status of oneiromancy and cartomancy should not obscure the fact that many took despised drawing-room pastimes very seriously. As the introduction to the cartomantic section in *The Book of Fate* (1838) observed: 'Some people read the cards out of idleness, and do not imagine they will find truth in them; but others believe in them in all seriousness and try to assure others that everything that has happened to them or to those whose fortunes they have read, was known to them in advance from the cards' (p. 255). Reading the coffee grounds, another popular form of divination among women, attracted even more serious attention, according to the *Book of Fate*: 'Many believe in reading the coffee grounds, even more than than they hold by reading the cards, and some think that this form of divination definitely possesses a good deal of the supernatural' (p. 286).

Belief and disbelief, seriousness and fun would not, however, have been the only responses to domestic fortune-telling. Many people, like Ol′ga in Goncharov's novel *Oblomov*, who began by having her fortune read in the cards for fun and, when it seemed to get too close to the truth, found it embarrassing (part 2, ch. 12), might not have described themselves as believers. A familiar process is at work here. Having agreed to a reading of some kind, the individual is then drawn in, and suspends his or her rational conviction that this cannot possibly reveal the secret of the future. Overcome by the desire to know, he or she drinks in the prediction, and, depending on its perceived relevance to the individual's own life, may retain some element of it afterwards. As an educated woman, Ol′ga was no doubt embarrassed not only by the apparent relevance, but also by her own 'weakness' in seeking to know her future. Obviously, in some people, rational scepticism overcomes hopeful belief more rapidly than others. It may be assumed that more of these would be men than women, and that few women in pre-Revolutionary Russia, if they were not already convinced of the efficacy of one or other type of fortune-telling, would have not found themselves drawn in to trying something that was so much part of women's culture. For doubters, fortune-telling would act as a form of social and gender solidarity, like discussing clothes, or, for men, sport.

Nineteenth-century fortune-telling was a vital part of urban and literate women's culture, a half-glimpsed sub-culture, which the sneers of ethnographers and intellectuals failed to stifle. In turning to fortune-telling these women were carrying on their traditional rôle of putting their skills towards the maintenance of family structures and welfare. A belief that the future is already mapped out might appear to reflect a hopeless fatalism. Women, it might be argued, were continuing the attitudes of the peasant, whose passive fatalism stemmed not only from his world view but also his life at the mercy of the weather and, before 1861, the landowner's whims. In so far as recourse to fortune-telling may divert an individual from present action, it can contribute to fatalism. Many women, and indeed men, however, had few opportunities to change their lives in pre-Revolutionary Russia. If we see fortune-telling simply as a reflection of fatalism or escapism, we fail to explain why it particularly attracted women. It would also be a mistake to regard fortune-telling merely as symptomatic of women's passivity, and fortune-telling books as fodder for passive consumers. Within the world of fortune-telling Russian women were by no means passive. They used fortune-telling as a way of gaining emotional support and of expressing their concern for those they loved. Luckman's description of fortune-telling as 'the invisible religion' appears justified when many Russian women, even those regarding themselves as Orthodox believers, relied on it to guide their every step.[34] Since divination formed an important part of women's domain in a traditional society, it is hardly suprising that women clung to it tenaciously even after leaving that world. Physically removed from a traditional setting, they sought psychological support in traditional practices, even when they came in a new guise. Counselling, emotional support, guidance all helped to make fortune-telling a vital part of women's culture. These serious functions were for many women more important than simply enlivening their spare time with amusing predictions. Even when fun predominated, fortune-telling that took place in groups within a domestic setting doubtless also served to bond family or female groups.

It may also be argued that despite men's control over publishing and, before about 1830, book consumption, women took steps to make the contents of fortune-telling books their own. The processes of oral transmission, particularly from mother to daughter, gave women some control over that tradition, with the freedom to accept or reject the contents of fortune-telling manuals, and to pass them down to others or not. The introduction of folk dream beliefs into dreambooks at the end of the nineteeth and in the early twentieth centuries may be a belated response to a process of intermingling oral and literate traditions, conducted almost entirely by women. Furthermore, the mainly female purchasers of fortune-telling books were certainly not passive stooges. The books demanded a much more active response than most, and were a stimulus to group or individual activity.

Men's role in domestic fortune-telling, by contrast, appears to have been much more passive than women's, taking the period as a whole.[35] In the period up till 1830, as a consequence either of the books' novelty, the paper-thin veneer of European attitudes among some men or a Romantic fascination with the irrational, they took a more active interest, purchasing and evidently using fortune-telling books. Subsequently, however, they were drawn into domestic fortune-telling mainly through their womenfolk, as participants in groups led by women. Some men took a more active rôle during later revivals of interest in the irrational, but, since these movements spurned traditional urban fortune-telling for spiritualism and, at the turn of the twentieth century, occultism, male involvement here is beyond the scope of this book.

It may be concluded that women made domestic fortune-telling part of their culture when they became literate or migrated to towns. Since fortune-telling books were generally concerned with offering answers to the major questions about an individual's future (both personal and economic), they exactly replicated the areas of women's concern in traditional rural life, if not the specifics of method. Little wonder that women treasured them so greatly. Fortune-telling books gained a measure of social respectability through their reduction to 'innocent amusement', but as educational levels rose men, and later increasing numbers of élite women, spurned them. In the transition from folk to 'literate' culture women thus lost one area of social esteem without acquiring another.

Despite all this, domestic fortune-telling not only survived but flourished, because it fulfilled a number of deep needs for its supporters: social bonding, entertainment and power over fate, all very important in a culture where women were associated with the private sphere and credited with rôles as possessors of intuitive (rather than acquired) knowledge, as well as social facilitators. These varied functions suggest that while definite conclusions about gender rôles and fortune-telling cannot be drawn, the situation in the fortune-telling 'world' was quite complex. On the one hand, fortune-telling devalued women, just as they were devalued in other contexts in Russia (and just as the scholarship on fortune-telling, such as it is, also devalues its devotees), but on the other, in certain instances, notably in oneiromancy, it empowered them. Nor is devaluation exclusively connected with gender; men who became involved in fortune-telling were derided as ignorant bumpkins, unless divination could be given a pseudo-scientific clothing or, as will be seen in chapter 6, linked with Orthodoxy.

CHAPTER 6

Fortune-tellers and their clientèle

The wide involvement of women in domestic fortune-telling did not deter Russian townsfolk from recourse to professional fortune-tellers. Their need was constant though the form it took was not. This chapter considers urban fortune-tellers in terms of their gender and skills, their clients and their rôle, as well as their status in the eyes of educated society, in particular men.[1] Though the sources are indecently skimpy, they corroborate each other sufficiently to allow for some general conclusions.

As was seen in chapter 2, rural divinatory specialists performed a valued rôle in the community, helping its members to cope with an essentially hostile world and a predetermined fate. Both white- and black-magic practitioners were involved in divination and were regarded with a mixture of fear and respect in the community. Only if they were thought to have caused harm would the community turn against them, but white-magic specialists, who included the fortune-teller (*vorozheia*) and the old women specializing in dream interpretation were generally respected. None demanded payment, for it was believed that this would nullify the effect of cures, charms and predictions, but they accepted, indeed expected, gifts.

In the pre-Petrine period, traditional divinatory specialists had flourished in Moscow and other large towns as well as in the countryside. Fragmentary evidence suggests that at this period practitioners of black magic took a larger rôle in divination than they did later, but this may only appear so because of their higher profile. Cases of 'spoiling' or the evil eye, especially when well-known people were the supposed targets, led to formal complaint or judicial action, whereas a fortune-teller predicting marital prospects from rows of beans naturally escaped censure or even comment. Existing sources deal predominantly with witchcraft: sorcerers, sorceresses, witches and their fateful predictions. They employed some divinatory methods not used by white-magic experts: Mikhail Chulkov, writing in the 1780s, refers to divination from the markings on a sheep's shoulder blade,[2] from dice or the movement of a ring on a tightly drawn drum, but others were common to both types of soothsayer, whether in town or country: divination with beans, using a psalter or from shapes formed by melted wax or tin are all attested from at least the seventeenth century, and continued to be rural practice in the nineteenth.[3] In the course of the eighteenth century, as their wealthy urban clients were educated out of magic belief, sorcerers gradually retreated to the countryside. Most references from the latter part of the century, such as in Ablesimov's comic opera of 1779, *The Miller as Sorcerer, Cheat and Matchmaker* or its imitators, are to country sorcerers. Chulkov is almost the only commentator to examine the categories of black-magic practitioners, implying that they were still an urban phenomenon. He states that both black- and white-magic specialists claimed to be able to identify thieves, pronounce on a wife's fidelity and offer guidance on personal matters such as the likelihood of pregnancy. Black-magic experts additionally made predictions about the weather, lucky and unlucky days and prospects for travel.[4] All commentators agree that folk-healers and fortune-tellers specialized in predictions about emotional and material prospects. As sorcerers retreated from towns in the course of the eighteenth century, fortune-tellers appear to have taken on some of their activities.

Apart from resident fortune-tellers, there existed other types of specialist who, being itinerant, might offer their services to townsfolk. Herbalists and healers (*lecheiki*), all women, are depicted by I. P. Sakharov as a special social group who 'wander the streets of villages and towns with bundles of herbs on their backs, and on Saturdays act as midwives in bath-houses'.[5] Their métier was or, rather, had been dream interpretation, for, in his view, they no longer existed in the 1830s. Tereshchenko, whose book came out in 1848, disagreed, saying that, while in olden days women used to visit houses to interpret dreams (performing the same function as rural dream interpreters), their place had now been taken by peripatetic healers, whom he, like Sakharov, describes as *lecheiki* with bundles of herbs, as well as toothless old women and gossips, who 'themselves strike up conversations about dreams and willingly set to interpreting them'.[6] He goes on to discuss their expertise which consisted of analysing the meaning of the whole dream, not just the separate dream objects as might be done by those using a dreambook. When it is also remembered that the Kindly Old Man of Duck Street was said to have practised dream interpretation for many years in Petersburg, it seems clear that dream diviners existed in pre-Revolutionary Russian towns. What is more, since commentators never refer to them as fortune-tellers (*gadalki* or *gadal'shchitsy*), they seem to have been viewed as a category entirely separate from professional fortune-tellers.[7] This hypothesis receives confirmation from the Welfare Ordinance of 1782, which included dream interpretation among banned black-magic practices, but put prediction (*predskazanie* and *predznamenovanie*) into a separate article.[8]

Another itinerant group offering divinatory services was the gypsies. Although gypsies had been in Ukraine as early as the fifteenth century, they did not move into many parts of Russia until the eighteenth century. As in Western Europe, they rapidly established a reputation for fortune-telling and charlatanism; Chulkov, for example, notes their involvement in fortune-telling, admitting that 'our simple folk firmly believe that gypsies are great experts at prediction'.[9] Vladimir Dal' stated in his dictionary (1863–6) that their specialty was reading palms,[10] and this is certainly the métier of the gypsy women who appear in Mariia Tsebrikova's 'Which one is better' (1865),[11] in paintings by Makovskii (1912) (see frontispiece) and Vrubel' (*The Fortune Teller*, 1895) as well as of today's gypsies in the Moscow metro. They also read the cards and interpreted dreams. Very little evidence about gypsy fortune-telling is available, since gypsy clairvoyants suffered from the double disadvantage of belonging to a hated ethnic minority and following a despised occupation, with the additional handicap of being female. They were considered beneath contempt and hence unworthy of scrutiny. Even a man with deep ethnographic interests like Dal' depicts a gypsy fortune-teller as a charlatan and thief ('The fortune-teller', 1848), while her Russian counterpart in 'The clairvoyant' (written in the second half of the 1830s) gets much more even-handed treatment. On the other hand, the gypsies themselves enjoyed repeating stories about their skill in extracting money and gifts from wealthy peasants by pretending to tell fortunes, suggesting that they were happy to mingle thieving with divination. Success depended upon finding a gullible dupe, probably much easier in the countryside.[12] It is unclear how active gypsy clairvoyants were in towns. In 1834, 8,000 gypsies were resident in urban areas, though not in St Petersburg, where they were banned from living between 1759 and 1917.[13] What sources there are on urban fortune-tellers do not mention gypsies after the end of the eighteenth century. Nonetheless, their prophetic skills were obviously well known and well used by both urban and rural populations, as the introduction to a book of moral precepts for young ladies of 1796 indicates. The book, a translation from German, came in the guise of a fortune-telling guide. The translator, N. P. Osipov, remarked in the preface that in order to tell the truth, he had adopted the seer's garb, by which he meant, he said, 'in Russian that of a gypsy, or in educated parlance, a prognosticator'.[14] But, though a different translation of the same book uses the word gypsy in its title, as do a handful of fortune-telling books which claimed to contain romany methods of interpreting dreams, cards or palms, the 'gypsy' stereotype may have been one borrowed from the West.[15] The relative rarity of such titles in Russia compared with Britain attests to the vigour of native Russian divinatory traditions, as well as the greater trust placed by Russians in home-grown exponents and translated fortune-telling books. Though many people certainly consulted gypsy clairvoyants, the rôle of gypsy fortune-tellers in large towns, if not elsewhere, was evidently modest.

It is not clear whether the numbers of fortune-tellers in cities were swelled by peasant immigrants from the neighbouring countryside, or by wandering healers who, finding themselves spending more and more time with urban clients, finally settled in town. Nikolai Novikov's casual remark of 1772 about coffee-cup readers that 'the whole bunch of old women is an assemblage of vagabonds, who should be deemed outcasts from the human race' implies that groups of homeless or itinerant women had banded together.[16] The picture suggests recent arrivals, who had caught on to the growing popularity of this new divinatory skill, but had yet to properly establish themselves in town. According to Novikov, by the 1770s they and other kinds of fortune-teller were supplying their services to a long list of his acquaintances. Many people, he declared, both wealthy as well as of more modest circumstances, summoned a fortune-teller whenever the occasion arose; in one instance that he knew of, this happened on a daily basis.[17] Clairvoyants appear to have become a constant feature of towns throughout the nineteenth century, though numbers are difficult to establish. One rare example of a survey was carried out by an anonymous gentleman calling himself Otshel'nik (Hermit), who visited a dozen male and female seers in 1894, and was told about a couple more.[18] Half did not describe themselves as fortune-tellers, though they all made predictions. It is very likely that Otshel'nik's selection is biased in favour of variety, since accounts of visits to several cartomancers, for example, would have proved less entertaining than his survey of the extraordinary practices of some he visited. In any case, his estimate of the numbers of fortune-tellers (as opposed to witches, magicians, holy fools and others) should probably be revised upwards, perhaps in the range of twenty to forty. Even so, given the size of the city in 1894, it would appear that numbers had dropped in proportionate if not absolute terms since the late eighteenth century. The reasons for this probably stem both from changed social attitudes and the more limited range of services offered, and will be considered later in the context of the fortune-tellers' clientèle.

Otshel'nik's report also provides confirmation about the disappearance of folk magic beliefs and practice from large towns by the end of the nineteenth century. Six of those he saw or heard about claimed to be black-magic practitioners: two witches, two sorcerers, one sorceress and a female magician. In contrast to the village sorcerer, who exerted power over his community through fear and general acceptance of his powers, these people had to make a living by attracting clients. Not suprisingly, they offered the same types of predictive and problem-solving services as the fortune-tellers, and could only be distinguished from them by the methods they used, which were idiosyncratic rather than traditional. One of the witches told fortunes using cards and witches' familiars. Since Otshel'nik's information in this case is not first-hand, but came from an elderly aunt, its accuracy may be questionable. According to the aunt, the witch made her predictions on the basis of the reactions of her twelve black cats, who came when called, then sniffed a pack of cards, the visitors and the corners of the room in turn![19] One of the sorcerers, who claimed to be clairvoyant, specialized in the laying-on of hands, while the second, a Greek, apparently asked young female visitors to undress so that he could sprinkle them with magic water![20] He was one of two foreigners: one of the witches, whose healing and divinatory activities suggest links with the figure of the folk healer, was, in fact, German. Since her treatments and her type of psalter divination were not of the folk Russian variety, it may be assumed that her adoption of the title of witch and the Greek's of sorcerer are explicable in terms of their own cultural background. As far as clients were concerned, consulting a foreign sage probably had a mystery value.[21] Of the other four, only one, the female sorcerer, here called *chernoknizhnitsa* (specialist in the arts of the black book) had links with tradition. The fact that her magic book turns out to be a geography textbook of the 1850s or 1860s does not nullify the connection with the Old Russian *chernoknizhnik*, though it immediately exposes her in Otshel'nik's eyes as a charlatan.[22] Since the other three had so little in common with rural black-magic exponents, their descriptive titles look like an attempt to attract customers by promising something exotic and therefore possibly more effective. The idea of consulting a black-magic figure may have given customers a frisson.

The problems in assessing fortune-tellers and their clientèle in pre-Revolutionary Russia are essentially the same as those bedevilling the study of domestic fortune-telling: regrettably little information, and that of a biased nature. But if educated men scoffed at domestic fortune-telling, at best regarding it with indulgence or as light entertainment, professional fortune-telling, by contrast, was little more than criminal; 'fortune-tellers live off the ignorant and weak-minded', remarked Tereshchenko sternly.[23] In general, commentators were only interested in condemnation or exposé. Their contempt is palpable. Novikov accompanied his discussion of readers of coffee grounds with scathing remarks, such as that 'a reader of coffee grounds is an elderly creature, who can no longer earn her living and does not wish to earn an honest crust'.[24] The information observers provide is often tainted by their view of fortune-tellers as out-and-out charlatans. The alternative sources of information, fictional references, have to be used with the same care as those on domestic fortune-telling.

The fortune-tellers who established themselves in towns from the 1760s followed traditional practice in almost every respect. Certainly the types of services they offered, predictions about emotional or material prospects, disclosure of marital infidelity and crime detection were identical. Over time, the range of their activities narrowed. In the 1770s, Novikov objected strongly to readers of coffee grounds on the grounds that they could shatter marriages by confirming a husband's vain suspicions about his wife's infidelity. A superstitious husband, he declared, would always believe the fortune-teller rather than his 'deceitful' spouse. Since later commentators do not mention this service, it must have lost favour even with the credulous.

Novikov is equally appalled that innocent servants can be ruined by false accusations of theft made by readers of coffee grounds, but crime detection continued to be part of the work of fortune-tellers until at least the 1840s.[25] To the contemporary eye, magical theft detection looks arbitrary and unjust, but in fact, when the suspects could be assembled, the ritual had the clear psychological function of putting pressure on the guilty person, who might betray himself, as in Vladimir Dal′'s story 'The clairvoyant' where two servants suspected of stealing some money visit a famous sibyl to establish which of them is responsible. One of the men disappears without trace before meeting her, leading to the inevitable conclusion that this was the guilty man. Since the guilty party did not actually conduct the divinatory session, and in the many instances when suspects were not present, fortune-tellers probably reinforced their client's own views by identifying the person strongly suspected by him. His suspicions once confirmed, the client then felt justified in acting on them, and received a degree of social support for his actions.[26] Sieve divination, as Chulkov notes, was used exclusively for this purpose. In the presence of all the suspects, a sieve was balanced on the fortune-teller's outstretched hand, and each suspect named in turn. If the sieve was seen to move at the mention of a certain name, that person was deemed the thief. Alternatively, in a method seemingly identical to that used in Britain, but perhaps used when the suspects could not or would not be present, shears were attached to the top of a sieve, and two people not involved placed the end of the shears on their middle fingers. In this case the aim was to identify the appearance of the thief, with the fortune-teller intoning 'a person with black hair, with fair hair' etc. Movements of the sieve indicated the thief's hair colour, and his or her other features could be similarly revealed.[27] It may be assumed that in Antonii Pogorel′skii's story 'The poppyseed cakeseller from Lafertovo', which is set in the

1790s, the cake-selling sibyl uses her sieve when identifying thieves. By the 1830s sieve divination was more of a village occupation, but working out a thief's identity was still a valid part of the fortune-teller's activities, albeit in new ways. Sakharov lists three reasons why people visit cartomancers, of which one is crime detection. However, by the 1890s, thanks presumably to a more sophisticated public and a more efficient police force, urban fortune-tellers no longer offered to detect crime, concentrating on what Sakharov regarded as the most important of their functions by the 1830s: matters of the heart and material circumstance.

In eighteenth-century towns, in accordance with rural folk custom, remuneration for fortune-telling services was voluntary, though cash was becoming the norm. Pogorel′skii's cakeseller accepts a contribution before beginning work, though she often receives further payment, twice as much as before, when her relieved and satisfied guests depart. Four decades on, Dal′'s fortune-teller is a conservative figure, who refuses payment. She does not even accept voluntary payments for herself, declaring that all contributions are for charity, though Dal′, whose depiction of the fortune-teller as a whole lacks the usual negative bias, does remark casually that no one ever knew whether these contributions ever reached the intended recipients. By the end of the century, according to Otshel′nik, fortune-tellers charged anything from twenty kopecks to a ruble, sometimes operating a sliding scale according to circumstance. By then, it was obviously no longer believed that the efficacy of the prognostication was negated by the open payment of fees.

The only significant innovation in the practice of urban fortune-tellers in the eighteenth century lay in the types of divinatory skill they practised. Apart from the traditional use of sieve, psalter or beans, they rapidly acquired the new arts of reading the cards or coffee grounds. By adopting these skills, fortune-tellers were acting as cultural intermediaries in familiarizing the urban population (who generally did not own books) with new, imported divinatory forms. They themselves had probably acquired them orally, since, as already noted, the first references to readers of cards and coffee grounds predate the appearance of printed instructions. Coffee-cup divination, which could only have caught on after coffee became fashionable in the 1740s,[28] is mentioned by Novikov in 1772, while cartomancy is attested from the 1770s, though playing cards were known well before this. But even if earlier cartomantic texts once existed, it is unlikely that fortune-tellers could have read them. All the references in fictional and non-fictional sources are to women of humble background and modest circumstances. Literacy was lamentably low in the eighteenth century, and always lower among women than men. Even at the end of the nineteenth century, as Otshel'nik reveals, some urban fortune-tellers were illiterate. Oral transmission doubtless accounted for their acquisition of these skills, with the source probably domestic servants in the houses of foreigners or aristocratic ladies who had travelled or purchased fortune-telling books in French or German.

Just as the functions of fortune-tellers altered over time, so too the skills they practised changed. Sieve divination, as has already been mentioned, had largely fallen out of the repertoire by the 1830s. Psalter divination seems to have passed out of fashion in towns in the course of the eighteenth century, though it was still used in villages in the nineteenth. The method used for detective purposes was similar to sieve divination in that a key was tied inside a psalter, which was then suspended from the ceiling. Names were read out and the guilty party held to be the one at whose name the book moved.[29] Sakharov remarked that this form of divination was usually performed by amateurs, and Tereschenko that it was a rural rather than urban aid to crime detection.[30] Bean divination, by contrast, was more enduringly popular, probably because it was directed towards elucidating the personal future of the individual, and the equipment was easily obtainable. Practitioners who used beans were so well known that sections on bean divination in fortune-telling books published before 1850 were almost always ascribed to an anonymous fortune-teller. Sakharov also makes a point of saying that professionals told fortunes with beans in the 1830s. However, by 1880 it was only a rural specialty,[31] judging by its omission from the array of skills offered by Otshel'nik's Petersburg fortune-tellers.

The best-known type of fortune-teller in the eighteenth and early nineteenth centuries was the reader of coffee grounds, thanks not only to Novikov but also to Ivan Krylov, whose comic opera *The Reader of Coffee Grounds* (1783) drew on Novikov's material and censorious attitudes; the conventionally structured plot revolves around the unmasking of a reader of coffee grounds who is in league with the servants in stealing the silver belonging to a gullible provincial lady. The fortune-teller who predicted the poet Pushkin's future in 1826 similarly told fortunes from coffee cups,[32] and it is one of the skills of Pogorel'skii's poppyseed cakeseller. She operates in secret because divination was banned at that point by Catherine the Great.[33] Apart from sieve and coffee cup, she also reads the cards. Even if it is assumed that this situation relates more to the date of the story (1825) than to the 1790s, it is clear that some time at the end of the eighteenth or early nineteenth century, fortune-tellers adopted cartomancy, which then became so popular that it had become the sole occupation of some by the 1830s.[34] Along with coffee-cup divination, cards thus became the favoured methods for fortune-tellers in pre-Revolutionary Russia. Whether they offered several methods, like Pogorel'skii's cakeseller or Dal''s clairvoyant, or just one, reading cards or coffee grounds was certain to be included.

Although spiritualism caught on in the third quarter of the nineteenth century, the medium occupied a different niche in the market, and spiritualism does not appear to have filtered down to fortune-tellers. Many of those visited by Otshel'nik, for example, used traditional methods; five read the cards or coffee cups or both.[35] Innovation was not what their clients wanted. If they did, they probably visited the dubious witches and sorcerers on Otshel'nik's list, or indeed a spiritualist medium.

It is perhaps more surprising that some of the fortune-telling skills described in countless printed guides did not become part of the professional repertoire. Reading palms was either left to gypsies, or remained within the domestic sphere. It is unclear why this should be, though possibly the link with physiognomy (they were almost always printed together) may have helped. Physiognomy, viewed as a 'pseudo-science', retained some credibility and adherents in polite society up to around 1840. It claimed to explain character rather than directly predict the future, and for that reason may not have attracted Russian fortune-tellers. Gypsies, on the other hand, had acquired chiromantic skills long before they arrived in Russia in the mid-eighteenth century, no doubt from vulgarized versions that saw chiromancy as divinatory. The absence of any skills involving astrology comes as no surprise, since even fortune-telling books, which were intended for the literate, had gradually rejected astrology as too complicated. The absence of dice divination, which was popular with black-magic practitioners in the seventeenth and eighteenth centuries, may perhaps be explained by the connections of dice with gambling, a male preserve. Since fortune-telling was, as I shall show, a female occupation, dice would not seem a natural choice.

Eighteenth- and nineteenth-century commentators are not primarily interested in the gender of fortune-tellers but they reveal it through the words they use for them; Novikov and Krylov refer only to female coffee-cup diviners,[36] while the editor of *The Wizard, No Idle Babbler . . .* (1792) refers disparagingly to fortune-tellers as *vorozhei* and *gadal'shchitsy*. While the second term refers only to women, the first could, in principle, also be applied to men. In actual fact, it almost always meant a female fortune-teller, as is clear from Sakharov's and Tereshchenko's use of the term. Pushkin's clairvoyant was a woman, as were all of Otshel'nik's. In this way, gender rôles both mirror traditional rural practice where men were more involved in black magic (including divination) and women more in healing and divination, and at the same time are stable throughout the period. Men neither read the cards nor, more understandably, given women's sway over the serving of light refreshments, scrutinized the coffee cups. The only area in which they seem to have participated at all is dream divination. The Kindly Old Man of Duck Street is an example. According to his nephew, he enjoyed great success as a dream interpreter up to his death in 1861. Tereshchenko, in his discussion of dream interpretation, also refers at one point to practitioners of both sexes. An explanation may be sought in the relative seriousness with which dream divination could be regarded since dreams were often deeply troubling affairs which could predict death and other tragedies, whereas much fortune-telling was concerned with matters of the heart, a traditional area of female concern. It is likely, nonetheless, that men were in the minority, since dream interpretation was a mainly female activity in traditional Russian life.

The only types of male clairvoyant and soothsayer, apart from village-style sorcerers, were holy fools, who were found all over Russia and were widely consulted either in asylums or in their own homes. Regarded as paranormal rather than abnormal, they were thought of as people of God who had special spiritual powers including clairvoyance.[37] Coming from dispossessed groups, whether women or disadvantaged men, holy fools had much in common with those described by Lewis as ecstatically possessed.[38] Despite obvious imbecility in some instances and a common refusal to observe elementary matters of hygiene, they enjoyed widespread respect, even adulation. Like fortune-tellers, they drew their support primarily from women, though they also attracted male supporters.[39] Female holy fools rarely attained the national prestige enjoyed by the most famous male holy fools, in a situation that paralleled rural culture, where the most powerful figure involved in divination was the sorcerer, usually a man.[40] Those that did were usually known for their powers of prediction. For example, on 6 September 1855, the poet Tiutchev's daughter Anna and her friend Aleksandra Dolgorukaia made a plan to visit a female clairvoyant holy fool, resident at Khot′kov monastery. The visit did not come off, but the intention reveals the respect for holy fools in the highest circles (these were ladies-in-waiting at the court of Alexander II).[41]

As in the village, fortune-telling was not a profession for the young. Fortune-tellers are always described as middle-aged or elderly, often as widows living on their own; Pogorel′skii, for example, declares with Romantic exaggeration that his old cake-seller was aged ninety. Coffee-cup readers in the 1830s were said to be 'elderly women, garrulous, quick-witted and often drunk, in Russian popular belief, "drinking as a consequence of their mental gifts"'.[42] From a historical point of view, the situation merely reflects the ancient equation of age and wisdom, especially where prophecy was concerned, but in purely practical terms, a middle-aged or elderly woman, widowed or without a family to care for her, had to find some means of support.

Their profession provided most of them with at least minimal subsistence. In the eighteenth century those who had access to great houses, like Krylov's coffee-cup diviner, probably did well, but others could barely scrape a living. Novikov observed that 'some coffee-cup readers may well not have a complete garment to their name, simply going around in tattered rags'.[43] Dal′'s clairvoyant enjoys fame but not great fortune. She has enough money for a servant, but her house on the outskirts of St Petersburg is modest. It may be that later in the century they could earn more, since Otshel′nik notes with outrage that five to ten rubles a day, even fifteen was normal. These sums were decent but not huge and his reaction is more a reflection of his view of them as charlatans, undeserving of remuneration of any kind. As he describes them, they live at best modestly, at worst in squalor. None could be said to be well-off.

Not only sex and age, but also *modus operandi* link fortune-tellers to their country counterparts. In order to fulfil the traditional female role of maintaining community structures and welfare, in this case through divination, rural clairvoyants needed to be familiar with the personalities and relationships of the members of their community, and their rôle was generally valued because of this knowledge. In towns, by contrast, the position of fortune-tellers was generally less enviable. The fragmented nature of urban society and the hostility of large sectors of the population made it harder for them to operate. Though they were unlikely to experience the open hostility or violence common in the countryside when magic specialists were believed to have acted malevolently, the climate was otherwise much less benign, not least because they frequently lacked prior knowledge of their clients simple to obtain in close-knit rural communities; the first stage in telling fortunes is always to gain a client's confidence by indicating a knowledge of his or her life and current problems.[44] Chulkov assumed that the attempt to acquire background knowledge of clients and their domestic circumstances merely indicated fraudulent practice. The women who read coffee cups, he declared, achieved their sordid ends by getting to know the servants in a house, so that they could find out what was what. Once they had made their predictions, or claimed to have detected the perpetrators of a crime, they split the proceeds with their informants.[45] Novikov suggests that they were easily flummoxed by customers who refused to furnish any information.[46] The editor of *The Wizard, No Idle Babbler . . .* (1792) declared that fortune-tellers were people who 'squeezed money out of people by deception'. Sakharov's comments about fortune-tellers are slightly less contemptuous. But, evincing a genuine interest in popular belief, he nonetheless makes it clear that they are charlatans. Women who practised cartomancy possessed, he said, an enormous network of acquaintances, mainly among servants, tradesmen and delivery boys. Thus 'the crowds of people who go to see fortune-tellers are always known to them' and consequently they 'are aware in advance who will be coming, for what reason and what needs to be said to them'.[47] Otshel'nik is gleeful at exposing fortune-tellers by giving them false information to work on. It does not occur to him that any skill or integrity was involved in their work.

The popularity of fortune-tellers is either explicitly stated by those who comment on them, or conveyed in their regret and irritation at the trust they enjoyed with so many people. Novikov notes that they were popular with all classes of society in the late eighteenth century. He reserves the greatest contempt for those social groups who should, in his view, know better, but concedes that nothing better could be expected of the 'stupid rabble'.[48] A century later, Otshel'nik states with disgust that one of his fortune-tellers received as many as ten clients in a single afternoon. Women, it appears, used their services more than men. Novikov does mention an instance where a man summons a fortune-teller; interestingly, it is not to glimpse his future, but to find out whether his wife is faithful. This service was probably largely used by men, at least where the spouse was openly confronted with the information. It is hard to imagine a humble fortune-teller agreeing to tell an irate husband from the noble or merchant classes to his face that she believed him unfaithful to his wife. Crime detection in a village environment was taken seriously by both sexes, and this continued to be the case in an urban setting, so long as the method found favour with clients. Sakharov notes that both men and women visited fortune-tellers for this reason, and in Dal''s 'The clairvoyant', it is two men (both of peasant origin) who visit a fortune-teller to sort out which of them is a thief.

Depending on the period, men did consult fortune-tellers about their personal futures. In the 1820s and 1830s it was modish for aristocratic young men to consult fortune-tellers; Pushkin went to a Petersburg fortune-teller and the Decembrists, Ryleev and Lunin, consulted the famous prophetess, Mlle Lenormand, in Paris,[49] while the fictional Pechorin in Mikhail Lermontov's novel, *A Hero of Our Time* (1840), is said to have been told by a fortune-teller that he would die through the fault of a woman. This trend may be regarded as another manifestation of the Romantic interest in fate and the processes of the unconscious. However, by no means all male clients of fortune-tellers in the 1820s and 1830s could have been world-weary young Romantics, who were not a numerous category of person. Dal''s fictional fortune-teller certainly sees men as well as women, and there is no suggestion that they were all young Byrons. Sakharov does not specify the gender of the visitors other than those seeking the return of their stolen property, but implies that more were women. This would accord with both rural and amateur urban practice.

Otshel'nik's statements of 1894 about the gender of the clientèle of professional fortune-tellers confirm Sakharov's assumptions. Whenever he refers to clients in general, he *assumes* they were female: 'lonely widows, merchant women or old maids'.[50] When he looks at the evidence furnished by waiting rooms, the picture is less clear-cut: it is true that the one he calls *chernoknizhnitsa* has only female customers, predominantly servants and simple folk, along with the occasional gentlewoman.[51] Yet Anna Karlovna Gren, a cartomancer and coffee-cup specialist, whose clientèle is rather better off, evidently sees men, judging by both the presence of cigarette butts in her waiting room and the emergence of a young man from her consulting room. Since crime detection was by this time not one of their services, this observation reveals that some men, including young ones, did seek personal guidance from fortune-tellers. Even so, the bulk of Gren's clients were evidently female, since the author spots one man to five women; two tradesmen's wives, two Swedes and a lady dressed up to the nines.[52]

Wealthy patrons of fortune-tellers preferred to summon fortune-tellers to their houses, but here they had to run the gauntlet of male disapproval. Like some kinds of domestic divination, professional fortune-telling was a discreet operation; the mistress of the house had to whisk the fortune-teller into a separate room in case her husband found out.[53] While Sakharov says that many fortune-tellers visited customers at home, Dal''s clairvoyant enjoyed such fame that, not merely did she not go to clients' houses, but she even sometimes refused to grant an audience, regardless of the client's status. In this way she neatly reversed the conventional situation in government offices where lower-class petitioners waited for days to see an official. Otshel'nik's fortune-tellers all received clients at home, but he was well aware that there existed other possibilities of meeting clients in their homes or the park. He further suggests that fortune-tellers preferred not to give their real names when they went to see clients, lest they be pursued by dissatisfied customers. Given his prejudices, it is not surprising that he should adduce fear of complaint as the reason for fortune-tellers' secretive behaviour, but since he at the same time notes that few customers were disenchanted, one may surmise that the answer lay in clients' own desire not to provoke ridicule or be seen in poor neighbourhoods. Dal′ depicts male and female visitors leaving their carriages at a distance and approaching the sibyl's house as discreetly as possible, with hats pulled down, collars up or faces veiled.[54]

Cartomancers, the most popular type of fortune-teller in the 1830s, relied on being able to gauge the emotional state of their visitors. According to Sakharov, clients fell into three categories: lovers who, if unhappy, gave themselves away by their distraught behaviour; those in difficult or straitened circumstances who hoped for deliverance and whose clothes or behaviour revealed their inner state, and finally men and women who had lost some property. Their absolute trust in the efficacy of the fortune-teller was an important factor in their being duped, he believed. Tereshchenko observes that with clients in extreme emotional distress (pale, their eyes red from crying, with shaking hands and incoherent speech), fortune-tellers could easily work out what was wrong, and since their predictions were deliberately ambiguous, they often hit the target.[55]

Tereshchenko adds that clients were prone to exaggerate and broadcast an accurate prediction, while a failure was blamed on fate. Both he and Otshel′nik observe that if clients did become disillusioned with one fortune-teller, they simply transferred their custom to another, who then rapidly acquired a crowd of devotees. 'Passions hold universal sway', remarks Tereshchenko, 'but they are best remarked in the cards.'[56] Otshel′nik ascribes the success enjoyed by fortune-telllers not only to the gullibility of their customers but also to their shame if predictions failed to come true. This point suggests that nothing would disabuse the credulous. Locked in their own contempt, the two commentators fail to perceive that visitors to fortune-tellers needed the hope and encouragement they offered.

It may be concluded that women's concern for matters of personal relations and family welfare together with their relative powerlessness and lack of job opportunity pushed them actively into fortune-telling as a profession, especially if they did not have, or no longer had family commitments. Clients undoubtedly took them seriously, though there must have been those from the moneyed classes who summoned a fortune-teller for fun. Novikov, Sakharov and Tereshchenko offer plenty of evidence about the desperation and distress of those who sought their help. It matters little whether many were careful to say only what clients wished to hear, or even that some were conscious charlatans. In a period when professional counsellors of other kinds were lacking, the fortune-teller performed the therapeutic rôle of offering hope and solace.

Conversely, the preponderance of women among clients is also attributable to gender stereotypes. Statistical evidence from Britain and other Western countries shows not only that women are more vulnerable to emotional stress and more willing to seek help than men, but also that this is not a modern phenomenon. The women patients who in the first part of the seventeenth century complained of stress and mental disorders to the astrological physician, Richard Napier, outnumbered men by approximately two to one. Analysing Napier's patients, Michael MacDonald hesitantly but plausibly speculates that the habit of seeking help 'was encouraged by a common prejudice that made it acceptable for women (but not men) to express their frustrations as sickness and for men (but not women) to express theirs as aggression and violence'.[57] One may observe that a visit to the fortune-teller should be regarded as a more active and positive response to distress than illness. Traditional female rôles obliged women to focus on family and community relationships, which were inevitably often problematical, while, as is often plausibly assumed, accounting for their 'superiority among the ranks of the troubled and insane'.[58] Women thus possessed both greater cause for emotional problems and the psychological mechanisms for bringing these into the open. When emotional problems hit Russian men, they may have reacted with violent or aggressive behaviour or, even more probably, taken refuge in the traditional remedy for a painful present and uncertain future, the bottle. It might be argued that the function of healers and fortune-tellers differ too greatly for any parallel to be drawn, but though fortune-tellers' clients did not present physical as well as mental symptoms and did not expect a cure, they can be aligned with emotionally distressed patients through their hope for some psychological relief.

This raises the question, of course, of why numbers of fortune-tellers should have declined in the late nineteenth century, just as towns swelled and, presumably, urban distress rose. One reason may be that the disappearance of services such as crime detection and the gradual abandonment of the traditional fortune-teller by the élite classes resulted in fewer visits by the high-born and by men, and so deprived fortune-tellers of their most affluent supporters, forcing many out of business as the profession became less lucrative. It may also be the case that, as literacy rose, and more people could purchase and make use of one of the huge numbers of handy printed guides, fortune-telling increasingly became a domestic or amateur pursuit. In any case, we have only Otshel'nik's estimate of the number of fortune-tellers in Petersburg to go on. There were very probably many others, particularly semi-professionals, who read the cards for neighbours or acquaintances and occasionally received some form of payment, as happens in Britain today.[59]

In some ways, the social history of fortune-telling mirrors that of divinatory books, in which imported skills became enormously popular and by the middle of the ninetenth century were so entrenched as to form their own tradition. Both fortune-telling books for the people and professional fortune-tellers in the second half of the century were deeply conservative, following types and patterns established in the late eighteenth or early nineteenth centuries. Upper-class repudiation of fortune-telling (books included) after about 1840 resulted in their becoming largely the property of the lower classes, who in general preferred familiar types of clairvoyant or guide. But while the fortune-telling book market underwent a renewal in the late nineteenth century to ensure it maintained its hold on the better-off, fortune-tellers did not change. Instead, traditional fortune-tellers lost ground to new kinds of sibyl (the medium, for example) catering for those in need of hope and guidance who no longer trusted the old fortune-teller.

CHAPTER 7

Sages and prophets

Eighteenth-century Russian translators usually translated the titles of fortune-telling books lock, stock and barrel, thereby introducing their Russian readers to a whole range of foreign luminaries, either previously unknown or familiar only to a select few. Since false attribution of divinatory works to illustrious sages, philosophers, alchemists, astronomers and others was commonplace practice elsewhere in Europe, fortune-telling books were acting not as tools of enlightenment, but of obfuscation. It was enough for figures like Aristotle or Albertus Magnus to comment on dreams, astrology or magic for editors and compilers of popular literature in the Latin Middle Ages and after to turn them into dream diviners, physiognomers and so on.[1] Additionally, figures such as Michael Scot or Albertus Magnus tended to acquire a pseudo-corpus of works, usually of a more popular, including popular divinatory, character. Since the processes at work in the development of popular literature in Russia echoed those in West Europe, but knowledge of Classical thought and medieval Western writings on science and magic were restricted to a tiny élite, it is far from surprising that publishers and editors acted at times with even less regard for accuracy than their Western counterparts, to the point of using names interchangeably. This chapter examines the careers of foreign divinatory luminaries in Russia as well as the rôle played by home-grown seers.

The first fortune-telling books in Russia (1760–90) were simple volumes containing a single text without reference to 'authorship' such as *A True and Most Simple Method of Reading the Cards* (Moscow, 1782,1785). By the 1790s, however, the large manuals issued by often semi-educated commercial publishers were enticing the reader to buy their large guides through titles listing a pick-and-mix assortment of astronomers, magicians, alchemists, mathematicians and others from Old Testament, Classical, Arabic, medieval and Renaissance times. The book, the reader was assured, had been penned by figures such as Plato, Ptolemy, Julius Caesar, Cagliostro (eighteenth-century magician and impostor), Albertus Magnus (medieval scholastic philosopher), Tycho Brahe (sixteenth-century Danish astronomer), Swedenborg, Artemidorus, Lavater (Swiss physiognomer), Regiomontanus (Renaissance mathematician, here called Ioann or Iogannes Kenigsberger), Michael Scot (medieval philosopher-bishop, reputed to be an alchemist, magician and physiognomer), Albumasar (ninth-century Arabic astrologer and astronomer), Apollonius of Tyana (ancient astrologer and mathematician), Zoroaster (Persian founder of Zoroastrianism), Giuseppe Moult (medieval political prophet), Haly (Arab astrologer, here called Aliia), Solomon, Plutarch, Hippocrates, Descartes, Aristotle, Pliny and others. Often when the reader opened the book he or she failed to discover any obvious relationship between text and most of the dignitaries listed on the cover; for example, *A New, Complete and Detailed Dreambook, Signifying the Amplified Interpretation and Elucidation of Every Dream, Such a Dreambook Not Being Previously Known in the Russian Language; With the Addition of Old Wives' Wisdom, Selected from the Works of Many Foreign Men Skilled in the Science of Dream Interpretation: Plato, Ptolemy, Haly, Artemidorus, Albumasar, Varlaam and Johannes Regiomontanus* (1802, 1808, 1818 with variants in 1829 and 1839) looks like a work full of contributions from the listed savants. In fact, the only one linked to the contents is the oneiromancer Artemidorus, since some of the dream objects and interpretations stem ultimately from his *Oneirocritica.* The others may be said to have been included, presumably as in the foreign original, merely to impress. Though fortune-telling publishers all over Europe used scholarly endorsements for their works, the adoption in Russia at this point may have something to do with the fashion for publishing anecdotes about famous people in the late eighteenth century, as well as the cultural authority awarded to West European figures in the new Westernizing culture of the élite.

Within the covers of these books, there was, in general, no concerted attempt to ascribe sections to a particular savant, such that the names on front covers frequently became simply symbols of an exotic, ancient tradition, designed to woo buyers. Exceptions are the lists of lucky and unlucky days in dreambooks which are always ascribed to Tycho Brahe, as well as Bruce's calendar and essays by

Michael Scot and Tavernier on the significance of dreams. Of these only two, Tycho Brahe and Bruce, warranted billing on the front cover; the others were evidently not deemed important enough, because their sections were subsidiary to the main alphabetical dreambook, and not strictly divinatory.

In the period to 1830, one of the most frequently misused names was that of Albertus Magnus (?1200–80), whose spurious reputation as an author of numerous works on divination and magic reached Russia in 1783 in *A Quantity of Useful Sections Selected From the Amazing Secrets of Albertus Magnus*, a fortune-telling volume translated from French. Between 1794 and 1822 at least fourteen books offered the secrets of happiness and misfortune in Albertus' 'Magic Mirror', another contained 'his' guide to physiognomy (1811), or 'his' pocket dreambook (1829).[2] Often merely a figurehead name on the front cover, he was occasionally presented inside as an expert in a given area. For example, Henri Decremps' *Focus Pocus* (1789), a collection of magic tricks based on an elementary knowledge of science, first appeared in Russian in 1791.[3] Decremps (1746–1826) was not a conjuror, but the first to penetrate and publicize the secrets of the famous conjuror, the self-styled Cavalier Pinetti, Marquis de Mercy (1750–1801).[4] Unsurprisingly, since Pinetti toured in Russia in 1799–1800 to great success, subsequent editions of conjuring tricks were usually attributed to him rather than to Decremps. Pinetti even featured from time to time on the title page of divinatory compilations right up to the Revolution. Despite their fame, the section on conjuring tricks was more often than not anonymous, while in one large compilation, *Soothsay, Do Not Jest . . .* (1808–27), it was attributed to Albertus, thus neatly illustrating how little names meant to editors, even just a few years after Pinetti reached the pinnacle of fame.

After 1830, as cheaper books began to be produced for a less educated market, so titles became simpler. For readers just discovering books, or whose horizons did not extend much beyond their own four walls, there was little point in listing ancient divinatory authorities. Even in the few types of fortune-telling compendium that continued publication, these lists shrank: the *Newest Complete Oracle, Divining and Predicting with Clear Answers the Fate of Young Lads and Lassies* . . ., put out by the firms of Smirnov/Smirnova and Sharapov between 1839 and 1880, mentioned just Bruce and Albertus, while only one of the many editions of *The Shop of All*

Delights . . . (published by Kirillov in 1850) enumerates the great authorities. Only when portmanteau editions became popular again in the 1890s do lists of names reappear, now used with even less relationship to contents than earlier: Albertus, for example, becomes the author of the list of unlucky days in a Sytin guide of 1912. During the nineteenth century certain types of book where one text predominated became attached to a particular name – King Solomon for the popular *lubok* and cheap printed Wheel of Fortune, Martyn Zadeka for dreambooks, though many more came without any attribution. Ancient authorities such as Aristotle, Pliny, or Albumasar tended to be jettisoned for more modern names: Cagliostro, Swedenborg, Bruce, Mlle Lenormand, Lavater. Cagliostro and Swedenborg (who had a following in Russia among Masons), for example, both acquired the reputation of experts on cartomancy and dreams.[5] Occasionally these attributions caught on with a humbler public, as is evident from the writer Aleksei Remizov's reminiscences about his mother's special fortune-telling cards.[6] In his childhood, he recalls, hardly an evening would go by without one of the workers at the factory where they lived dropping in and urging his mother: 'Swedenborg's cards!' 'The Swedenborg cards!' 'Tell us our fortune with Sivenborg.' This scene, which would have occurred in the 1880s or early nineties, demonstrates that spurious reputations could flourish in family or local groups thanks to incorrect attributions and the perceived efficacy of a particular text.

An alternative to the use of named authorities was adopted by many publishers of longer fortune-telling books in the period after 1830. They ascribed their texts to anonymous sages such as Egyptian and Indian wise men and astronomers.[7] In so doing they were simply taking the most comprehensible part of the attributions in many of the fortune-telling books published before 1830.[8] These too were characteristic of Europe; *The Old Egyptian Fortune-Teller's Last Legacy* was published in London in the eighteenth century, *The Egyptian Dream Book and Fortune-Teller* in New York in 1866, and even today Polish dreambooks claim to be Egyptian oracles.

In any case, the continuing use of 'famous names' to lend authority to compendia remained characteristic of Russian fortune-telling books. By contrast, English and American fortune-telling books often do not bother (Erra Pater in England, and the

American *Universal Dream-Book . . .* (four editions, 1797–1817) which listed fourteen authorities are obvious exceptions). Where they do, they prefer local prophets such as Mrs Bridget, Mother Carey, Policy Sam,[9] Old Gypsy Madge or Nan, who may or may not ever have existed, or else, especially in America, authors whose authority is emphasized by the title of Dr or Professor.

It may be that the greater insistence in Russia on ascribing dream interpretation to foreign luminaries partly reflects the state of publishing in the first half-century of their existence on Russian soil. Whereas English eighteenth-century guides were chapbooks, in Russia they were designed, as all printed books had to be, for upper-class readers, who wished to demonstrate their alienation from folk 'superstition'. Its influence on them was too recent, and on others too apparent for such things to be treated with indulgence. The very vitality of the indigenous folk tradition appears to have encouraged the new printed divinatory literature to insist on its foreign origins. At the same time, its massive popularity ironically depended on the continuing existence of parallel oral traditions. More generally, things foreign, literature included, bore the imprint of respectability and sophistication; there was obvious mileage in keeping the names of foreign savants and seers, even if they were mumbo-jumbo to most readers. Once entrenched in the conservative traditions of popular literature, the names of sages and prophets continued to help distinguish and elevate printed divinatory literature in the eyes of its increasingly more humble readers. In particular, long lists were deemed essential in promoting the virtues of pantechnicon works designed for those with more income and pretensions.

The need to use a sage to boost the credibility of fortune-telling books was not simply a matter of mere copying of titles. Russian dreambooks illustrate clearly how cultural transmission is complicated by chance factors and local conditions, for they are rarely attributed to the great authorities on oneiromancy like their Western equivalents; Achmet ben Sirin is quite unknown in Russia (although some of the entries in the dreambook of Artemidorus, mentioned above, stem from Achmet), while Artemidorus, after the five editions of his dreambook between 1800 and 1830, simply fades from sight. Far more startling is the absence of the name of the Prophet Daniel, the supremo of West European and Scandinavian dreambooks. In Russia his name, like that of

Achmet, never appears on the title page of printed dreambooks, as a consequence of which, even though 'his' dreambook was constantly reprinted, Russians did not know him as an interpreter of dreams. Sheer chance explains the absence of Daniel; the dream texts arbitrarily selected for translation simply happened not to be attributed to him. Perhaps his name might have become known a little later if his place had not been usurped by Martyn Zadeka.

In the nineteenth century, almost any Russian asked who was the best known interpreter of dreams would have unhesitatingly named Zadeka. To this day his is the only name that Russians know. If pressed, they can sometimes supply the information that he compiled the manual favoured by Tat'iana in Pushkin's *Eugene Onegin.* They rarely know more, but this does not prevent their rejection of any suggestion that he might have been foreign.

The 'career' of Zadeka in fact displays a number of features characteristic of the development of popular culture and its interrelationship with élite culture in Russia, though it should be added that it is distinctively Russian in its form and timing rather than its essence. It is, firstly, not untypical that the figure of Zadeka should be of foreign origin; figures in popular culture, once absorbed locally, are frequently adopted and adapted to local conditions. There is, for example, an obvious parallel with the figures of Eruslan Lazarevich and Bova Korolevich, who despite the Indian origin of one and the West European provenance of the other, were regarded as Russian heroes by the end of the eighteenth century, and even entered Russian folk-tale repertoire. In this particular instance the first appearance of the 'Russian' sage was in Switzerland where, in 1770, a pamphlet appeared in Basle containing the political predictions of the 'famous 106-year-old hermit Martin Zadeck' from Solothurn, delivered on his deathbed to a faithful group of friends on 20 December, 1769. The genre of political prophecy was a well-developed one in German-speaking areas, and the prophecy seems to have excited little interest.[10] Only one copy has come to light (though it cannot be excluded that others may lurk in libraries elsewhere), and it seems unlikely that it ran to more than one German edition.[11] The Swiss sage was saved from rapid extinction by the lucky accident of a Russian translation of his predictions. The Russian Zadeck, a generally accurate translation by one KN, appeared a year later in 1770. The translator was probably Nikolai Kurganov, best known for *The*

Epistolary Art, but also the translator of a number of other works.[12] Evidently Kurganov regarded political prophecy with respect since he did not preface the work, as he did in the case of his translation of a fortune-telling text, with a statement that the contents were not to be taken seriously. The predictions of Zadeck, in his Russian garb now transformed into Martyn Zadek, proved instantly appealing to Russian readers. Among other things the Swiss sage predicted the decline of the Turkish empire and the loss of its European territories in 1770. With a Russian victory over the Turks in the campaign of 1769–70, and the *St Petersburg Herald* in its issue of 12 January 1770 predicting the demise of Ottoman power in Europe, the prophecy struck a chord with readers. Interestingly, the passing of 1770 without major loss of territory for the Turks did not undermine trust in Zadek.[13] His popularity among Russian patriots was in any case assured by his prediction of a shining future for Russia, while his warning of the French conquest of Italy must have given him credence in the Napoleonic period. For Russians watching their country's emergence onto the international stage, the Swiss sage's pronouncements were soothing or even inspirational. The work was reprinted in separate editions in 1785, 1798, 1807, 1820, and in response perhaps to the Greek War of Independence, again in 1828 and 1830. Furthermore, judging by the existence of no less than seven manuscript copies, it was highly regarded by those without access to bookshops. At the same time, it achieved the widest possible social currency by appearing in cheap woodcut form, which brought it to a reading public that included servants, merchants, the urban lower middle classes as well as the less sophisticated country gentry. All these editions declared on their title pages that Zadek was Swiss. This was not, however, always the case with another group of publications of the prophecy, those published in a variety of fortune-telling compendia (even though the text of Zadek made it clear that the ancient hermit's abode was the Alps). Between 1800 and 1830, almost all such books included Zadek. Two published in 1807 advertised the prophecy on their title pages as the chief item. The others, with a couple of exceptions, mention Zadek's name in the descriptive titles but mostly along with a varied assortment of luminaries such as Ptolemy, Albertus Magnus, Tycho Brahe and Bruce. This development removed Zadek from his specifically Swiss setting into the category of international sages.

Between 1770 and 1830 Zadek's prophecy appeared in print no less than twenty-one times, plus an unknown number of woodcut editions. After this it came out more rarely, mostly issued by publishers who were trying to maximize their profits by republishing tried and trusted texs.[14] Zadek's prestige seems inflated, especially as some of his prophecies (famine in Germany and Switzerland, or the cataclysmic destruction of much of the New World, for example) were not very credible. Sceptics emerged, and not only among the highly educated; Matvei Komarov, the author of the immensely popular tale of the Russian bandit Van'ka Kain, himself of relatively humble background, declared in 1779 that his own tale contained 'indubitably more truth than the empty prophecy of Zadek'.[15] This was evidently a minority view. Nonetheless, by the 1820s, sophisticated and educated young men did not know Zadek as a political prophet. For the Decembrist Baten'kov, he was a soothsayer who predicted a rather more personal kind of future. As he jocularly remarked in a letter, he would definitely get married in 1825, because Martyn Zadeka, Albertus Magnus and Mr Bruce had unanimously predicted the birth the following year of an extraordinary child, who would, naturally, be his.[16] Pushkin, on the other hand, connected Zadek, whom he too called Zadeka, exclusively with dream divination; in the fifth canto of *Eugene Onegin* Tat'iana seeks elucidation of her disturbing dream in her favourite book, a guide to oneiromancy ascribed to the 'chief of the Chaldean sages, the diviner and interpreter of dreams', Martyn Zadeka.[17] In response to comments from the minor critic Fedorov, Pushkin subsequently appended a corrective note: 'Fortune-telling books are published in Russia under the name of Martyn Zadeka, an honourable man who did not compile divinatory books, as B. M. Fedorov has pointed out.'[18] He was at least prepared to grant the political prophet the epithet 'honourable', though the extent to which this was tongue-in-cheek can only be guessed at.

Thus by 1825 Zadeck had been transmuted into Zadek and the switch to Zadeka was under way, while his reputation as political prophet was being overlaid by that of dream interpreter. This reincarnation is perhaps appropriate for a man who was probably an invention. There is no evidence that the 106-year-old recluse ever existed and it seems likely that the name was taken from Voltaire's *Zadig ou la Destinée* (1748) which similarly purports to be the account of a venerable sage and makes allegorical reference to Turkey.[19] 'Zaddik' is a rabbinical title meaning the 'specially righteous'. *Zadig* had been translated into Russian a few years earlier in 1765, which may possibly have assisted the prophecy's favourable reception. An alternative suggestion made by the writer Vladimir Nabokov is that the name derives from Zadok, a high priest in the time of Solomon.[20] The close association of Solomon with Freemasonry and other mystical cults so popular in the eighteenth century make this a credible hypothesis.

The actual identity of the anonymous author remains a secret, though there was one attempt in Russia to provide an answer to the mystery, and incidentally develop Zadek's career as a political prophet. In 1833 the Romantic writer A. F. Vel'tman published a Utopian novel *The Year MMMCDXLVIII. A Manuscript by Martyn Zadek*. In the introduction the author claims that, while in Jassy in Bessarabia, he made the acquaintance of a jolly Swiss pieman.[21] After a while he decides to ask him about his illustrious fellow countryman. With an exclamation of surprise the man tells him that Martin Zadeck is his ancestor, his own name being Werner Zadeck. He goes on to elaborate on his ancient lineage stretching back through Zadok the high priest, and then solicits a ruble before telling Martin Zadeck's story of the year 3448, recorded by one Ernst Roder, preserved in Zolotur (for Solothurn) and known as Martin Zadeck's manuscript. This device permits the inventive Vel'tman to present his own novel as the work of the famous prophet, a mystification typical of this Romantic writer. It was a subterfuge to fit the repressive 1830s, since the work depicted a social utopia of the thirty-fifth century, destroyed by a tyrant and only restored after his death. It might well have attracted official opprobrium. The setting, the mythical state of Bosphorania, has some links with Turkey which looms large in the prophecy. Nonetheless, there is no need to conclude, as has been done, that the author of the prophecy was Ernst Roder.[22] The statement in the introduction to the book that this is not a verbatim account 'because Werner Zadeck's language approached that of the time of the tower of Babel and consisted of all the dialects on earth' leaves no doubt that this is fantasy. We are asked to believe that Vel'tman deciphered Werner Zadeck's garbled rendering of Ernst Roder's record of Martin Zadeck's utterances. The roving pieman can only be an invention, like Zadeck himself. It may also be concluded that in the social milieu of small-time officialdom in which Vel'tman had grown up,[23] Zadek retained his position as prophet, whereas in Pushkin's high-society circles he had become a dream interpreter rather earlier, and in so doing ended with a different spelling of his name.

The new career of Zadeck as a writer of three-volume social utopias did not take off; Vel'tman's novel was not a success. On the other hand, since 1800 Zadeka had been branching out in the direction of fortune-telling. His reputation was launched by a Moscow merchant cum publisher called Semen Komisarov in *The Ancient and Modern Permanent Divinatory Oracle, Discovered After the Death of a Certain One-Hundred-and-Six-Year-Old Man Martin Zadek* . . . (1800). Here the sage was still Zadek but now Martin instead of Martyn. The contents of the book were fairly typical of the time; Komisarov combined well-known divinatory texts, geomancy, physiognomy and palmistry as well as magic tricks and humorous riddles. The title led the reader to think that Zadek was the author of all of these, but the headings for each section ascribe only dreams, physiognomy, palmistry and magic tricks to him, though these are certainly the most substantial.[24]

In the three following decades Zadek's name continued to be attached to sections in divinatory books. Responsibility for the promotion of Zadek as multi-purpose sage lay exclusively with the publishing firms of Reshetnikov and Glazunov, and primarily with the former. The error was repeated in two large fortune-telling guides put out by Auguste Semen in 1824–5. Editors made no attempt to be consistent; while some of Reshetnikov's books, *The Magic Mirror* . . . of 1818 and the *Ancient and Modern Permanent Divinatory Oracle* . . . of 1821, ascribed the physiognomy and palmistry sections to Zadek, others such as the 1814 edition of *The Ancient Astrologer or The Oracle of Those Most Skilled in Divination, Martyn Zadek, Guiseppe Moult, Tycho Brahe and the Physiognomer Lavater and Others* . . . did not. This may perhaps be explained by Reshetnikov's known preference for printing books to order,[25] but equally plausibly by the cavalier attitude of publishers to popular texts. It may simply have depended upon the edition from which the various sections were pirated.

Zadek was less often presented as palmist and physiognomer at this time because of the contemporary fame of Lavater. Nikolai Il'in in his one-act comedy of 1816, *The Physiognomer and*

Chiromancer, condemned the heroine's husband for his foolish obsession with reading character from physical appearance, and poured venom on Lavater. There were, therefore, presumably enough people who knew that Zadek had nothing to do with these forms of divination to prevent the attribution from sticking. The same was not true for conjuring tricks, which were very popular in Russia at that time. As already mentioned, most texts were anonymous, even though they were taken from Pinetti or Decremps, leaving open the possibility of false attribution. Fortune-telling books published in 1807, 1817, 1820, 1824–5 and 1826, as well as the popular *Shop of All Delights* . . . (1830–50), contained 'Martyn Zadek's magic tricks'. Now Zadek could tell the reader how to teach his or her cat to write in Latin, French and Russian in twenty minutes flat (thanks to some invisible ink, a docile cat and a knowledge of Latin, the last doubtless being the most problematic for Russians of the time). At this period, he was more widely presented as conjurer than dream interpreter, in which guise he made only four appearances, in 1807 (twice), 1820 and 1824–5.

Should then the image of Zadek as Zadeka the dream interpreter be attributed to Pushkin? Certainly the spelling seems to owe a good deal to *Eugene Onegin*, but the position with the dreambook is more complex. Whereas magic tricks were occasionally attributed to famous conjurors, the first dreambooks in Russia were anonymous.[26] On the other hand, since compilers and publishers of dream manuals and other forms of fortune-telling books liked to attribute their predictions to venerable or exotic sages, a wise 106-year-old was a perfect candidate. In Russia, the choice of the venerable Martyn Zadek was conditioned by his successful career as a political prophet. Political prophecy enjoyed considerable popularity in Europe in the sixteenth to eighteenth centuries, and appealed to newly Europeanized Russians. Furthermore, as the only type of divination that was entirely within the male sphere, it possessed a greater degree of respectability. As noted in chapter 4, the Academy Press and other high-brow publishers would stoop to political prophecy if not to cartomancy, and it is notable that most of the separately printed editions of Zadek's prophecy came out in the intellectual centre of Petersburg rather than Moscow. Age, respectability, foreign origins – the choice of Zadeka was almost a foregone conclusion. When it is also borne in mind that in Komisarov's fortune-telling guide the dreambook ascribed to

Martyn Zadek normally preceded other sections, reflecting the greater popularity and importance for Russians of dream divination, it is not so surprising that the name stuck.

In the years after 1825, as books began to be produced for a wider readership in both town and country, Martyn Zadeka's name attached itself to one of the standard short dreambooks. *The Interpretation of Dreams by the Venerable 106-year-old Man Martyn Zadek* seems to have been published first by the merchant I. I. Smirnov in Moscow in 1848,[27] and revived by his widow, M. Smirnova in 1865, 1870, 1877 and 1903 (and various years in between). The use of the spelling Zadek suggests that the inspiration for this publication was not Pushkin but an earlier divinatory compendium, although it is not possible to say exactly which. The Smirnov firm's title caught on with other Moscow publishers, who also issued multiple editions. A rival edition, likewise intended for peasants and semi-literate workers at the bottom end of the market, was put out by Abramov for two decades from the late 1860s. *The Interpretation of Dreams of the Well-Known Old Man Martyn Zadeka* may well have taken its cue from Pushkin, since the title dispenses with the words '106-year-old', and uses the Pushkinian spelling of the name. It was pirated by Sytin who had put out at least fourteen editions by 1915, when the print run was 30,000.[28] By the Revolution, Martyn Zadeka had become the accepted form of the name and 'his' dreambook had been produced in such quantities that there can hardly have been a village where he was not a household name. In Zamiatin's *A Provincial Tale,* it is dreams, the dreambook and Martyn Zadeka that the two main characters discuss over breakfast, while Marina Tsvetaeva's poem of 1924, *Dream,* makes reference to Martyn Zadeka's oneiromantic skills.

If this facet of Zadeka's reputation flourished, the brief career he had enjoyed as a multi-purpose sage was over by 1830. Though magic tricks were ascribed to Zadek (or Zadeka) in compendia published 1831, 1836, 1850 and 1866, these were a small proportion of the total of such texts. Furthermore he was never again presented as a physiognomer and chiromancer, though guides to chiromancy and physiognomy were popular components of fortune-telling manuals, particularly up to 1850.

Zadeka's career did not end, however, in a mass of cheap dream books with gaudy covers. He has made a reappearance in Russian literature, though not with any distinction. His name has been taken as a pseudonym by a number of Russian writers: one Iakov

Petrovich Davydov, who produced two books in Khar'kov in the 1920s, Vasilii Stepanovich Kurochkin in the journal *The Spark* (no. 32, 1862), Mikhail Ksenofontovich Sevin in a miscellany *The Fire* (Moscow, 1905), and a Ukrainian émigré writer (novel published in Neu-Ulm in 1947).[29] N. F. Shcherbina, the minor poet and satirist discussed in chapter 3, not only published the parodic *Dreambook of Contemporary Russian Literature* which he said served as an appendix to Martyn Zadeka, but also in his *Album of a Hypochondriac* described himself as 'Martyn Zadeka, son of Arcadia', a reference to his position as Russia's bucolic poet. The use of the pseudonym owes a great deal if not everything to Pushkin. Even if popular culture in the form of fortune-telling books seems not to have taken notice of Pushkin with any consistency until well into the second half of the nineteenth century, and even though it is likely that at the Revolution a larger number of ordinary people knew Martyn Zadeka from 'his' dreambook rather than from *Eugene Onegin*, it is probable that publishers like Sytin were aware of the Tat'iana connection. Writers who adopted the pseudonym of Zadeka were similarly following common Russian literary practice of referring to great writers of the past. In some instances, writers may have been aware of both connections; Remizov, for example, a writer particularly interested in Russian popular cultural traditions and the author of a story about dreams entitled *Martyn Zadeka*, was probably making a dual reference.

Who then dreamt up this sage? To some extent it was some unknown Swiss citizen, who created the political prophet. To some extent it was Komisarov who took this respected seer and launched him on a career as an all-purpose luminary, of which only the title of dream diviner stuck. To some extent it was the firm of I. I. Smirnov, who first produced the simple dreambook attributed to Zadek. Most of all, it was Pushkin who, ignorant of Zadek's origins, immortalized him as the great interpreter of dreams, and ensured the change from Zadek to Zadeka. Others tried and failed to launch him on a variety of careers as novelist, author of political Utopia, essays and stories. No single one of these can claim sole credit in a process in which the Russians took an imaginary old Swiss gentleman to their hearts, and transformed him into the most respected interpreter of their dreams.

Not a single sage so far discussed is female. A primarily female activity like fortune-telling might be expected to seek its authority in female figures, but in a male-dominated society authority figures tend to be male. Fortune-telling thus mirrors the situation in official religion where all positions of power and authority are in the hands of men but where much of the day-to-day practice and support of the official religion is performed by women.[30] The real sages are not only male but non-Russian. Nonetheless as time went on, and fortune-telling books became primarily women's books, it might be assumed that female authorities would appear. This is not generally the case. Where new sages appear, they continue to be male and foreign (Martyn Zadeka is the prime example).

There is only one famous female clairvoyant in Russia, and she, like Zadeka, is not Russian. Marie Anne Adelaide Lenormand enjoyed enormous success in Napoleonic and post-Napoleonic France as a visionary, predicting the futures of the great (the Empress Josephine, and possibly both Napoleon and Alexander I, for example). Her fame, both contemporary and posthumous, is partly to be attributed to her involvement in political prediction. Politics was even more part of a male world in the eighteenth and nineteenth centuries than now. Political prophecy is the only type of divination that falls clearly outside the female sphere of influence. In this it parallels village divinatory practice where men were actively involved in predictions involving spheres other than the personal and family. Mlle Lenormand combined straight political prophecy with predictions about the future of rich and famous clients. The process that transformed Zadek into Zadeka the arch-commentator of dreams also operated in Mlle Lenormand's case. Once she had made her name in the male sphere of political prophecy, and with predictions about the future political rôle of various illustrious figures, she was rapidly appropriated by the world of popular fortune-telling books. There are differences between the two. Mlle Lenormand enjoyed success as a fortune-teller for over forty years, employing a range of mantic skills (palmistry and cartomancy in particular), while Zadeka, if he existed, simply produced the one prophecy. Furthermore, Mlle Lenormand was addicted to self-promotion, writing volumes of self-congratulatory *Souvenirs prophétiques* and bombastic eulogies of rulers.[31] Her claims to have been patronized by members of the Russian nobility in Paris, even including Alexander I, together with her panegyric on his death, would certainly have brought her to the attention of élite circles in Russia; she was sufficiently well-known in Russia by 1825 for the narrator in Pogorel'skii's *The Double* (1825) to describe a supposed visit to her. He may well have been making an oblique reference to the Decembrists, Ryleev and Lunin, who consulted her during their time in Paris.[32] Her rapid debut as the sibyl of Russian fortune-telling books is a natural consequence of her métier and her involvement with Russians. It does not follow that the books, either translated or original, which appeared under her name in Russian were versions of her own books. Like Zadeka, her name became detached from her own activities. In France, her reputation as a cartomancer proved the most enduring, and various special sets of fortune-telling cards were attributed to her, almost certainly falsely.[33]

Unsurprisingly, the first Lenormand book in Russian (1843) presented the sibyl as a cartomancer, teamed up with Cagliostro and the unlikely figure of Swedenborg: *Cagliostro or Fortune-telling with Cards. A New and Hitherto Totally Unknown Method of Divination Fully Satisfying All Desires of those Persons Participating, Approved by the Famous Oracles Lenormand and Swedenborg* (Kirillov Press, Moscow). The volume may not have been a translation from French,[34] since it does not refer to the symbolic figurative cards ascribed to her in France. The first fortune-telling books attributed solely to Mlle Lenormand (1850 and 1862) are certainly translations. A similar guide to reading the cards came out in 1850 with further volumes in (at least) 1885, 1896, 1911, as well as sections in some large fortune-telling handbooks in the 1880s and 1890s.[35] She even briefly became an all-purpose sibyl when in 1874, in Moscow, there appeared *The Drawing-Room Soothsayer and Diviner. A Fortune-Telling Book for the Inquisitive . . . A New Method of Divination by the Famous Mademoiselle Lenormand.*

Mlle Lenormand was, however, less often presented in Russia as a dab hand with a pack of fortune-telling cards than as an interpreter of dreams. She first appeared in this guise in 1862 (linked again with Swedenborg and also with Bruce),[36] with further editions in 1865, 1875, 1892, 1896, 1897, 1899 and 1913 (at least). As time went on, she seems to have lost her pull with readers. Thus her name was tacked on to the end of a long list of prophets (none of them oneiromancers) in a dreambook published in slightly differing forms by various publishers in Moscow, Petersburg and Kiev (at least ten editions between 1890 and 1912). It was prefaced by the epithets 'the well-known French dream-interpreter, Mlle

Lenormand'. Only by the use of these epithets and titles could the semi-literate buyer understand that this was a prophetess not a prophet. Clearly her gender did not prevent her being held up as an authority, but when male authorities were also to be listed, she came last. She never acquired the broad fame of Zadeka.

Whereas named divinatory authorities are overwhelmingly male in both Russia and Western Europe, the same is not true where home-grown prophets are concerned. This is presumably in recognition of the dominant rôle played by women in professional fortune-telling. In England, for example, some fortune-telling books are attributed to Dr Trotter (London, 1708 and after) or 'a late celebrated wizard' (Newcastle 1850), but far more boast of their connection to 'wise women' like Mother Shipton (also famous as a political prophetess) and Mrs Bridget (alias the Norwood Gypsy) (London, 1790 and many times after). Local prophets are among the most popular. American dreambooks are sometimes attributed to figures such as Solomon, Mlle Lenormand or Aristotle, but they too see contemporary local specialists as a selling point. A high proportion of these are women, including a number with the title of Madame or Mother.[37] Thus both in an old country like England and a new society like America, home-grown clairvoyants, commonly but by no means exclusively women, were accorded sufficient respect to propel their names onto the front covers of fortune-telling books. In Russia by contrast, local seers were almost totally absent. True, there are sporadic references to anonymous female specialists, the Finnish fortune-teller or the wise woman of Murom.[38] The Finns, or rather Finno-Ugrian peoples of north European Russia, generally termed *chukhontsy*, were widely known for their divinatory skills. The true identity of the 'wise woman of Murom' is unknown, but her name was used to promote translated texts without the slightest attempt at credibility; for example, in a book published in 1824–5, the 'Incredible Enchantress, Astounding Sibyl, the Magician, the Wise Woman of Murom' was credited with a fortune-telling section that included zodiacal interpretations and the names of famous Roman emperors and Greek philosophers![39] A few books are also attributed to (or entitled) 'The Gypsy Woman', but these may just as well be translations as a reference to the fortune-telling skills of Russian gypsy women.[40] Male prophets did slightly better, so long as they were old. *An Interpretive Dreambook or Collection of Interpretations of Various Dreams, from the Experience of My 100-Year-Old Relatives* became one of the popular types of cheap dreambook in the 1870s–90s. Its author, as it turns out, was Mikhail Evstigneev, the prolific writer for lower-class urban readers. Given the tongue-in-cheek title and his reputation for attacking superstition in his other writings, this has to be a cynical commercial move on his part, something doubtless lost on the many folk who paid out their few kopecks for a copy.

On the other hand, a dreambook attributed to a home-grown specialist, whose book came complete with biographical details, was not a success. In 1863 in St Petersburg there appeared the *Reference Guide and Encyclopedic Lexicon of Dreams* of the Kindly Old Man, former resident of Duck Street in the Petersburg outskirts. His nephew, who edited the book, carefully attempts to equate him with Akakii Akakievich of Gogol′'s famous tale *The Overcoat* by commenting that his uncle had been a titular counsellor, who at one time 'had worked in a certain department'. Like Akakii he caught his death of cold in the ferocious Petersburg winter as a result of a hopelessly worn-out greatcoat (the word *shuba* is used rather than the Gogolian *shinel′*). Despite these affecting details and assertions of the old man's great local reputation, venerable old age (he was eighty-three) and piety (he left a library of Church books), as well as assurances that each interpretation had proved correct at least twenty times, when the book was republished seven years later all reference to the old man was omitted.[41] However touching the story, the old man's failure to gain enduring fame stems, firstly, from the inherent conservatism of the dreambook market and, secondly, his publication in St Petersburg, rather than the centre of popular publishing, Moscow. In the Russian context, his gender would not have been a disincentive factor.

The only Russian linked to fortune-telling books to become a household name was, in fact, neither a fortune-teller nor strictly speaking a Russian. James Bruce, known in Russian as Iakov Villimovich Brius, was the son of a Scots nobleman who had escaped Cromwellian Britain and settled in Russia during the reign of Aleksei Mikhailovich. A professional soldier who rose to the rank of general under Peter the Great, he was put in charge of printing and in 1710 supervised the production of the first

Russian almanac, known as the Bruce calendar. Its instant and enduring success was discussed in chapter 1. The adoption of the Bruce calendar by editors of fortune-telling books is partly to be explained by the popular failure to distinguish between scientific and non-scientific knowledge, but Bruce's own activities, which ensured him an enduring reputation as a sorcerer, may have encouraged this. Apart from his interest in astronomy (he was astronomer to Peter the Great), he liked to conduct chemical experiments. His strange instruments, bubbling glass retorts and large leather-bound books, led ordinary folk to believe that he dabbled in sorcery and black magic. Legends about Bruce and his supernatural skills still circulated in Moscow in the 1920s,[42] and may well have stimulated the appearance of volumes like *A New Book. Household Remedies. The Bruce Calendar for 200 Years. A Course in Folk Healing. Magic, Sorcery, and a Complete Collection of Russian Folk Spells* (three editions 1916–17), in which Bruce's calendar sits alongside sections on magic. The conjunction of Bruce and magic at this particular point in time probably owes something to the fad for occultism and black magic at the turn of the century. Earlier, when Bruce was still remembered and his Russified descendants still influential, any attempt to publicize his reputation as a wizard would not have found favour with the censor.[43] Nor is it likely that editors and publishers would have wished to link his name with sorcery, since they presented their books as respectable light entertainment, not aids to black magic.

Bruce's name became firmly attached to the calendar. The sole example of a false attribution before the second half of the nineteenth century seems to be *Bruce's Pocket Oracle, or A New Fortune-Telling Book (in Verse)*, published in Moscow in 1846, which turned the astronomer into a fortune-teller. However, in the second half of the century, and with increasing frequency in the early twentieth century, Bruce was presented as an interpreter of dreams. The first book to do so was *A Dreambook or Guide to the Elucidation and Interpretation of Dreams, Compiled According to the Guidance of the Famous Seers Lenormand, Swedenborg, Briuss (sic!) and Others* (St Petersburg 1865). Subsequently his name became one of those regularly included in the litany of famous names in the titles of dreambooks aimed at a somewhat more affluent market.[44] James Bruce's name on the front of dreambooks which also contained the calendar led to less scrupulous publishers taking his name in vain.

Throughout the period, it remained the case that foreign sages, either venerable themselves or from a past age, were perceived as the best guarantee of an effective prediction. Since native prophets (male) enjoyed so little success, it is clear that foreign origin was more important than gender. Nonetheless, with one exception, all named authorities were male, making gender a significant factor. Russians may have consulted home-grown clairvoyants who were predominantly women, but when it came to books, authority resided in tradition, age, exotic origins and patriarchal attitudes. The attributions to ancient sages, alchemists and others were often spurious, and had long been so in the West European originals. So long as a figure like Martyn Zadeka or James Bruce was well known some effort was made to stick to the facts. As soon as precise information ceased to be common currency, whether through the course of time or because publication fell into the hands of the semi-educated, names turned into simple stamps of authority. Of all the types of fortune-telling books dreambooks were the most likely to be falsely ascribed to sundry luminaries, possibly because they had to compete with parallel folk oneirocritical traditions for the loyalty and kopecks of rural purchasers and needed to assert their superiority. Among other social groups and earlier in the century before books reached the peasantry, it may be that the lure of the foreign and exotic as well as competition between publishers stimulated the imposing roll-call of foreign names. In any case, it made some surprising figures famous, in contexts they could never have imagined or approved.

While some became famous, others, renowned throughout Europe, never achieved fame on Russian soil. One notable absence is Nostradamus, whose obscure work *Centuries*, written in a mixture of Latin, Greek, French, Italian and Provençal, and first published in 1555, has managed to survive to this day, generating a full-length biopic feature film about him as recently as 1994. The very ambiguity of his prophecies allows for perpetual varieties of interpretation. There are those who feel he successfully predicted the French Revolution, the rise of Hitler and even the assassination attempt on the Pope in 1981. His absence from the gallery of prophetic luminaries in Russia can only have been pure chance, but one that serves to illustrate, along with the contrary example of Zadeka, the extent to which a borrowed popular tradition acquires its own distinctive features in a particular country.

CHAPTER 8

Disappearance and revival

The Revolution and then the exigencies of the Russian Civil War put paid to cheap commercial publishing, and cultural centralization after 1925 and especially 1928 totally changed the character of the book market. The new régime maintained and developed the cultural orientation of the pre-Revolutionary educated élite, likewise emphasizing the worthlessness of popular culture and prescribing literature designed for positive educative effect. The difference lay, of course, in the message. According to what was a strongly materialist philosophy, fortune-telling books did not simply propagate false values, but also encouraged irrationality and superstition. Hence they had nothing at all to recommend them. The advancement of socialism required that peasants be wrenched away from an archaic world view via literacy and political education. And so, after their swan song in 1919 in the dreambook published by the *Sport and Science* newspaper in Odessa, Russian fortune-telling books disappeared until 1987 (the occasional émigré edition excepted).[1] In the countryside folklorists and ethnographers continued to study calendrical rituals, while largely ignoring folk beliefs in divination and the supernatural, which they presumed would wither away in the face of advancing rationality and secularism.

It is one thing to stifle books and dismiss beliefs, and another to banish the human desire to seek clarification of the future. Though Marxists would have rejected the idea of a parallel between Marxism and fortune-telling, and indeed any link was undoubtedly subconscious, their concept of an inevitable succession of stages, through which all societies must pass on the way to a communist utopia, meant that its supporters could and did declare with confidence that the problems of the future had been solved, at least conceptually. Communists are like fortune-tellers in their efforts to clarify and control the future. Their supporters and others may object that this is a crudely cynical view of a philosophy that presented the future as predetermined by scientific laws and attainable sooner rather than later by dint of human effort (socialism was, it will be remembered, to be 'built' or 'constructed'). They might point out with some justice that this is a far cry from peasant fatalism, which ruled out forward planning. According to this world view, the future was predetermined and malleable less through one's own efforts than by the application of counter-sorcery or ritual. Such objections ignore the position of ordinary people, mere cogs in the wheel of history. For them, the utopian vision of a communist society with its harmonious relations and universal prosperity could appear more attractive than the fortune-teller's predictions which sometimes presaged doom. It justified the hardship of the present in terms of the shining future awaiting children and grandchildren, so channelling the impulses behind fortune-telling or Christian belief in eternal life into social aims. This is not to suggest that the true communist society was any less remote to the average peasant or worker than the happy vistas peddled by the fortune-teller. Indeed the reverse may be true. Political education notwithstanding, belief in the attainment of a communist ideal was a huge leap of faith for most people. Combined with the emphasis on the communal good of society, Soviet women in particular were exhorted to extend their concern with the fates of self, family or friends to that of society as a whole. Individual interests were subsumed in the broader ones of the country as a whole. The shining future laid out for the Soviet state, it was incessantly declared, would bring individual happiness in its wake. The relative success of this ploy relied both on the desire for a better and clearer future and the familiarity with communal activities and ties that had been so much part of the peasant society to which the majority of Russians belonged on the eve of the Revolution.

If political dogma had hijacked the future, then the politicians and economists who put theory into practice acted as the purveyors of the future, in a sense, therefore, as fortune-tellers. The architects of the five-year plans laid down the targets for human effort in the immediate future in the cause of more distant glittering prospects. Even more obviously than planners, it is scientists who stand out as the modern equivalent of the magic practitioner/fortune-teller. In Mikhail Bulgakov's *Heart of a Dog* (1925), the medical scientist who features in the story is called *mag* (magician), *charodei* (enchanter), and *kudesnik* (wizard) by an ecstatic patient.[2] Though the story is satirical, the terms capture the actual position of scientists at various stages of Soviet history with uncanny accuracy. With their empirical approach to knowledge scientists would seem the antithesis of the fortune-teller, but clear parallels exist. Although scientists did not perform the counselling rôle of the fortune-teller, they promised that their discoveries would bring progress, happiness and a better life, and in this way distracted attention from a dismal present. Perhaps the best example was the agronomist Lysenko, who not merely managed to survive the attacks on scientists but was almost deified because he promised miracles.[3] In their experiments they manipulated nature in a manner quite beyond the understanding of the ordinary person, who generally acquires scientific knowledge in the same way as traditional belief knowledge through instruction rather than experiment. Thus magic on the one hand and scientific experiment and discovery on the other have much in common for the non-specialist. It requires only for the individual to be taught that one is true and the other not. Reactions may be the same to both, on the one hand admiring and, because both are mysterious and powerful, at the same time fearful.

These ambivalent attitudes underlie the history of science and technology in the USSR. In the immediate post-Revolutionary period, elaborate millenarian claims were made for science, which, in Trotsky's view, was going to transform both the environment and man himself.[4] But idealization of the scientist and technological specialist was always likely to conflict with the class struggle and the desire for a proletarian-dominated society. As Katerina Clark remarks, 'there has been a tension in Soviet history between the impulse to privilege the scientists and technocrats and a mistrust of them, coupled with a tendency to favour either the proletariat or the warrior class (in the Soviet context, the military and security forces)'.[5] Towards the end of the 1920s, suspicion of specialists intensified and the thirties was dominated by the switch of emphasis from pure science to technology, in which quantity of specialists replaced quality, and scientists were at best regarded with mistrust, and at worst terrorized. After the War, and with increasing momentum up till the 1970s, this tendency was reversed and a cult of science developed.[6] The alternation between admiration and mistrust echoes the ambivalence felt towards magic practitioners in pre-Revolutionary rural Russia. In village society those who claimed supernatural powers evoked fear or respect depending on whether they were viewed as benign. Fear turned to active hostility when peasants believed that they were the victims of 'spoiling'; sorcerers were blamed for unfavourable prophecies when they came true. White-magic practitioners, on the other hand, were generally respected. In hovering between these two extremes, the Soviet régime was merely repeating the ambivalent attitudes of the village towards its own interpreters of the future. Indeed, it may be argued that some of the mechanisms of the totalitarian state, conspiracy theories and show trials in particular, betray the influence of popular culture. The traditional 'taste for reallocating responsibility for difficulty and disaster' and fear of 'spoiling' led to the demonization of opponents.[7] The infamous *History of the All-Union Communist Party. Short Course* (Moscow, 1945) poses white Stalinist magic against black Trotskyite and Bukharinite magic, describing history in terms of spoiling, black deeds and alien forces in contrast to revelation, moulding of the future and certainty. Though the term *porcha* (spoiling) is not used and the derogatory terms for the enemies of the state are not the traditional images of evil, the Manichean tenor of the whole replicates the old world view.

One aspect of the pre-Revolutionary interest in divination, the occult and the paranormal, did acquire a degree of official approval, albeit clandestine. During the cold war the KGB followed the CIA into research in the uses of the paranormal in counter-espionage. Though inspired by its cold war rivalry with the US, for the USSR this move represented the clear victory of Realpolitik over ideology,[8] in which distaste for the supernatural and irrational could be overcome by giving it a scientific clothing. Success in learning to read minds would certainly have lent a chilling reality to the term 'thought police'.

However strong the impulses sublimated into ideology and government policy, rural divination and ordinary domestic fortune-telling did not wither away after 1917. For example, the vitality of beliefs in dreams is demonstrated by a satirical dreambook published in 1989 in the 1 January issue of the newspaper *Moskovskic novosti.* Its comic effect depended on awareness of the genre as well as familiarity with Soviet life; thus, dreaming of *matreshki* (wooden nesting dolls) meant the arrival of tourists, a new television meant a fire (based on the propensity of Soviet televisions to explode), while woodpeckers meant night visitors (i.e. the KGB, based on the popular term for an informer *stukach*, the one who knocks). Dream beliefs have survived among women of all social groups (and to a lesser extent among men). In 1989–90 I conducted a survey among 130 people from different towns in the Russian Federation. Seventy per cent of the women questioned believed that their dreams might provide information about the future but only thirty-five per cent of the men. By contrast in a survey I conducted among seventy-seven people living in Britain, only four per cent said that dreams could be prophetic, though a further sixteen per cent thought they might provide information about the future as well as about the present, the past and their own personalities. There were no gender differences in the British replies.

Dream beliefs remain widespread among those over fifty and among the rural population. In the summer of 1994, I interviewed a group of women (all over fifty-five) in a village in Karelia, all of whom believed dreams could be prophetic. Asked about dream interpretations, they produced not separate symbols but dramatic stories of how death, serious illness and marriage had been foreseen in their dreams. These dreams were clearly key moments in their lives, and some wept as they told how the predictions came true. The happiest dreams were those in which the dreamer had encountered her future husband. Some were connected with Yuletide customs, as one woman explained: 'When you got to a marriageable age, you put a well made out of matches under your pillow, locked the door and sewed the key to your nightdress. The year I was expecting to get married, I dreamt my future husband came to see me. It was a man I didn't know. When I woke up, I just dismissed it as rubbish, and thought no more about it. But it turned out my husband did have a slight limp, just like in the dream . . . In a different dream he was wearing exactly the same clothes as when I first met him.'

The Karelian dreams were of two traditional types, those which exactly presaged an event or encounter, and those that veiled their meaning in symbols. Both are widespread in modern Russia, judging by the accounts of prophetic dreams collected from 1992 on by the fledgling Institute of Dreams in Moscow, a private research institute funded by American money. Admittedly, however, this group is self-selecting, having responded to newspaper and radio requests for dream accounts.[9] Those over fifty naturally focused on dreams which, in their view, were prophetic, and wanted to explain how they came true. Like the women in Karelia, they remembered dreams from decades before. The commonest type of dream predicted the death of a loved one, but a number had political dreams, notably about Stalin, Khrushchev and Gorbachev, perhaps not surprising in a country with a history of powerful rulers. These dreams were often interpreted by informants as foreshadowing political events; a thirty-six-year-old waitress from Volgograd foresaw the casting down of Lenin in two dreams, in 1964 a seventy-eight-year-old man from Iaroslavl dreamt of the fall of Khrushchev two days before it happened, and in 1943 a pensioner from Belgorod dreamt that she was walking down a dark street when the sun came out and with it Stalin appeared. Within ten days the area was freed from German occupation. The belief, as much ingrained among Russians today as in the nineteenth century, that rulers and other powerful authority figures will help ordinary folk if only they can be told of the problem can also be reflected in prophetic dreams. These dreams may also act as incitements to action if their impression is sufficiently strong. In 1990, a mother of four children, describing herself in folkloric style as an old woman, wrote to the Queen and Princess Anne care of London University explaining that they had told her in a dream to write to them and ask for 10,000 dollars, some second-hand furniture and a car, giving their address as the University of London. This variant combines both the traditional appeal to the ruler and the modern cry to the foreigner, who is regarded as a bottomless purse.

Younger informants among the material from the Institute of Dreams tended either to offer a highly unusual dream as interesting artistic material in its own right or hoped the Institute would provide a personalized dream-interpretation service by return of post. Such a reaction suggests that they were not in touch with either printed or oral tradition, but were responding out of curiosity, either idle or serious. It is notable that in my survey, slightly over a quarter of those who interpreted their dreams said they relied on personal experience and observation, rather than tradition of any kind. Their own interpretations, when they offered them, bore little relation to the traditional meanings of dream symbols. Those that were close to tradition tended to apply popular stereotypes to conventional symbols, such as a gypsy variously meaning a thief, wild entertainment, travelling or being deceived (some of which coincide with printed dreambooks). Almost no one, regardless of age, mentioned Freud or Jung or attempted to view their dreams in the light of psychoanalysis. The absence of popular psychology in the mind-set of Russians distinguishes them from Europeans and Americans, and allows them to continue thinking that dreams tell the future rather than reveal information about their subconscious or their lives. It will be interesting to see how soon the current interest in Western psychoanalysis reaches the popular consciousness.

Many of those in the survey as well as some of those who wrote in to the Institute of Dreams knew one or more traditional dream symbols. The belief that a corpse signifies a change in the weather, blood means relatives, a fish pregnancy or illness, a dog a friend, teeth falling out a dead relative and small coins tears but large notes or coins good luck were all very widespread regardless of where the informant or his/her mother came from. More than a quarter of those who did not believe in prophetic dreams knew some of these traditional symbols. The majority were women, clear evidence of the vitality of Russian oneirocritical traditions among urban women. Where they were men, they seemed to have picked them up from their families. In the countryside oral dream beliefs are much more alive and elderly women with an extensive knowledge are not uncommon.[10]

The evidence from the survey is that most well-known dream symbols come from folklore rather than the secondary oral tradition of dreambooks. Though a few informants in the survey stated that their family had owned a dreambook, in general, between 1917 and 1987 knowledge of dream beliefs was acquired less from print than from a female member of the older generation or a friend. By contrast with trends in urban fortune-telling in the Tsarist era, in Soviet times there was a major swing towards primary and secondary oral transmission. For example, in the survey a sizeable number of informants knew the folk interpretation for girl as miracle or surprise. This is based on similarity in the roots of the words involved (dev*ochka* and div*o* or *u*div*lenie*). On the other hand, others knew the dreambook interpretation for cats (connected with betrayal and adultery) rather than the oral one, and sometimes presented it along with well-known oral interpretations, evidence of the intermingling of the two traditions.

The process was as much a consequence of the hostile climate as the unavailability of fortune-telling books. Whereas women had earlier adopted subterfuge to keep fortune-telling away from the scorn of educated men, after the Revolution they had to redouble their efforts, but now for political as well as gender reasons. Unlike the esoteric sciences, which survived clandestinely,[11] fortune-telling had the option of operating more openly, provided it resorted to one of its tried-and-trusted strategies, trivialization. As light entertainment for social gatherings, it could stand its ground against charges of pernicious influence. The professional urban fortune-teller became a creature of the past, but anecdotal evidence in abundance reveals that fortune-telling refused to die.

Although dreams went on being elucidated in many households at breakfast time, the survey suggests a swing towards discussing them with friends rather than family. Such a move allowed dream interpretation to move towards social entertainment, evident in the high proportion of respondents in the survey who had tried dream interpretation with friends, but strictly for fun. Such declarations should, however, be taken with a pinch of salt. For many people brought up under a social system that banned the metaphysical and supernatural, admitting that even a part of oneself wants to believe in prediction would have been difficult in 1989–90, so soon after change began. Whatever their personal motivation, their replies gave solid evidence of dream divination in groups in the Soviet and post-Soviet period.

Reading cards and coffee cups had no need of printed texts to survive the Soviet period. Cartomancy had settled into the pattern of thirty-six and fifty-two cards for the Russian and gypsy methods respectively, implying a continuous oral tradition and widespread familiarity.[12] It rarely gets an overt mention in the Soviet period though the film *Bed and Sofa* (in Russian *Tret'ia Meshchanskaia*), a film by Avraam Room made in 1925, is an interesting exception. In one scene the heroine Liuda, a petit-bourgeois housewife whose values are apparently unchanged by the new social order, sits over the cards. Their lodger, Volodia, her husband's friend, decides to take over, and ends by showing her herself as Queen covered by the Jack, a symbol of himself. Before they turn to love-making, she comes back to the table and aligns the King on one side of the Queen with the Jack on the other, indicative of the *ménage à trois* that results after her husband Kolia returns. Though card-laying is conventionally seen as symbolic of woman's passivity – note that it is Volodia who uses it to indicate his intentions towards Liuda and force events – ultimately the card scene is the beginning of Liuda's active search for a meaningful life. Both her husband and Volodia are part of the new socialist order, but their transformation does not apply to their private lives. In the end it is Liuda who has the courage to strike out for a new life and a new future. The film's director and the scriptwriter, Viktor Shklovskii, obviously knew they could rely on the audience's understanding of cartomancy and its cultural connotations.

One of the combined effects of trivialization and oral transmission was the adaptation of familiar divinatory techniques of long standing. For example, most townsfolk gave up Yuletide divination, but the well-known method of seeing whether a chicken chooses grain, water or a girl's ring metamorphosed into the schoolgirl's pastime of releasing a guinea pig to see whose piece of paper it will choose (a method not restricted to New Year). The divinatory psalter, still used by the poet Akhmatova in the 1920s, was replaced by Pushkin's *Eugene Onegin*, opened at random, with prophetic meaning assigned to the first lines to catch the eye.[13] Given that divining from Pushkin may be taken seriously, especially by young women, nothing better illustrates the deification of great writers in Russian culture. One wonders what the poet with his strong sense of irony would have made of it!

With the disappearance of the Soviet state interest in all aspects of the irrational has expanded hugely; apart from Russian Orthodoxy, religious groups of almost every hue as well as occultism and supernatural belief flourish. Probably best known in the West are the faith healers or hypnotherapists, generally termed in Russian *extrasens*, who address huge audiences or cure patients over the television. Sorcery and witchcraft have also re-emerged, with their practitioners more often operating from the typical Soviet-style flat than the peasant hut. Whereas in the countryside the folk healer existed throughout the Soviet period,[14] in towns this tradition has had to be revived. How much contemporary sorcerers owe to native Russian traditions is hard to gauge, but probably not a great deal. Just as the fortune-tellers in Petersburg at the end of the last century had only faint connections with oral tradition, it would appear that latter-day urban sorcerers draw their knowledge from a variety of traditions, many of them Western. One such, Tamara Lan'kova, who offers healing and support to those with emotional problems, physical ill-health and even psychic illness, relies on her innate psychic skills, but discusses her work almost entirely in Western terms.[15] She does not see herself as a fortune-teller.

It is far from surprising that ordinary Russians, deprived of the pseudo-religion of communism, should seek alternatives, or released from a rational intellectual straitjacket grab at all manner of dubious alternatives. It is more startling to learn that the current fascination with the paranormal and occult has been harnessed to El'tsin's security. General Georgii Rogozin (a KGB general not a battle-scarred hero), currently second in command of the presidential security services, apparently continues to foster research into the applications of the paranormal to counter-espionage, just as he had in the KGB research institute where he worked formerly.[16] His extraordinary influence on the Kremlin rests upon what may be a unique combination of old-style KGB professionalism and paranormal expertise. Both evoke fear. Their efforts throughout the first part of 1996 were directed not towards security but to getting El'tsin re-elected, one might say, with evident success. After the first round, the Russian sorcerer and *extrasens* Iurii Longo declared that El'tsin would win the run-off because he 'has a team providing extra-sensory help and cosmic force'.[17] He would, however, have to leave office in 1997 because of ill-health, not a very risky prediction given El'tsin's physical condition. Although other societies such as Burma use divination at the highest levels and both Nancy Reagan and Hillary Clinton have been reported to tap into cosmic forces, the official use within a country which is largely Western in its cultural orientation is much more unusual and indicates the high level of credibility attached to various divinatory, faith healing or paranormal activities in today's Russia, coupled with the intense desire to glimpse the very uncertain future.

In the lower echelons of society many people who would not consider visiting a professional sorcerer nonetheless believe in 'spoiling' or the evil eye. For the Western observer, perhaps the most interesting aspect of this phenomenon is the number of highly educated people who not only believe, but can cite 'proofs' of its existence. In the article on Tamara Lan'kova, a highly respected woman journalist praises the sorceress for removing a spell cast by her husband's first wife which had resulted in a serious psychic illness and the theft of most of her money and property. Numerous books on witchcraft and sorcery also testify to the public's fascination with magic. The earliest (c. 1989–90) tended to be translations or reprints of pre-Revolutionary ethnographic material, often outdated, but recent publications indicate a growing interest in contemporary ethnographic material, though these are less popular than do-it-yourself guides to sorcery. For example, those who purchased *Russian Sorcery, Witchcraft and Folk Healing* (St Petersburg, Litera, 1994), a partial reprint of a 'best-seller' of 1904, were informed in the preface that the book was intended not just as cultural history but also for those 'interested in the practice of sorcery'!

Fortune-telling forms an important part of the current obsession with the irrational. On the pedestrianized Staryi Arbat in Moscow cartomancers offer their services, joined occasionally by others, such as the man claiming to be a good Orthodox believer who was offering the public the divinatory services of his guinea pig in the summer of 1995. Fortune-telling books have also made a dramatic reappearance. Since 1988 private publishers in all corners of the former Soviet empire have been reissuing old texts or new translations in huge print-runs. In 1988 tiny hand-written or typed dreambooks, reproduced on a single sheet of photographic paper (see ills. 5 and 6), began to be sold in kiosks or on suburban trains by people who can have had no idea that they were the modern equivalent of the nineteenth-century colporteur. By the end of 1989 they were appearing in journals and soon bookstalls and then bookshops began stocking a range of fortune-telling books. Some were published on the presses of old institutions, others by enterprising individuals operating on a shoestring, but print runs rivalled the huge numbers for Marxist classics in the Soviet period; for example, 300,000 copies of *One Million Dreams. A New and Complete Dreambook* and 500,000 of Miss Hussey's dreambook of 1912, both in 1990.[18] Four years later the fad looked to have passed its peak, though probably not because of market saturation; difficulties in the publishing industry (paper

СОННИК

Арбуз-радостная
жизнь
Альбом-неожиданн
ная встреча
Акула-неприятные
хлопоты
Акушерка-долгая
болезнь
Абрикосы-исполне-
ние желаний
Ангел-успех в
делах
Апельсин-успех,
нечаянный подаро
Банан-удар
Барабан-сплетни
Бархат-приятная
новость
Булка-счастье
Башмаки-дорога
Берет-неожидан-
ность
Бездна-разорени
Бить кого-нибудь
вражда
Бирюза-известие
о любимом
Блины-болезнь
Блохи-неприятные
новости
Болезнь-долгое
здоровье
Борода-прибыль
Бороду брить-
убыток
Бородавка-неожи-
данность
Брод у реки-
неприятный случа
Берег-спокойная
жизнь
Бутылка-новость
Вагон-нездоровье
Варенье-сладость
Ведро с водой-
прибыль
Ветер-любовь
Ветка-успех в
любви
Вишня-слёзы
Виноград-обвине-
ние
Волк- враг
Ворона-горе
Вода-болезнь
Водка-неожидан-
ность

Волны-внезапный
отъезд
Волосы густые-
прибыль.
Волосы стричь-потер
Гроб-удивительное
известие
Гребенка-дорога
Груша-удовольствие
Грязь-болезнь
Гуси-любовь
Гадюка-злость
Гитара-веселая жизн
Газеты-расстройство
Голуби-удачная жизн
Деньги-
радость
Деньги мед
ные-слёзы
Дети-успех
в делах
Дождь-непр
ятность
Дом-новая
жизнь
Дуб-прибыл
Еж-разгово
с лжецом
Ель-чужая
сторона
Жаба-ковар
ство,
Жемчуг-слёзы
Забор-неудача
Заря-радостная вест
Заяц-утрата
Зеркало-перемена в
делах
Зима-охлаждение
в любви
Золото-разлука
Изумруд-свидание
Иголка-влюбиться
Икона-благополучие
Индюк-друг
Искры-замешательство
Кал-деньги
Кастрюли-воровство
Кино-разбор дела
Кирпич-успех удача
Карты-ссора
Клоп-досада
Корыто-счастье
Колокол-счастье
Кошка-враг
Комар-опасность
Кудри-богатство

Купаться-неожи-
данность
Кукла-удивление
Лампа-удивление
Ландыш-признание
Лебедь-удовольствие
Лестница вверх -
успех
Лестница вниз-
неудача
Лес-чужая сторона
Лекарство-обида
Лиса-обман
Лимон-измена друга
Лук-
огорчение
Луг-
прибыль
Лошадь-
ложь
Люди голые
Мак-
благополу
чие
Малина-
ускорение
дела
Магазин-
Интерес
Мёд-наслаждение
Могила-забвение
Молоко-прибыль
Мороженое-веселье
Морковь-стыд
Музыка-известие
Нитки-сплетни
Носки-интересное
знакомство
Озеро-спокой
Одеяло-разлука
Орехи-оскорбление
Одеколон-признание
Огонь-ссора
Огурцы-волнение
Пение-новость
Помидоры-стыд
Полотенце-письмо
Портфель-надежда
Почта-сюрприз
Парк-волокита
Пьяный-боль
Радио-слух-сплетни
Резать-терять
Ручей-радость
Рыбу ловить-прибыль

Сметана-прибыль
Снег-смех
Сахар-удовольст-
вие
Сумка-возмущение
Стол-предложение
Сыр-прибыль
Табак-огорчение
Таз-пустота
Театр-радость
Улыбка-о вас меч-
тают
Утюг-разлука
Ураган-перемена
в жизни
Ухабы-досада
Уху есть-радость
Фартук-ложные
вести
Филин-неприят
ность
Фиалки-радость
Флаг-уважение
Хвастать-хлопоты
Ходить по мосту
опасность
Хромой-неожидан-
ность
Целовать-непри-
ятность
Цепочку купить-
удача
Церковь-воля
Цыган-быть
обманутым
Цветы-богатая
жизнь
Цыплята-радость
Чай пить-радость
Чулок-дорога
Щетка-измена
Шкаф-тоска
Шоколад-радость
Эхо-письмо
Юбка-свидание
с любимым
Яд-обман
Яйца-визит
Якорь-надежда
Яма-горе
Яхта-радость
Ящик-пустая жизнь
Ясное небо-
улучшение вжизни
Яблоки-исполнение
желаний

5 An example of the first dreambooks to appear in 1988, produced on one sheet of photographic paper.

ГАДАНИЕ НА КАРТАХ

ГАДАНИЕ I — ВЗЯТЬ ПРЕДВАРИТЕЛЬНО ПЕРЕТАСОВАННУЮ КОЛОДУ КАРТ, СНЯТЬ ЛЕВОЙ РУКОЙ К СЕБЕ И РАЗЛОЖИТЬ КАРТЫ ВЕЕРОМ КРАПОМ ВВЕРХ, ЗАГАДАВ ЧТО-НИБУДЬ, ВЫНИМАТЬ ПО КАРТЕ И СМОТРЕТЬ ОТВЕТ В ТОЛКОВАТЕЛЕ.

ГАДАНИЕ II — ВЗЯТЬ ПЕРЕТАСОВАННУЮ КОЛОДУ КАРТ И СНЯТЬ ЛЕВОЙ РУКОЙ К СЕБЕ ВЫНУТЬ ИЗ КОЛОДЫ КАРТУ И В ЗАВИСИМОСТИ ОТ ЕЕ МАСТИ ВЫБРАТЬ ЭТОЙ ЖЕ МАСТИ КОРОЛЯ ИЛИ ДАМУ (СМОТРЯ КТО ЗАГАДЫВАЕМЫЙ - МУЖЧИНА ИЛИ ЖЕНЩИНА). ЭТОГО КОРОЛЯ ИЛИ ДАМУ КЛАДУТ НА СЕРЕДИНУ СТОЛА И ОКРУЖАЮТ КАРТАМИ, ОТСЧИТЫВАЯ ЧЕРЕЗ ШЕСТЬ НА СЕДЬМУЮ, ЧИСЛОМ ДЕСЯТЬ, ЗАТЕМ ГАДАЮЩИЙ ПО ТОЛКОВАТЕЛЮ УГАДЫВАЕТ ЕГО ИЛИ ЕЕ СУДЬБУ

ГАДАНИЕ III — ВЗЯТЬ ПЕРЕТАСОВАННУЮ КОЛОДУ КАРТ И СНЯТЬ ЛЕВОЙ РУКОЙ К СЕБЕ. ЗАТЕМ ГАДАЮЩИЙ, ЗАДУМАВ НА КОРОЛЯ ИЛИ ДАМУ ЛЮБОЙ МАСТИ, РАСКЛАДЫВАЕТ В ЧЕТЫРЕ РЯДА ПО ДЕВЯТЬ КАРТ В РЯДУ. КАРТЫ, ОКАЗАВШИЕСЯ ВОЗЛЕ ЗАДУМАННОГО КОРОЛЯ ИЛИ ДАМЫ, ПО ТОЛКОВАТЕЛЮ ОПРЕДЕЛЯЮТ СУДЬБУ ЗАДУМАННОГО.

ГАДАНИЕ IV — ВЗЯТЬ ПЕРЕТАСОВАННУЮ КОЛОДУ КАРТ И СНИМАТЬ НА СТОЛ ОДНУ КАРТУ НА ДРУГУЮ, ПРИГОВАРИВАЯ В ТАКОМ ПОРЯДКЕ: ШЕСТЕРКА, СЕМЕРКА, ВОСЬМЕРКА И Т.Д. ДО ТУЗА. КАРТЫ, КОТОРЫЕ ВЫХОДЯТ СОГЛАСНО СО СКАЗАННЫМИ СЛОВАМИ (Т.Е. ПРИ СЛОВЕ „ШЕСТЕРКА" ВЫПАДАЕТ ШЕСТЕРКА) - ОТЛОЖИТЬ В СТОРОНУ. ПРОДЕЛАТЬ ЭТО ТРИ РАЗА И, РАЗЛОЖИВ ОТОБРАННЫЕ КАРТЫ В РЯД, ОПРЕДЕЛИТЬ СУДЬБУ ПО ТОЛКОВАТЕЛЮ.

ТОЛКОВАТЕЛЬ

МАСТЬ	ТУЗ	КОРОЛЬ	ДАМА	ВАЛЕТ	10-КА	9-КА	8-КА	7-КА	6-КА
♠	ПЕЧАЛЬНОЕ ПИСЬМО	ВРАГ	ИСПОЛНЕНИЕ ЖЕЛАНИЯ	НАПРАСНЫЕ ХЛОПОТЫ	БОЛЕЗНЬ	ПОТЕРЯ ДРУГА	ОСТЕРЕГАЙТЕСЬ ОПАСНОСТИ	ССОРА	НЕСЧАСТЛИВАЯ ДОРОГА
♦	ЖЕЛАНИЕ НЕ СБУДЕТСЯ	ОСТЕРЕГАЙТЕСЬ ОБМАНА	НЕОЖИДАННОЕ ОСКОРБЛЕНИЕ	ДЕНЕЖНЫЕ ХЛОПОТЫ; РЕВНОСТЬ	ПОДАРОК	ПРЕПЯТСТВИЕ	РАДОСТНАЯ ВЕСТЬ	НЕВЕРНОСТЬ	ВЕСЕЛАЯ ДОРОГА
♣	ЛОЖНЫЙ ШАГ	ВЕРНЫЙ ДРУГ	ДОСТОЙНАЯ НАГРАДА	ПЕЧАЛЬ, УДАЧА В ПРЕДПРИЯТИЯХ	БОЛЬШИЕ ДЕНЬГИ	ПЕЧАЛЬНАЯ ВЕСТЬ	БОЛЕЗНЬ БЛИЗКОГО ЧЕЛОВЕКА	ИЗВЕСТИЕ ИЗ КАЗЕННОГО ДОМА	БЕСПОЛЕЗНАЯ ДОРОГА
♥	ВАС ЛЮБЯТ	НЕ ТРЕВОЖТЕСЬ ВСЕ ПОЛУЧИТЕ	СКРЫВАЙТЕ ЧУВСТВА	ПРИЯТНЫЙ ГОСТЬ	ИЗВЕСТИЕ О ЛЮБВИ	ЛЮБОВНОЕ ОБЪЯСНЕНИЕ	НОВОЕ ЛИЦО РЕШИТ ВАШУ УЧАСТЬ	БЕРЕГИТЕСЬ, НЕ ИГРАЙТЕ С ОГНЕМ	НЕПРИЯТНОСТИ

ЗНАЧЕНИЕ СОЕДИНЕНИЯ КАРТ

ДАМА ПРИ КОРОЛЕ - ЗАМУЖНАЯ ЖЕНЩИНА ИЛИ ТАЙНАЯ НЕВЕСТА.
КОРОЛЬ В НОГАХ КАРТЫ, ИЗОБРАЖАЮЩЕЙ ДАМУ - ВЕРНОСТЬ ВОЗЛЮБЛЕННОЙ.
ДАМА МЕЖДУ ДЕСЯТКАМИ - ПРЕДЛОЖЕНИЕ ИЛИ ЛЮБОВНОЕ ОБЪЯСНЕНИЕ.
ЕСЛИ КОРОЛЬ, ДАМА И ДЕСЯТКА ТОЙ ЖЕ МАСТИ, ТО ЭТО ЗНАЧИТ, ЧТО КОРОЛЬ ПОЛУЧИТ ОТВЕТ НА СВОЮ ЛЮБОВЬ, ЕСЛИ ПРИ ДАМЕ, КОРОЛЬ И ДЕСЯТКА - ТО ЖЕ САМОЕ.
ВОСЬМЕРКА ВОЗЛЕ ДАМЫ - СПЛЕТНИ.
ПИКОВОЙ ТУЗ ПРИ СЕМЁРКЕ - БОЛЕЗНЬ РОДСТВЕННИКА.
КОРОЛЬ МЕЖДУ ТУЗОМ И ДЕСЯТКОЙ - ПОВЫШЕНИЕ ПО СЛУЖБЕ.

ЧЕТЫРЕ ТУЗА - ИСПОЛНЕНИЕ ЖЕЛАНИЕ.
ЧЕТЫРЕ КОРОЛЯ - БОЛЬШОЕ ОБЩЕСТВО.
ЧЕТЫРЕ ДАМЫ - РАЗГОВОРЫ, СПЛЕТНИ.
ЧЕТЫРЕ ВАЛЕТА - БОЛЬШИЕ ХЛОПОТЫ.
ЧЕТЫРЕ ДЕСЯТКИ - СВАДЬБА.
ЧЕТЫРЕ ДЕВЯТКИ - ПЕРЕМЕНА В ЖИЗНИ.
ЧЕТЫРЕ ВОСЬМЁРКИ } НЕПРИЯТНОСТИ.
ЧЕТЫРЕ СЕМЁРКИ }
ЧЕТЫРЕ ШЕСТЁРКИ - ДАЛЬНЯЯ ДОРОГА.

6 A guide to cartomancy from 1990 printed on photographic paper.

shortages, liquidity problems, and the absence of marketing and distribution networks) cut back print runs and reduced the number of titles. Nonetheless in a publishing climate in which a print run of 5,000 is considered large, such books are still evidently very popular. *Stars and Fates*, a collection of different kinds of horoscopes, and *The Dreambook or Interpretation of Dreams* by Gustavus Hindman Miller were published in print runs of 100,000 in 1994 and 1996 respectively, though by 1996 the average was 30–35,000.[19]

The fascination with magic and the irrational is not the only factor determining the immense popularity of these books. No less important is nostalgia for the culture of the Tsarist era, something reflected in various cultural phenomena in Russia today. The new commercial publishers, ever on the look-out for a quick ruble (or nowadays a quick twenty or thirty thousand rubles) have seen this as a way of keeping afloat financially. Inevitably they are not concerned with reissuing the most interesting or typical texts.[20] Whatever old edition is at hand will do. Furthermore, just as in the nineteenth century, the first private publishers had no scruples about copyright; Miss Hussey's dreambook of 1912, which has been issued by at least three different publishers since 1990, was almost certainly pirated from the first contemporary edition. Were Russian readers to judge on the basis of reprints of the last few years, they would assume, wrongly, that the commonest type of Russian dreambook grouped objects by category, and that Miss Hussey was well known in early twentieth-century Russia.[21] Conversely, except by reading *Eugene Onegin*, they would have no conception of the authority Martyn Zadeka wielded among nineteenth-century Russians. The failure of Martyn Zadeka to reach a contemporary audience probably stems from the association of his name with the simplest and shortest dreambooks. Just as the longer texts before the Revolution tended to avoid his name, so now readers prefer editions with a multitude of dream objects. The result is that republished dreambooks only mention him as one of a list of divinatory authorities, and this not often.

Unable or unwilling to rely on traditional oral or printed material, modern editors and compilers sometimes still like to lend authority to their books by giving them a scholarly preface. Though the old divinatory authorities, Albertus, Mlle Lenormand and others have lost both appeal and significance, the learned preface found in expensive dreambooks before 1830 occasionally still survives. In one instance, a publisher has reproduced unaltered the preface from a pre-Revolutionary dreambook, which discussed the significance of prophetic dreams and added accounts of the dreams of the famous, which had come originally from seventeenth-century Europe. Nonetheless, the majority of cheap editions of all kinds of fortune-telling books as ever dispense with preambles, sticking to the briefest possible instructions for interpreting dreams, reading the coffee grounds or the cards. Where prefaces do exist, they tend to offer potted views of psychologists such as Jung (*Dreambook*, Ekaterinburg, 1994) or contemporary discussions of dreambooks (E. Tsvetkov's *Dreambook* of 1990).

The contents of the contemporary dreambook depend on many of the same strategies as adopted by pre-Revolutionary publishers. A few pad out the contents by collating dream objects from a variety of sources without checking for repetition; 'horse', for example, will appear under the letter K as *kon'* and under L for *loshad'*, each with a different interpretation.[22] Other modern dreambooks bear little or no relation to Russian literary or oral tradition, probably because they are translated from modern Western texts. The advantage of the latter is their inclusion of a wide range of modern dream objects.

Russian versions appearing before 1995, just like their pre-Revolutionary counterparts, opted not to label themselves as translations. What, for example, was the source of the *samizdat* dreambook circulating among the actors of the Moscow Art Theatre in 1990? Or the full dreambook published in Ekaterinburg in 1994? As ever, pinpointing their origin is difficult; for example, *The Complete Dreambook* (Tallinn, 1990) declares itself a reworking of various ancient works, but this piece of information is belied by dream objects like electricity and cars. The book is, in fact, an unattributed reprinting of an émigré Russian dreambook.[23] It, in its turn, was taken from a pre-Revolutionary text, or possibly translated. From 1995 publishers increasingly began to turn to translation, resulting in the appearance in Russian not only of Hindman's dreambook but also one by Tony Crisp as well as one containing interpretations from Artemidorus to Zadkiel (Richard Morrison, the Victorian astrologer).[24] These generally offer fuller interpretations and explanations, a return to the trends of 1780–1825.

One rarity in the earlier period, the dreambook created by an individual, is now much more common.[25] The contents of these owe something to printed and oral traditions, just like the Kindly Old Man's. It should not be assumed that their creation is a cynical commercial ploy, even if the profit motive is certainly present. In a culture that stresses innovation and individual endeavour rather than tradition, compilers of new dreambooks feel no compunction in proffering their own experience to a wider audience. Now that widespread attachment to the traditional dreambook has melted away, contemporary dreambook users are bound to find some of the traditional dream objects in a standard nineteenth-century text bizarre and dated. What relevance can hunting blackcock have to the life of a modern Russian woman, and how likely is she to dream about them? Far better to learn the significance of dreams about trams, macaroni or *pel'meni* (Siberian ravioli).

One obvious source has been neglected, just as it was earlier. It may seem surprising that village dream beliefs have not got into print, especially as there are numbers of scrupulous scholarly collections, but once again the pressures of commercial publishing militate against them. What is more, most folklorists and ethnographers do not wish to sully genuine folk belief by laying it out for sale along with commercial popular culture. If they can overcome their fastidiousness, they may persuade publishers to put folk dream beliefs into wider circulation at long last.

The composition of other fortune-telling books in Russia today, like dreambooks, corresponds only partially to their pre-Revolutionary counterparts. Guides to reading the cards, palms or coffee grounds and discussions of physiognomy correspond very closely both to earlier manuals and to the secondary oral tradition of the Soviet period. The relative popularity today of these old forms of fortune-telling has changed; card, coffee-cup and palm reading remain popular, but physiognomy has only survived by the skin of its teeth, as a couple of pages in a few longer fortune-telling books.[26] Rather surprisingly, the Bruce calendar with its unscientific weather predictions has been reissued, though it is hard to imagine it replacing conventional weather forecasts.[27] On the other hand, astrology has at last caught on, becoming along with dreambooks the commonest type of fortune-telling text. Its widespread acceptance is not restricted to fortune-telling books; individuals can buy horoscopes for their birth sign in the Moscow metro, consult an astrologer, read their horoscopes in mass-circulation magazines or learn astrology from a published guide.[28] The clearest indicator of its success in modern Russia is the part it plays in the deliberations of the Kremlin. In a manner reminiscent of the Reagan era in the White House, astrologers attached to the Academy of Astrology in Moscow regularly draw up horoscopes for President El'tsin and other important government figures, and pronounce on the most favourable dates for the presidential elections.[29] How seriously these are taken is not clear, but evidently it is not just the unsavoury General Rogozin who thinks astrology may help the El'tsin team remain in power. Its influence is also creeping into new areas of everyday life including the kitchen, judging by *Astrological Cuisine* (1995) which provides recipes and lists of herbs suitable for each birth sign.

Popular astrology in Russia, as elsewhere, considerably simplifies the intellectual complexities of judicial astrology. Its adoption might imply a merger between Russian and West European fortune-telling traditions, but evidence to the contrary comes with the recent publication of Chinese astrological texts as well as of the I Ching and Japanese horoscopes. Fads for Eastern divination occur in the West as well, but only among certain groups – the obvious example is the popularity of the I Ching in the late 1960s and 1970s which failed in the long run to achieve the acceptability of palmistry, crystal balls, tarot and horoscopes. It is unclear whether current Russian fashion reflects an enthusiasm for innovation (witness also tarot cards, 'druid' horoscopes and tables of birthsign gems),[30] or a response to Russia's geographical location. Probably, as before the Revolution, accident played a large rôle in the choice of texts for translation. Tarot is an example. Having had some limited success at the turn of the century, it looks ripe for rediscovery, especially in view of both its pretensions and its popularity in the West. So far this has not happened, and the only book whose title uses the word tarot (spelt incorrectly as 'torot') turns out to be a guide to the Russian gypsy cartomantic method using fifty-two cards.[31]

Clear parallels exist between the current renaissance of fortune-telling books and their first manifestation in the late eighteenth century. In both instances texts appeared as soon as the state slackened its grip on the printing industry, and caught on rapidly despite rationalist disapproval. Just as fortune-telling books in the

7 Cartoon published in the newspaper *Komersant* (31.12.90–7.1.91) illustrating the ongoing debate between 'scientific' and irrational forms of predicting the future in the new post-Soviet Russia. It depicts a group of businessmen awaiting the predictions of a fortune-teller who advertises her services as 'Consulting and Gadalking' (the last word a combination of the Russian word for fortune-telling with a trendy English ending).

eighteenth century appealed to an educated as well as a semi-educated readership (in so far as the latter had access to them), so in contemporary Russia purchasers range from academics to office workers and peasants. In both instances, curiosity seems to have been an important motivating force for some, while others are responding to a deep-felt need or personal conviction. Where the two processes differ is in the speed and size of the contemporary revival. Modern technology, universal literacy, the lack of restrictions on the number and location of publishers and a group of people already familiar with fortune-telling books ensured that the print explosion occurred almost instantaneously. Since small publishing houses sprang up all over the former Soviet Union from Tallinn to Kiev, Iaroslavl to Tiraspol′, a receptive public in both urban and rural areas had access to fortune-telling literature almost immediately, problems with distribution notwithstanding. A further difference is that nowadays fortune-telling books are firmly women's books, whereas in the late eighteenth century they had yet to become so. For the first time, women have played some rôle in publishing their own literature, though a surprising number of male names appear as compilers, editors or publishers, suggesting that, as in the West, the profit motive overrides the gender divide.[32]

It may be assumed that, barring a return to a hostile government, fortune-telling will enjoy a long and happy life in Russia, though perhaps not at the same levels as today. At the same time, the eternal human desire to predict the future that in Soviet times was channelled into politics and science is being transmuted into phenomena such as the current interest in futures research or business techniques like forward planning. A cartoon published at the beginning of 1991 in the business newspaper *Komersant* (see ill. 7) shows businessmen learning the future from a fortune-teller who offers 'consulting and divining'. Plus ça change!

Conclusion

As Russia goes through a major crisis in which the evaporation of the socialist goal of the 'shining future' has engendered a deep need for reassurance and a shift to basic concerns about family and individual welfare, fortune-telling demonstrates its ability to resist attempts at ridiculing it out of existence. But is it enough to attribute the revival and popularity of fortune-telling solely to social factors? It might be argued that similar socio-psychological factors underpin the New Age revival in Britain in the late eighties and early nineties. When recession followed a period in which social emphasis had been switched from service to self-advancement and the protective cover of the welfare state was seen to be diminishing, the result was widespread insecurity. One of the specific consequences was a revived enthusiasm for crystal ball and horoscope. A survey in Britain in 1993 found that a quarter of those questioned had consulted a fortune-teller, a fifth believed their horoscope completely, while half thought it possible to predict that something was going to happen before it actually did. Much more than the British, the Russians have reason to feel insecure about the present and fearful for the future. Gone are the days of stable prices, guaranteed jobs and a cradle-to-grave welfare system. Problems always existed, of course, but the average citizen knew he or she could get by. Now the individual is forced back on his or her own resources in providing for self and family. With dialectical materialism replaced by rampant consumerism, another element in the current popularity of irrational belief is a reaction against the contemporary obsession with money. For many, not least for the elderly and women with children, the world is a terrifying place. In this context, the sharp turn towards non-material belief is understandable.

But there are two problems with this argument. The first is that social factors can be of varied kinds. As was argued in chapter 3, the success of fortune-telling literature in the eighteenth century should be attributed to factors no longer relevant today; to the needs of newly literate groups embracing a facet of fashionable West European culture which replaced folk divination. Social factors, therefore, vary according to context, period and location, indicating that they define the level of popularity of fortune-telling and the forms it takes at a given time rather than explain its perennial popularity.

Secondly, the argument fails to explain the survival of traditions of fortune-telling in the Soviet period, when social disapproval was intense and the problems of the collective future had, it was claimed, been solved. Perhaps these should be explained as a reaction to science and materialism? Taken to its limit, this view would imply that in the USSR an attachment to fortune-telling was a sign of political dissidence, albeit sub-conscious. If this is a major reason, then fortune-telling should have been even more popular than it was and is in the West. The reaction theory is better seen as a contributory factor to the level of popularity in a given situation. Alternatively, perhaps, the popularity of fortune-telling among the Russians should be attributed to national cultural characteristics? Can Chekhov's view of the Russians as a people who adore the past, hate the present and fear the future explain their ongoing need to take a glimpse into the future?[1] Partially, maybe, but only in so far as a high proportion of Russians are close to the peasant culture of their parents and grandparents, where such attitudes are ingrained.

Looking behind the specific social situation is ultimately more helpful, since it reveals the existence of general human factors. Thus the popularity of fortune-telling books in the eighteenth century may have depended upon their replacing a specific oral cultural tradition, whereas in modern Russia they replace a materialist philosophy, but the need for reassurance about the future continues. The British survey of 1993 probably would have produced similar results if conducted in, say, 1978. Worries about the future of friends, family or self can be soothed by a sympathetic fortune-teller or by a prophecy that gives hope when at best the future is unknown and at worst bleak. Whatever the social, political and economic situation, the daunting problems of life remain, though the perception of helplessness in the face of larger forces may be less acute at some periods than others.

The question of the relationship between the popularity of fortune-telling in a modern society and scientific thinking also requires further examination. It has been pointed out that the differences between scientific knowledge and belief knowledge are often less clear to ordinary people than they are to specialists, allowing elements from a traditional world view to coexist with modern rational thought. Evidence both from modern Western and totalitarian societies like the Soviet Union suggests that, however effectively knowledge that nature is governed by impersonal laws percolates through society, people do not relinquish irrational belief. The drive for success in particular tends to prompt recourse to all manner of techniques or devices thought to be beneficial; sportsmen and actors everywhere are well known for their attachment to talismans and to fortune-telling, probably because they feel that, despite their best efforts, chance plays a determining rôle in the success of a play, race or contest. In another sphere of life the financial service industry in Britain is known to use astrology in its targeting of potential customers.[2] The popularity of fortune-telling goes further; France today, for example, is a country where twenty per cent of the population have consulted a clairvoyant, and practitioners of the paranormal have an estimated annual turnover of more than a billion pounds. One commentator, Gérard Miller, a Paris psychiatrist, has even gone so far as to claim the reverse of the view that science will overcome superstition and divination, when he declared recently that 'the astonishing thing is that the more science progresses, the less it affects obscurantist phenomena such as clairvoyance'.[3] He is here employing a variant of the argument that fortune-telling is a reaction to rational thought, but just as it is highly dubious that science will vanquish fortune-telling so too the popularity of fortune-telling and faith-healing does not seem to depend on *advances* in science. One might add that, in any case, his own field of psychiatry is one that demands belief and acceptance from those who use its services rather than scientific understanding.

More relevant is that science is no longer regarded as a cure-all. Few now see it as a form of secular religion, as something that can solve the problems of mankind. Nor is religion seen by many in

Western society as a valid alternative; fortune-tellers and faith-healers outnumber priests in Catholic France, thereby revealing the deep human need for a magical resolution to problems of the present or the future. The exhortations to trust in God may not be sufficient solace. As Judith Devlin shows, nineteenth-century French peasants drew enormous comfort from the magic rituals attached to the cult of various saints,[4] something that has been downplayed by the Church in this century. In that sense the Catholic Church in France is proceeding in a similar direction to the Communist Party in Russia in preferring a non- or less magical approach to belief.

The rational process appears to go only so far; man cannot live by rational scientific explanation alone, though modern culture accepts the superiority of rational thought over irrationality. In the 1860s Dostoevskii's Underground Man asserted that man preferred irrationality to scientific reason, because this gave him individual freedom of choice, whereas scientific laws predetermined his behaviour and so enslaved him. However exaggerated and dangerous when taken to extremes, this view appears less perverse today than it seemed in the nineteenth century with its optimism about scientific progress. An essential psychological continuity ensures that social change often merely transmutes patterns of society into new forms. Without ignoring the major differences between pre-modern and modern societies, I suggest that in this respect they have been much exaggerated. Fortune-telling, a reflection of man's magical dialogue with reality, illustrates the continuity, though it must be set against the recognition that the notion of self-help and greater control over the environment has greatly diminished the reliance on magical views in the modern world.[5] By looking at fortune-telling in one culture over a period of two centuries, I hope to have shown that science and superstitious belief differ less than is commonly assumed and that the desire to foretell the future constitutes a basic human urge, stronger than an education that emphasizes the empirical. This desire is channelled and focused differently in different times and places.

Once the view of divination as a basic human need is accepted, the study of its reception and rôle in a given country, in this case Russia, reveals distinctive features. Not surprisingly, the parallels between Russia in the late eighteenth and nineteenth centuries and early modern Europe are considerable. In both we find a widespread fascination with divining the future. In sixteenth- and early seventeenth-century England, the magical world view still held sway over even the educated, but ceased to be intellectually respectable as the seventeenth and eighteenth centuries advanced. In late eighteenth-century Russia the principles of a rational Enlightenment had only been grasped by a small élite, while the mind-set of other literate groups differed little from that of the illiterate majority and conditioned their positive reaction to Western fortune-telling books, which arrived simultaneously with Enlightenment ideas. Some members of that tiny élite despised superstition and irrationality of any kind, fortune-telling included, though others favoured the esoteric or pseudo-sciences like freemasonry or physiognomy, which were not always clearly distinguished from humble fortune-telling. Whereas in Western Europe it took fortune-telling books centuries to become exclusively part of low culture, with a long period in which the élite was seriously interested in magic and the more complex forms of divination (while spurning popular manifestations of the art), in Russia this process was telescoped and changed by the much later period in which this process occurred. A mere sixty-five years after the appearance of the first fortune-telling book, Russian culture began to separate ever more clearly into high and low, with fortune-telling consigned to low culture. The Enlightenment emphasis on reason and the next century's on empirical study and science combined to ensure that fortune-telling enjoyed a much briefer period of respectability than it had in Western Europe. It was not, however, the Orthodox Church and the State who led the fight against fortune-telling, both tending to locate their enemies elsewhere. Their attacks were extremely sporadic. Instead, as the intelligentsia emerged in the 1830s, it increasingly took on the rôle of defender of cultural values, scourge of backwardness and purveyor of enlightenment to the people, ensuring that, as the century progressed, cultural stratification intensified and the climate for fortune-telling worsened. The condemnation of professional fortune-tellers in the eighteenth century by the educated élite demonstrates that they were extremely widely patronized, whereas the relative paucity of references for the period beyond 1840 suggests increasing marginalization.

This contempt did not stop the traffic between the two cultural zones. It may have weakened male participation, but it did not seriously limit the role of fortune-telling in the culture of women, nor prevent the spread of books to the peasants. As the contents of fortune-telling books turned into a secondary form of folklore, the natural conservatism of oral tradition helped stabilize the contents and type of books. Urban and rural purchasers shared essentially conservative tastes, a point of contrast with popular commercial fiction, which responded to the changing aspirations of the urban classes. The new fiction (kopeck dreadfuls and others) embodying attitudes characteristic of a modernizing society was by the Revolution gradually filtering down to the peasants who began to reject the old *lubok* tales which in many instances were medieval or at least eighteenth century in origin.[6] In the case of fortune-telling books the whole social range of urban buyers from wealthy merchant women to semi-literate workers opted for essentially the same types of fortune-telling as the peasants, with the only differences being the modest level of expansion and innovation in dreambooks and the reproduction in the 1890s of the types of omnibus edition that had sold so well in the first couple of decades of the nineteenth century. Once fortune-telling books or the standard fortune-teller had ceased to interest the élite, who instead channelled their divinatory impulses into spiritualism or occultism as fashion dictated, the skills they presented remained remarkably stable. Thus, unlike popular fiction and later Soviet popular culture which responded to an industrializing modernizing Russia, fortune-telling books are much more characteristic of the essentially conservative popular culture of pre-modern societies, of the type elaborated by Peter Burke.[7] Their survival in a modern society reveals that not all Russian popular culture is, as Richard Stites suggests, both contemporary and often temporary.[8] The differences stem from the rôle different types of popular culture have had. While a serious message may be concealed in a popular film or novel, success depends, as Stites argues, as much on the ability of the work to strike a contemporary chord in terms of theme or characters and on its capacity to absorb and entertain. While entertainment was uppermost in the minds of some participants in fortune-telling, it managed to maintain and still maintains a range of serious functions, whatever the declarations made by some people that their interest went no further than having fun.

The analysis of gender and fortune-telling reflects a similar continuity, with differences explicable in terms of the specifics of time and place. The socio-psychological function of fortune-telling as an extension of women's traditional caring role is one factor that remains unchanged throughout time. This does not preclude men's interest and involvement, but it tends to be more haphazard. Apart from a general tendency in patriarchal societies for men to take a leading rôle in divination where it allows the exercise of power, or has prestige (for example, as divinatory sages), social factors seem to determine the level of male participation. When men were the readers and women the defenders of oral culture in Russia, fortune-telling books were more the property of men than women. In the eighteenth century men visited fortune-tellers particularly for magic thief detection or to discover whether their wives were faithful, and tended to go less as these functions were lost. The exception to this general trend is the product of cultural factors, when Romantic interest in the irrational led young élite men to consult fortune-tellers in the 1820s and 1830s. As women and people from outside the élite classes acquired literacy, fortune-telling books reached these groups and, in so doing, lost credibility with élite men. Such a development was entirely in keeping with contemporary attitudes to women as intellectual inferiors, incapable of logical reasoning. Women in Russia continued to support fortune-telling throughout the pre-Revolutionary period, and the varied uses they made of it reveal that it made an active contribution to their world and their lives. Offering hope, solace or guidance as well as, in various contexts, enjoyment, fortune-telling also served to bond families, friends and broader social groups. Though women have often been seen as passive victims of circumstance, in fortune-telling they were actively continuing their caring rôle, especially when acting as professional or amateur interpreters.

Fortune-telling equally demonstrates clearly the active rôle played by consumers in some facets of popular culture. Though both fortune-telling books and the skills of professional fortune-tellers changed very little in the course of the nineteenth century, this conservatism should not be confused with consumer passivity. If the contents of books altered little, it was because users did not want them to. The purchaser of a fortune-telling manual was much more active than a conventional reader, in that he, or more likely she, was a co-interpreter of the material. The book was only the raw material for a session in which its users applied the material to particular circumstances. On the other hand, it may fairly be objected that clients of fortune-tellers or users of books were passive in a different way, escapists seeking a beautiful future. If the desire to escape from drab reality and seek clarification of the future is a natural human impulse, such passivity is part of human make-up. Hopes and visions of the future may impel the individual to make certain choices, and do not necessarily indicate a passive approach to life. Fortune-telling, judging by its cult status in Russia today, has an important rôle to play in helping individuals cope with their lives. There is every reason to believe that Russian fortune-telling has a future as much as a past and a present.

Notes

INTRODUCTION

1 T. Luckman, *The Invisible Religion*, London, 1967.

2 I owe a considerable debt to Jeffrey Brooks, *When Russia Learnt to Read: Literacy and Popular Literature, 1861–1917*, Princeton, NJ, 1985, and to two other major studies, Richard Stites, *Russian Popular Culture: Entertainment and Society since 1900* (Cambridge Soviet Paperbacks 7), Cambridge, 1992, and Catriona Kelly, *Petrushka – the Russian Carnival Puppet Theatre*, Cambridge, 1990.

3 Key studies of pre-modern popular culture are Keith Thomas, *Religion and the Decline of Magic*, London, 1971, and Peter Burke, *Popular Culture in Early Modern Europe*, London, 1978. The inclusiveness of the term popular culture varies. Burke, for example, argues for varieties of popular culture according to social groups which combined traditional oral and literate elements. It is generally agreed that the dichotomy between urban culture and rural folk culture becomes more distinct with time, though Roger Chartier (*The Cultural Uses of Print in Early Modern France*, trans. Lydia C. Cochrane, Princeton, NJ, 1987) argues that this was the case in France as early as the seventeenth century.

4 Russian scholars have spent little time discussing the function of divination, largely because 'superstition' was deemed to have perished after the Revolution. In my consideration of this question, I was most helped by Keith Thomas' *Religion* and Judith Devlin's *The Superstitious Mind: French Peasants and the Supernatural in the Nineteenth Century*, New Haven–London, 1987, as well as the work of various French social historians whose views and achievements are discussed by Robin Briggs, *Communities of Belief: Cultural and Social Tensions in Early Modern France*, Oxford, 1989.

5 D. A. Nechaenko, *Son zavetnykh ispolnennykh znakov*, Moscow, 1991, for example, opens his book with a sneer at printed dream books before leaving them out of further discussion (pp. 4–6).

6 The arguments advanced against the binary model are summarized neatly by Tessa Watt, *Cheap Print and Popular Piety, 1550–1640*,

Cambridge, 1991, pp. 2–5. Old élitist attitudes die hard; for example, E. Heier derides popular books on physiognomy in *Studies on Johann Caspar Lavater (1741–1801) in Russia*, Berne–Berlin–Frankfurt–New York–Paris, 1991.

7 Stites, *Popular Culture.* As Robert Edelman points out in his review of Stites' book (*Slavic Review*, 52, 1993, pp. 568–76), his position brings him closer to the work of Stuart Hall and Raymond Williams, who, distinguishing popular culture from the mass culture generated by the entertainment industry, considered the former to possess a variety of responses to mass culture, ranging from uncritical acceptance by the public to a negotiated response as well as outright rejection.

8 *Superstitious Mind*, especially pp. 215–30.

9 The position changed in the early twentieth century, when Symbolist women poets drew on folk spells, incantation and divination, because, as Catriona Kelly remarks, 'they conferred on the speaker the right to command the spiritual world through the power of language' ('Life at the margins: women, culture and narodnost' 1880–1920', in Marianne Liljeström, Eila Mäntysaari, Arja Rosenholm, eds., *Gender Restructuring in Russian Studies: Conference Papers – Helsinki, August, 1992* (Slavica Tamperensia, 2), Tampere, pp. 148–9).

10 For example, Iu. M. Lotman's fascinating *Besedy o russkoi kul'ture. Byt i traditsii russkogo dvorianstva (XVIII-nachalo XIX veka)*, St Petersburg, 1994, concentrates, as the title suggests, on élite culture, largely that of men.

11 N. I. Tolstoi, 'Slavianskie narodnye tolkovaniia snov i ikh mifologicheskaia osnova', *Son – semioticheskoe okno. Snovidenie i sobytie. Snovidenie i iskusstvo. Snovidenie i tekst* (XXVI-e Vipperovskie chteniia, Moskva, 1993), ed. D. Iu. Molok, Moscow, [1994], p. 89.

12 N. I. Tolstoi, *Etnolingvisticheskii slovar' slavianskikh drevnostei. Proekt slovnika. Predvaritel'nye materialy*, ed. N. I. Tolstoi et al., Moscow, 1984, p. 11. My point is not to denigrate the considerable achievements of the ethnolinguists, whose position since the death in June 1996 of Nikita Tolstoi is deeply insecure.

13 Kelly, *Petrushka*, p. 4, quoting James Clifford, *The Predicament of Culture: Twentieth Century Literature, Ethnography and Art*, Cambridge, MA–London, 1988.

14 N. I. Tolstoi, 'Nekotorye problemy slavianskoi etnolingvistiki', *Zeitschrift für Slavische Philologie*, no. 2, 1990, pp. 238–53.

15 The concept of the third estate, on which the term presumably relies, is not widely known in Russia.

16 *Svodnyi katalog russkoi knigi grazhdanskoi pechati XVIII veka, 1725–1800*, Moscow, 6 vols., 1962–75.

17 In particular, N. Obol'ianinov, *Katalog russkikh illiustrirovannykh*

izdanii 1725–1860 gg., 2 vols., Moscow, 1914–15; V. I. Mezhov, *Piatoe pribavlenie k sistematicheskoi rospisi knigam prodaiushchim v knizhnykh magazinakh Ivana Il'icha Glazunova, 1883–7*, St Petersburg, 1889; M. D. Ol'khin, *Sistematicheskii reestr russkim knigam s 1831 po 1846 god*, St Petersburg, 1846; *Bibliograficheskie pribavleniia k Zhurnalu Ministerstva narodnogo prosveshcheniia. Ukazatel' knig, vyshedshego v Rossii i v Tsarstve pol'skom*, 5 vols., St Petersburg, 1837–55. Other sources are noted when they crop up in the book.

1 DREAMBOOKS AND OTHER FORTUNE-TELLING GUIDES

1 Fortune-telling books are listed in Section A of the bibliography in both English and Russian, with, for eighteenth-century books, the appropriate number from the Union Catalogue, *Svodnyi katalog russkoi knigi grazhdanskoi pechati XVIII veka, 1725–1800*, 6 vols., Moscow, 1962–75. General references to the catalogue use the abbreviation *Svodnyi katalog*.

2 See Harry B. Weiss, *Oneirocritica Americana: The Story of American Dreambooks*, New York, 1944.

3 See the introduction and appendices to *A Collection of Russian Folk Songs by Nikolai L'vov and Ivan Prach*, ed. Malcolm Hamrick Brown, Ann Arbor–London, 1987.

4 For a discussion of political prophecy, and Martyn Zadeka in particular, see chapter 7.

5 Editions in 1794, 1799, 1801, 1808, 1816 and possibly 1814.

6 Tommaso Giuseppe Moult, sometimes known by the French version of his name, Thomas-Joseph Moult, was a thirteenth-century seer. The Russian version (1778) was translated from the Paris edition of 1771.

7 Twenty-six compendia to twenty-four single texts, though these figures must be regarded with caution.

8 *Svodnyi katalog*, vol. 5, p. 136, lists nine for the eighteenth century, but to this must be added SK add. 198 plus two non-extant editions, SK n-e 681 and 775, as well as SK3077, which the catalogue lists incorrectly under *gadanie*. In fact, SK8840 and add.681, which the *Svodnyi katalog* lists as dreambooks, are, like SK3077, compilations, where the dreambook is one of several divinatory texts.

9 On the existence of dream beliefs and their reflection in texts in pre-Petrine Russia, see chapter 2. I am grateful to N. A. Kobiak of the Rare Books Department of Moscow State University Library for the information about indexes.

10 H. Kapełus, 'Senniki staropolskie. Z dziejów literatury popularnej XVI-XVIII wieku', *Studii z dawniej literatury czeskiej, słowackiej i polskiej*, Warsaw–Prague, 1963, p. 303, quoting Simoni, notes the similarity between the title of the mid-eighteenth-century MS and a frag-

mentary Polish dreambook (Craców, 1717). Polish dreambooks were part of a regular stream of printings of the *Somniale Danielis*, the first of which was probably translated from German (pp. 301–3). The Russian MS of 1700 is described by A. Sobolevskii, *Perevodnaia literatura Moskovskoi Rusi XIV-XV vekov*, St Petersburg, 1903, p. 226.

11 See B. A. Gradov, B. M. Kloss, V. I. Koretskii, 'K istorii arkhangel'skoi biblioteki D. M. Golitsyna', *Arkheograficheskii ezhegodnik*, 1978, pp. 238–53; on the *Fortuna* see Kapełus, 'Senniki', pp. 303–4.

12 N. A. Baklanova, 'O sostave bibliotek moskovskikh kuptsov vo vtoroi chetverti XVIII veka', *Trudy otdela drevnerusskoi literatury*, vol. 14, 1958, pp. 644–9. Indeed, of the 299 volumes listed, both printed and manuscript, no less than 174 were Church books, though this may have been because some of the owners were Old Believers. Despite their strict opposition to secular culture, Old Believers copied and used some divinatory texts that were highly dubious from a Christian point of view. On the composition of libraries in Russia in the seventeenth and eighteenth centuries, see Max J. Okenfuss, *The Rise and Fall of Latin Humanism in Early-Modern Russia: Pagan Authors, Ukrainians and the Resiliency of Muscovy*, Leiden–New York–Cologne, 1995.

13 A. Leo Oppenheim, *The Interpretation of Dreams in the Ancient Near East with a Translation of an Assyrian Dream-Book* (Transactions of the American Philsophical Society), vol. 46, pt 3, Philadelphia, 1966, pp. 179–373; also his 'Mantic dreams in the ancient Near East', *The Dream and Human Societies*, ed. G. E. von Grunebaum and Roger Caillois, Berkeley–Los Angeles, 1966, pp. 341–50.

14 For example, Gregory of Nyssa in the fourth century accepted dreams as divine messages, while both St Augustine and Thomas Aquinas were much interested in prophetic dreams.

15 The attribution of a dreambook to ben Sirin (d. 728), widely seen as the incarnation of Arab oneiromancy, probably occurred in the ninth century (see Toufy Fahd, 'The Dream in Medieval Islamic Society', Grunebaum and Caillois, *Dream*, pp. 360–1). The text of Pseudo-ben Sirin may be found in *Das Traumbuch des Achmet ben Sirin*, trans. with a commentary by Karl Brackertz, Munich, 1986. On Artemidorus, see *The Interpretation of Dreams by Artemidorus*, trans. with a commentary by Robert I. White, Park Ridge, NJ, 1975; C. Blum, *Studies in the Dreambook of Artemidorus*, Uppsala, 1938. Other important studies include Maurice Hélin, *La Clef des songes*, Paris, 1925; Bernhard Büchsenschütz, *Traum und Traumdeutung im Altertum*, reprinted from the edition of 1868, Wiesbaden, 1967; Naphtali Lewis, *The Interpretation of Dreams and Portents*, Toronto–Sarasota, 1976; Stephen Michael Oberhelman, 'The Oneirocritic Literature of the Late Roman and Byzantine Eras of Greece: Manuscript Studies, Translations and Commentaries to the Dream-Books of Greece

during the First Millennium AD, with Greek and English Catalogues of the Dream Symbols and with a Discussion of Greek Oneiromancy from Homer to Manuel the Palaeologian', PhD thesis, University of Minnesota, photocopy version Ann Arbor, MI, 1983.

16 See S. R. Fischer, 'The dream in Middle High German epic', *Australian and New Zealand Studies in German Language and Literature*, vol. 10, Berne–Frankfurt–Las Vegas, 1978, p. 28; Hélin, *La Clef*, p. 65 ff.

17 Chaired by Annikki Kaivola-Bregenhøj (see NIF *Newsletter*, 1–2, 1988, pp. 24–6). See also *Drömmar och kultur*, ed. Ulf Palmenfelt and Annikki Kaivola-Bregenhøj, Copenhagen, 1992. The *Somniale Danielis* also had an enormous impact on oral oneirocritical beliefs in Belgium according to Hélin (*Clef*, p. 90).

18 See Palmenfeldt and Kaivola-Bregenhøj, *Drömmar*, especially pp. 187–272.

19 *The Prediction Worthy of Note of the Renowned Martyn Zadek* . . . and *The Curious Prediction of the Venerable One Hundred and Six Year Old Renowned Swiss Man Martyn Zadek* . . ., both Moscow, 1807.

20 E.g. *Soothsay, do not Jest* . . ., 3 pts, Moscow, 1808 (vols. 1 and 2) and 1827 (vol. 3); *The Ancient Astrologer or Oracle* . . ., Moscow, 1814 and 1820; *The Ancient and Modern Astrologer or A Complete Divinatory Oracle* . . ., Moscow, 1814, and 1824–5.

21 The first (SK6700) was republished in 1787 (SK6701), 1843 and 1846; the second (SK n-e 775) reappeared in 1791 (SK add.198) and 1820). The problems of studying dreambook redactions are exemplified here: the 1784 edition of the second book is not extant, the 1791 edition (SK add.198) is only found in Kostroma. I have therefore relied on the defective copy of the 1820 edition in the Russian National Library, which declares it is based on the 1791 St Petersburg edition. An inscription on p. 83 implies the date 1820. Though claiming to be a new corrected edition, the total number of pages was the same. It is likely that the declaration is merely an attempt to boost its chances with prospective buyers.

22 These two sets of interpretations for dreaming of diamonds alternate consistently in pre-1825 dreambooks, suggesting two basic redactions. It may be, therefore that the 1784 and 1787 dreambooks were translated from different variants of the same European dreambook.

23 *A Dreambook or The Interpretation of Dreams Arranged in Alphabetical Order* . . ., 1784, 1791 and 1820 (SK. n-e 775, add.198).

24 Book 3, no. 11.

25 The 1831 edition retained the original title (more or less), whereas the 1839 version was called *The Sibyl or Morning Teller of Dreams*. . . . The variations in title suggest independent adaptations.

26 For example in the *Interpretation of Dreams of the Venerable 106-Year-Old Man, Martyn Zadeka*, Moscow, 1885. Instances of this practice crop up

occasionally in early dreambooks, such as in the *The Ancient and Modern Permanent Divinatory Oracle . . .*, Moscow, 1800, but became more common with time.

27 *A Dreambook of 215 Dreams or The Interpretation of Dreams by Various Egyptian and Indian Sages and Astronomers.*

28 For example in *The Interpreter of Dreams by the Well-Known French Dream Diviner, Mlle Lenormand...*, St Petersburg, 1862.

29 Ancient dream categories took a long time to disappear entirely; the purchaser of a short dreambook of 1865 was still able to discover that dreaming of eating camel meat meant a long illness, and in *1,500,000 Dreams . . .* (Moscow, 1896), that eating lions signified honour and riches.

30 *Azbuka* is commonly found in dreambooks from 1802, *ananas* from 1839, and *arab* or *arap* in 1859.

31 *The Popular Dreambook for 1915*, Petrograd, 1915, quoted by D. A. Nechaenko, *Son zavetnykh ispolnennyi znakov*, Moscow, 1991, p. 4.

32 Folk influence is discussed in chapter 2.

33 The interpretation for the Englishman is clearly based on the common nineteenth-century Russian perception of the English as both social hypocrites and possessors of an acute business acumen.

34 *3000 Dreams. A Detailed Elucidation of All Manner of Dreams*, St Petersburg, 1870.

35 The Dzhagatai text with Russian translation, Kazan′, 1901. The sole exception is an attempt to draw on local Tatar traditions, which appeared in Kazan′ in 1902: N. G. Mallitskii's *Muslim Dreambook.*

36 Published by N. P. Pantusov in *Materialy k izucheniiu narechiia taranchei Iliiskogo okruga*, no. 7.

37 The figures of Madame Blavatsky, the founder of the Theosophical Society and the mystic, G. I. Gurdjieff illustrate the impact of Russians on the popularity of occult philosophy both in Russia and worldwide.

38 Peter Burke, 'L'Histoire sociale des rêves', *Annales*, vol. 28, 1973, pp. 329–42; Philippe Descola, 'Head-shrinkers versus shrinks: Jivaroan dream analysis', *Man*, vol. 24, 1989, pp. 439–50.

39 Dice divination appears in a text mistakenly entitled 'rafli' in A. N. Pypin, *Lozhnye i otrechennye knigi russkoi stariny*, pt 3 of *Pamiatniki starinnoi russkoi literatury izdannye G. Kushelev-Bezborodko*, St Petersburg, 1862, pp. 161–6, as A. A. Turilov and A. V. Chernetsov, 'Otrechennaia kniga Rafli', *Trudy otdela drevnerusskoi literatury*, vol. 40, 1985, pp. 260–344, point out. They publish a genuine geomantic *Rafli* text, whose complexity ensured that its popular impact was negligible (only one copy is extant).

40 *A Newly Appeared Wizard, Recounting the Divination of the Spirits . . .*, St Petersburg, 1795.

41 D. A. Rovinskii, *Russkie narodnye kartinki*, 5 vols., Moscow, 1881, vol. 5, p. 9, thinks *Solomon* may have been translated from French in the first

half of the century, though he does not explain how the text came to be in a heavily Church Slavonicized Russian. A possible explanation is a clerical translator, though few of these can have known French. More likely, the text arrived in manuscript form via a neighbouring Slav-speaking area.

42 For example, the State Historical Library in Moscow contains eight different copies dating from between the 1810s and the 1830s.

43 *A True and Most Simple Method of Reading the Cards*, St Petersburg, 1782 (SK add.24). A.V. Tereshchenko, *Byt russkogo naroda*, pt 7, St Petersburg, 1848, p. 262, suggests that cartomancy developed in the Empress Elizabeth's reign (1741–61) as a direct consequence of the popularity of card-playing, but without offering any corroboration.

44 Rovinskii, *Russkie kartinki*, vol. 5, p. 95.

45 For example, two sets of cards with the same title *The Newest Fortune-Telling Cards Replacing All Oracles . . .*, Vsevolozhskii (1814), and Moscow University Press (1816), offered sixty-four and seventy-two boxed cards respectively .

46 *The Book of Fate . . .*, Moscow, 1838, p. 259.

47 Tereshchenko, *Byt*, p. 262.

48 Mlle Lenormand is discussed in chapter 7.

49 A pack of this kind, based on memories of packs of cards known to her mother and an old émigré, was published in San Francisco in 1992 by Svetlana Aleksandrovna Touchkoff as *Russian Gypsy Fortune-Telling Cards*. Touchkoff is undoubtedly wrong in thinking they are of gypsy origin, though gypsies in Southern Russia may indeed have adopted them. M. I. Lekomtseva and B. A. Uspenskii, ('Opisanie odnoi semioticheskoi sistemy s prostym sintaksisom', *Trudy po znakovym sistemam*, vol. 2, Tartu, 1965, p. 100), observe that Russian gypsies today use all fifty-two cards of the conventional pack.

50 For example, *The Magic Fortune-Telling Cards . . .*, Moscow, 1885, which had seventy-seven cards, though the early Lenormand types had sixty-four.

51 A. Balov, 'Son i snovideniia v narodnykh verovaniiakh', *Zhivaia starina*, no. 4, 1891, p. 209, notes that this was not very common.

52 A book with the same title was published by Stepanov in 1843. I have not seen this book, but incline to think that the word *strelka* which means, *inter alia*, a clock hand indicated that the contents were the same.

53 Michael Dummett, *Twelve Tarot Games*, London, 1980, pp. 1–2.

54 See, for example, Gérard Encausse, *Predictive Tarot or The Key to Cartomancy of All Kinds . . .*, St Petersburg, 1912.

55 Keith Thomas, *Religion and the Decline of Magic*, London, 1971, pp. 282–3.

56 On the *Secretum secretorum*, see W. F. Ryan, 'The Old Russian version of the pseudo-Aristotelian *Secretum secretorum*', *Slavonic and East European Review*, vol. 56, 1978, pp. 242–60.

57 E. B. Smilianskaia, '"Suevernaia" knizhitsa pervoi poloviny XVIII v.', *Zhivaia starina*, no. 2, 1994, pp. 33–6.
58 S. P. Mordovina and A. L. Stanislavskii, 'Gadatel'naia kniga XVII v. kholopa Pimena Kalinina', *Istoriia russkogo iazyka. Pamiatniki XI-XVIII vv.*, Moscow, 1882, p. 322.
59 E. Heier, *Studies on Johann Caspar Lavater (1741–1801) in Russia* (Slavica Helvetica 37), Berne–Berlin–Frankfurt–New York–Paris, 1991.
60 The first use of Lavater's name on a divinatory physiognomy text was in 1808 (further editions in 1809 and 1817).
61 Heier, *Lavater*, p. 97.
62 On astrology in England, see Patrick Curry, *Prophecy and Power: Astrology in Early Modern England*, Cambridge, 1989, and *A Confusion of Prophets: Victorian and Edwardian Astrology*, London, 1992; Ann Geneva, *Astrology and the Seventeenth-Century Mind: William Lilly and the Language of the Stars*, Berkeley, CA, 1993; Thomas, *Religion*, chs. 10–12.
63 For a bibliography of literature on astrology, see O. P. Khromov, 'Astronomiia i astrologiia v Drevnei Rusi. Materialy k bibliografii', *Estestvennonauchnye predstavleniia Drevnei Rusi*, Moscow, 1988, pp. 290–310.
64 Curry, *Prophecy*, pp. 96, 128.
65 Smilianskaia, 'Knizhitsa', pp. 33–4, discusses one such manuscript (c.1730).
66 *The Systematic Astrologer or Scientific Divination.*
67 *Astrological Horoscopes and Their Significance in the Life of Man*, Moscow, 1912, was a relative rarity.
68 Gary Marker, *Printing, Publishing and the Origins of Intellectual Life in Russia, 1700–1800*, Princeton, NJ, 1985.
69 Ibid., p. 189. English almanacs, by contrast, were 'characterised by political, religious and social speculation' (see Bernard Capp, *Astrology and the Popular Press: English Almanacs 1500–1800*, London, 1979, p. 271).
70 A. Pokrovskii, *Kalendari i sviattsy*, Moscow, 1889, pp. 16–17.
71 Ibid., p. 57.
72 Iu. Ovsiannikov, *Russkie narodnye kartinki XVII-XVIII vekov*, Moscow, 1968, pp. 25–6.
73 For an example of a lubok version, see Iu. Ovsiannikov, ed., *Lubok. Russkie narodnye kartinki XVII-XVIII vv.*, Moscow, 1968, pp. 25–6, and of one in a fortune-telling omnibus, see *The New Complete Oracle and Magician . . .*, Moscow, 1912 etc.
74 Smilianskaia, 'Knizhitsa', pp. 33–4.
75 An example of the latter is *The Genuine Fortune-Teller . . .*, 1787, 1792, 1793.
76 For example, in the *The New Complete Oracle and Magician . . .*, Moscow, 1912.

77 From *The Magic Mirror*. . ., Moscow, 1794.
78 For example in *The New Complete Oracle and Magician* . . ., Moscow, 1912.
79 R. E. F. Smith and David Christian, *Bread and Salt. A Social and Economic History of Food and Drink in Russia*, Cambridge, 1984, p. 179.
80 It is not clear why this volume is described in the *Svodnyi katalog* as not extant (SK n-e440). It is in the catalogue of the Muzei knigi in the Russian State Library and a defective version exists in the Russian National Library.
81 M. Zabylin, *Russkii narod: ego obychai, obriady, predaniia, sueveriia i poeziia*, Moscow, 1880, reprinted Moscow 1992, notes that bean divination was banned in a secular *Potrebnik* of the early seventeeth century.
82 As with other texts, it was revived in some of the late nineteenth-century compendia.

2 DIVINATION IN RUSSIAN TRADITIONAL CULTURE

1 L. N. Vinogradova, 'Devich'i gadaniia o zamuzhestve v tsikle slavianskoi kalendarnoi obriadnosti (zapadno-vostochnoslavianskie paralleli)', *Slavianskii i balkanskii fol'klor*, Moscow, 1981, p.13.
2 As such it had something in common with incubation, the ancient method of secluding an individual in a sacred place in order to induce a cure. See Carl Alfred Meier, 'The dream in Ancient Greece and its use in temple cures (incubation)', *The Dream and Human Societies*, ed. G. E. von Grunebaum and R. Caillois, Berkeley–Los Angeles, 1966, pp. 303–19.
3 Vinogradova, 'Devich'i gadaniia', pp. 21–3.
4 On Yuletide rituals, see Mikhail Chulkov, *Slovar' russkikh sueverii, idolopoklonicheskikh zhertvoprinoshenii svadebnykh, prostonarodnykh obriadov, koldovsta, shamanstva i proch.*, Moscow 1782; S. V. Maksimov, *Literaturnye puteshestviia*, Moscow, 1986, pp. 244–5, 263–7; M. Zabylin, *Russkii narod. Ego obychai, obriady, predaniia, sueveriia i poeziia*, Moscow, 1880, reprinted 1992, pp. 1–34. For a discussion in English, see W. F. Ryan and F. Wigzell, 'Gullible girls and dreadful dreams: Zhukovskii, Pushkin and popular divination', *Slavonic and East European Review*, vol. 70, 1992, pp. 647–69. On the activity of the unclean force at Yuletide, see V. I. Chicherov, *Zimnii period russkogo zemledel'cheskogo kalendaria XVI–XIX vekov* (Trudy instituta etnografii AN SSSR, 40), Moscow, 1957, p. 36. Yuletide divination was performed throughout the Twelve Days of Christmas, whereas the smaller number of divinatory rituals connected with the summer solstice were performed on one day only, when other traditional activities took precedence.
5 A. Makarenko, *Sibirskii narodnyi kalendar' v etnograficheskom otnoshenii.*

Vostochnaia Sibir', Eniseiskaia guberniia (Zapiski Imperatorskogo russkogo geograficheskogo obshchestva 36), St Petersburg, 1913, pp. 94–5, 123, notes that in Eniseisk province, girls put herbs under their pillows on 23 June (St Agrafena's day) to ensure a prophetic dream, while on the Feast of St Philip (14 November), which was the beginning of the Christmas fast and the day when recruits joined the army, divination was about life expectancy. Rituals varied from region to region.

6 I. P. Sakharov, *Skazaniia russkogo naroda, sobrannye I. P. Sakharovym*, Moscow, 1990 (reprinted from the Moscow edn. of 1885), pp. 118, 120.

7 For example in I. Shchegolev, 'Sviatochnaia vorozhba v Olonii', *Olonetskie gubernskie vedomosti*, no. 136, 1906.

8 Known as mythological tales in Russia. See N. A. Krinichnaia, *Domashnii dukh i sviatochnye gadaniia (po materialam severnorusskikh obriadov i mifologicheskikh rasskazov)*, Petrozavodsk, 1993, pp. 5 ff.; Vinogradova, 'Devich'i gadaniia'.

9 My use of the word 'specialist' rather than 'professional' is deliberate. The word 'professional' may mislead, since although such people received gifts for their efforts, it was considered wrong to demand or offer payment. Similar practices are normal elsewhere in Europe, e.g. in Portugal (João de Pina-Cabral, *Sons of Adam, Daughters of Eve*, Oxford, 1986, pp. 194–5).

10 M. M. Gromyko, *Traditsionnye normy povedeniia i formy obshcheniia russkikh krest'ian XIX v.*, Moscow, 1986, pp. 109, 112–13. An extract in English may be found in Marjorie Mandelstam Balzer, *Russian Traditional Culture: Religion, Gender and Customary Law*, Armonk, NY–London, 1992, pp. 225–35.

11 Linda J. Ivanits, *Russian Folk Belief*, Armonk, NY–London, 1992, p. 111.

12 Samuel C. Ramer, 'Traditional healers and peasant culture in Russia, 1861–1917', *Peasant Economy, Culture and Politics in European Russia, 1800–1921*, ed. Esther Kingston Mann and Timothy Mixter, Princeton, NJ, 1991, pp. 207–32. There are no reliable figures for gender representation among folk healers; Nadezhdinskii suggested that there were more male than female folk healers in Siberia ('Narodnoe zdravie', *Tobol'skie gubernskie vedomosti*, 1863, no. 48, p. 420, quoted by N. A. Minenko, 'The living past: daily life and holidays of the Siberian peasant in the eighteenth and first half of the nineteenth centuries', Balzer, *Russian Culture*, pp. 187–8), but figures given by N. A. Kogan for Samara province at about the same period ('O znakharstve v Novouzenskom uezde', *Vrachebnaia khronika Samarskoi gubernii*, 5, no. 7, 1898, pp. 1–11) imply the contrary. Nowadays casual references are more often to women; for example, O. F. Fishman ('Sotsiokul'turnyi status i ritual'noe povedenie

"znaiushchikh" v Tikhvinskom krae', *Zhivaia starina*, no. 4, 1994, p. 24–5), indicates that folk healers not only flourish in the contemporary village but that they are predominantly women.

13 N. A. Krinichnaia, *Lesnye navazhdeniia (mifologicheskie rasskazy i pover'ia o dukhe-"khoziaine" lesa)*, Petrozavodsk, 1993, pp. 43–4.

14 B. A. Uspenskii, 'Antipovedenie v kul'ture drevnei Rusi', *Izbrannye trudy*, 2 vols., Moscow, 1994, vol. 1, p. 328.

15 On English cunning folk, see Keith Thomas, *Religion and the Decline of Magic*, London, 1971, pp. 253–300; on their French counterparts, see Judith Devlin, *The Superstitious Mind: French Peasants and the Supernatural in the Nineteenth Century*, New Haven and London, 1987, pp. 108 ff. On blurring between categories outside Russia, see [Augusta] Lady Gregory, *Visions and Beliefs in the West of Ireland [1920]*, Gerrards Cross, 1992, pp. 31–79.

16 Gromyko, *Traditsionnye normy*, p. 111, cites material from the Tenishev archive of the turn of the century about the Gzhatsk area of Smolensk province. Sakharov, *Skazaniia*, pp. 130–2, refers exclusively to *female* dream interpreters.

17 A. Balov, 'Son i snovideniia v narodnykh verovaniiakh', *Zhivaia starina*, no. 4, 1891, p. 210, notes this for Iaroslavl province, but it applies elsewhere.

18 Balov, 'Son', p. 210; A. Tereshchenko, *Byt russkogo naroda*, St Petersburg, 1848, pt 7, p. 274.

19 Sergei Aksakov, in the first 'fragment' of his family history, published 1846 describes the old-style life of his grandparents. Every morning his grandmother asks her husband whether he had any dreams. See *A Russian Gentleman*, trans. J. D. Duff, Oxford, 1982, p. 21.

20 Leea Virtanen, 'Dream-telling today', *Studies in Oral Narrative*, ed. A-L. Siikala (Studia Fennica 33), 1990, pp. 137–45. See also chapter 8.

21 Jovan E. Howe, *The Peasant Mode of Production, as exemplified by the Russian 'Obshchina-mir'*, Tampere, 1991, p. 40.

22 Pp. 118–19, and 18–50 in the second edition, *Abevega russkikh sueverii* (1786).

23 Tereshchenko, *Byt*.

24 See the memoirs of the poet Tiutchev's daughter: A. F. Tiutcheva, *Pri dvore dvukh imperatorov. Vospominaniia, dnevnik 1853–55*, trans. from French by E. V. Ger'e, ed. S. V. Bakrushin, 2 vols., Moscow, 1928–9, vol. 1, p. 132.

25 Tamara Talbot Rice, *Tamara: Memoirs of St Petersburg, Paris, Oxford and Byzantium*, ed. E. Talbot-Rice, London, 1996, p. 23.

26 *The Berlin Diaries of Marie ('Missie') Vassiltchikov 1940–1945*, London, 1985, p. 2.

27 For example, *The Interpretation of Dreams: A Complete Collection of Yuletide Pleasures*, 3rd edn., Moscow, 1865, 9th edn., 1897, a combination of dream and Yuletide divination.

28 V. A. Lipinskaia notes this with regard to the Altai region ('Narodnye traditsii v sovremennykh kalendarnykh obriadakh i prazdnikakh russkogo naseleniia Altaiskogo kraia', *Russkie: semeinyi i obshchestvennyi byt,* ed. M. M. Gromyko, T. A. Listova, Moscow, 1989, p. 118). Its wider relevance is suggested by my own conversation with a group of middle-aged and elderly village women in Karelia.

29 Sakharov, *Skazaniia,* pp. 118–19, notes two methods, the last of which (opening the psalter at random) survived into the twentieth century. Sakharov mistakenly thinks psalter divination arrived from Germany. See chapter 6 for discussion of urban professional fortune-tellers' practice of psalter divination.

30 Pp. 303–4 in the 1818 edition.

31 P. 306 in the 1818 edition.

32 They also appeared in scholarly works such as A. N. Afanas'ev, *Poeticheskie vozzreniia slavian na prirodu,* Moscow, 1865, vol. 1, p. 648, or Dal''s dictionary, e.g. s.v. '*koshka*'.

33 For an interesting discussion, see N. I. Tolstoi, 'Slavianskie narodnye tolkovaniia snov i ikh mifologicheskaia osnova', *Son – semioticheskoe okno* (XVI-e Vipperovskie chteniia Moskva, 1993), Moscow, 1994, pp. 91–3.

34 I have been unable to discover the date of the first edition.

35 Sakharov, *Skazaniia,* p. 130.

36 Noted by S. Derunov, 'Materialy dlia narodnogo snotolkovatelia. III. (Iaroslavskoi gubernii)', *Etnograficheskoe obozrenie,* vol. 36, no.1, 1898, p. 151. The saying is repeated in a recent dreambook. Numbers of other beliefs detailed methods for remembering or nullifying a dream, or instructed whether to lie on one's right or left side: see N. Ia. Nikiforovskii, 'Materialy dlia narodnogo snotolkovatelia. I. (Vitebskoi gubernii)', *Etnograficheskoe obozrenie,* vol., 36, no. 1, 1898, pp. 134–5.

37 N. A. Krinichnaia, *Nit' zhizni: Reministsentsii obrazov bozhestv sud'by v mifologii i fol'klore, obriadakh i verovaniiakh,* Petrozvadsk, 1995, pp. 11 ff.; Joanna Hubbs, *Mother Russia: The Feminine Myth in Russian Culture,* Bloomington–Indianapolis, 1988, pp. 116–23.

38 I. Snegirev, *Lubochnye kartinki russkogo naroda v moskovskom mire,* Moscow, 1861, p. 50; V. I. Dal', *Tolkovyi slovar' zhivogo velikorusskogo iazyka,* s.v. 'piatnitsa', 'ponedel'nyi', gives various sayings about these days. See also B. A. Uspenskii, 'K simvolike vremeni u slavian: "chistie" i "nechistie" dni nedeli', *Finitis duodecim lustris: Sbornik statei k 60–letiiu prof. Iu.M. Lotman,* ed. S. G. Isakov et al., Tallinn, 1982, pp. 70–5, who points out that odd-numbered days are unlucky and even lucky, though which these are depends on which day is deemed the first in the week. S. M. Tolstaia discusses evidence from Poles'e in Belorussia in 'K sootnosheniiu khristianskogo i narodnogo kalendaria u slavian: shchet i otsenka dnei nedeli', *Iazyk kul'tury i problemy perevodimosti,* ed. B. A. Uspenskii, Moscow, 1987, pp. 154–68.

39 For example, in Josephus, *De bello judaico* or the *Dreams of Shakhaishi* (or *Mamer*) (Ia. N. Shchapov, 'Arkheograficheskaia ekspeditsiia v Gor'kovskuiu oblast'', *Trudy otdela drevnerusskoi literatury*, vol. 14, 1958, pp. 613–18).

40 D. A. Nechaenko discusses the *visio* and *somnium* in early Russian literature in *Son zavetnyi ispolnennyi znakov*, Moscow, 1991, pp. 56–99.

41 Mainly in translated works, though this does not mean that their message was not relevant. See V. N. Peretts, *Slovo o polku Ihorevym*, Kiev, 1926, pp. 244–5, and Iu. A. Iavorskii, 'Karpatorusskoe pouchenie o snakh', *Karpatskii svet*, vol. 8, 1928, pp. 282–5.

42 Over and above the unresolvable question of the authenticity of the *Tale of the Campaign of Igor'*, Sviatoslav's dream remains problematical, since Russian court circles may have retained some Scandinavian influences even as late as the end of the twelfth century. Both dream-telling and the emphasis on the totality of a dream characterize Scandinavian as well as Russian traditions.

43 V. Peretts, *Slovo o polku Ihorevym*, Kiev, 1926, pp. 244–5; Sakharov, *Skazaniia*, pp. 131–2.

44 Chapter 23 also condemns soothsaying, making magic, sorcery and witchcraft.

45 For discussion of sources and their relationship with each other and with the printed tradition, see below.

46 Grunebaum, *Dream*, especially pp. 10–20.

47 Tolstoi, 'Slavianskie tolkovaniia', pp. 90–1, and E. P. Romanov, 'Opyt belorusskogo narodnogo snotolkovatelia', *Etnograficheskoe obozrenie*, no. 3, 1889, pp. 54–5.

48 Balov, 'Son', p. 210. Chulkov also says blood means relatives. Dreambook examples come from two variants of the standard text, published nearly a century apart: *The Magic Mirror*. . ., Moscow, 1794, pp. 3–54, and *The Interpretation of Dreams by the Venerable 106-Year-Old Man Martyn Zadeka*, 10th edn, Moscow, 1885. Each is indicated by the date of publication. Oral dream beliefs are taken from Balov, 'Son'; Derunov, 'Materialy I and III'; Nikiforovskii, 'Materialy I'; Romanov, 'Opyt', as well as E. Liatskii, 'Materialy dlia narodnogo snotolkovatelia. II. (Minskoi gubernii)', *Etnograficheskoe obozrenie*, vol. 36, no. 1, pp. 139–49. Where possible, I have used Russian rather than Belorussian examples, though differences in the traditions are not great.

49 The characteristics of the fox and the hare in Russian animal tales conform exactly to the European pattern, but they do not feature in Russian folk dream beliefs or at least, not in the available printed collections.

50 Tolstoi, 'Slavianskie tolkovaniia', p. 91; 1794 dreambook, p. 20.

51 D. A. Rovinskii, *Russkie narodnye kartinki*, 5 vols., St Petersburg, 1881, vol. 5, p. 95, notes that the book had acquired a spiritual character, becoming an essential item of domestic life among peasants, mer-

chants and small tradesmen. The quoted interpretation is taken from a recent republication of *Solomon* (*Novyi i polnyi sonnik . . .*, Moscow, 1994, p. 153).

52 Gromyko, *Traditsionnye normy*, p. 111.

53 Sakharov, *Skazaniia*, p. 115, says that cartomancy was little known in the 1830s whereas Tereshchenko, *Byt*, p. 260, declares that in the 1840s it was ubiquitous. Sakharov's prejudices against imported types of fortune-telling may have led him to underestimate, though differences may also be regional ones.

54 For details, see chapter 1.

55 M. Georgievskii, 'Sviatki v derevniakh Olonetskoi gub. i razlichnye gadaniia', *Olonetskie gubernskie vedomosti*, no. 46, 1898, p. 496.

56 V. N. Marakuev, *Chto chital i chitaet russkii narod*, speech delivered on 9 March in the Polytechnical Museum, Moscow, 1886, p. 34.

57 Unfortunately it is not possible to concur with his argument, which uses the criteria of consistency of method and interpretation to demonstrate folk origin. These features are not unique to folk tradition; Russian dreambooks are generally as consistent as folk interpretations, though admitttedly oral tradition lacks the conscious efforts to innovate characteristic of one segment of the book market in the second half of the nineteenth century.

58 Sakharov, *Skazaniia*, pp. 124–5.

3 READERS AND DETRACTORS

1 From Alexander Pushkin, *Eugene Onegin*, trans. Charles Johnston, London, 1977.

2 E. Nekrasova, 'Narodnye knigi dlia chteniia v 25–letnei bor'be s lubochnymi izdaniiami', *Severnyi vestnik*, no. 6, 1889, p.13.

3 In his lightly fictionalized account of his family (1846), Sergei Aksakov describes his grandfather as barely able to read or write his native language.

4 N. Chechulin, *Russkoe provintsial'noe obshchestvo vo vtoroi polovine XVIII veka,* St Petersburg, 1889, p. 35.

5 Ibid., p. 36.

6 Ibid., pp. 34–5.

7 For a sober estimate of the range of reading among Russians in the eighteenth century, see Max J. Okenfuss, *The Rise and Fall of Latin Humanism in Early-Modern Europe: Pagan Authors, Ukrainians, and the Resiliency of Muscovy*, Leiden–New York–Cologne, 1995, especially chs. 2 and 3. See also P. I. Khoteev, *Kniga v Rossii v seredine XVIII veka. Chastnye knizhnye sobraniia,* Leningrad, 1989, pp. 28–35.

8 There are instances of the ownership of manuscript miscellanies among townsfolk and peasants, but these should be regarded as exceptions. See M. Speranskii, *Rukopisnye sborniki XVIII veka*, Moscow, 1963, pp. 99–102.

9 Gregory L. Freeze, *The Russian Levites: Parish Clergy in the Eighteenth Century*, Cambridge, MA–London, 1977, pp. 78–106, 210–16; Chechulin, *Russkoe obshchestvo*, pp. 37–8.

10 R. Jones, *The Emancipation of the Russian Nobility 1762–85*, Princeton, 1973, pp. 58–60, 78; R. Givens, 'Servitors or Seigneurs: The Nobility and the Eighteenth Century Russian State' (thesis submitted for PhD, Berkeley, 1975), Ann Arbor, Michigan, 1984.

11 Chechulin, *Russkoe obshchestvo*, pp. 61–3.

12 Charles Stewart, *Demons and the Devil: Moral Imagination in Modern Greek Culture*, Princeton, 1991, pp. 117–20.

13 See Patrick Curry, *Prophecy and Power: Astrology in Early Modern England*, Cambridge, 1989. For a discussion of the male and female spheres of activity in this area, see ch. 4.

14 Edmund Heier, *Studies on Johann Caspar Lavater (1741–1801) in Russia* (Slavica helvetica 37), Berne–Berlin–Frankfurt–New York–Paris, 1991, chs. 1, 4 and 7.

15 See Heier, *Lavater*, chs. 2 and 3. Not all famous contemporary seers enjoyed the same success in Russia. Cagliostro, for example, was suspected of charlatanism by the small intellectual élite, and his welcome in Petersburg in 1779 was muted. Once he had been rejected by masonic circles, and pilloried in one of Catherine II's plays, *The Swindler*, no one remained to champion him (see Charles Neilsen Gattey, *Visionaries and Seers*, Bridport, 1988, p. 123; Heier, *Lavater*, pp. 18–19). Cagliostro's name only reappears in Russia much later in the titles of translated fortune-telling books (see chapter 7). Thus, even if Catherine II disapproved of anything connected with the occult and irrational, it remained an object of attraction to others in court circles, so long as it could be justified intellectually.

16 See chapter 4.

17 Khoteev, *Kniga*, p. 33.

18 See chapter 5.

19 A Russian version of the West European tale about (in his English guise) Bevis of Hampton.

20 Cited by Shklovskii, *Matvei Komarov, zhitel' goroda Moskvy*, Leningrad, 1929, pp. 13–15.

21 Antonii Pogorel'skii, *Dvoinik. Izbrannye proizvedeniia*, Kiev, 1990, p. 88.

22 For example, the treatment of Yuletide divination in Zhukovskii's *Svetlana* and Pushkin's *Eugene Onegin*. See W. Ryan and Faith Wigzell, 'Gullible girls and dreadful dreams (Zhukovskii's *Svetlana* and Pushkin's *Evgenii Onegin*)', *Slavonic and East European Review*, vol. 70, 1992, pp. 647–69.

23 M. O. Gershenzon, 'Sny Pushkina', *Stat'i o Pushkine*, Moscow, 1926, pp. 96–110. On the general interest in dreams, see D. A. Nechaenko, *Son zavetnykh ispolnennyi znakov*, Moscow, 1991, pp. 104–61.

24 T. Grits, V. Trenin, M. Nikitin, *Slovesnost' i kommertsiia (knizhnaia lavka*

A. F. Smirdina), ed. V. B. Shklovskii and B. M. Eikhenbaum, Moscow, 1929, p. 13; V. Shklovskii, *Chulkov i Levshin*, Leningrad, 1933, pp. 32–43.

25 The first is ultimately of Indian origin, the others are all West European.

26 Shklovskii, *Chulkov*, p. 43.

27 Grits, *Slovesnost'*, pp. 87–9.

28 Both copies are in the Russian State (formerly Lenin) Library in Moscow.

29 M. N. Speranskii, 'Odin iz starykh rukopisnykh sbornikov snotolkovanii i pesen'', *Etnograficheskoe obozrenie*, nos. 1–2, 1906, pp. 98–101, reaches these conclusions from his scrutiny of the linguistic features and contents of the song book.

30 Shklovskii, *Chulkov*, pp. 31–7, argues that favourable economic circumstances at the end of the eighteenth century stimulated the development of big towns. He suggests that perhaps forty per cent of serfs were on *obrok*, which brought them to towns to participate in trade and manufacturing, giving them greater freedom and a modicum of money. Economic decline in the early nineteenth century forced them back onto *barshchina*, in which they worked the landlord's land. This then became the norm in pre-Emancipation Russia.

31 Titles often indicate that the book is either intended to entertain and/or while away the boredom hours (SK446, 619, 2121, 2842, n-e.440, 681), or is harmless (SK446, 619, 2121, 2842, add.10, n-e 299, 400). For a consideration of the relationship between trivialization and gender, see chapter 5.

32 R. N. Kleimenova, *Knizhnaia Moskva pervoi poloviny XIX veka*, Moscow, 1991, p. 167.

33 'Otvet molodogo knigoprodavtsa staromu knigoprodavtsu', *Literaturnye listki*, no. 1, 1824, p. 421, cited by Grits, *Slovesnost'*, pp. 32–3. They quote another similar complaint.

34 N. S. Sokhanskaia (Kokhanovskaia), 'Avtobiografiia', *Russkoe obozrenie*, vol. 40, no. 8, 1896, p. 466. By this time the term 'oracle' could be applied to a general fortune-telling book, whether or not it contained an oraculum.

35 Vol. 61, section 6, p. 25, quoted by Grits, *Slovesnost'*, p. 44.

36 See Catriona Kelly, *Petrushka, the Russian Carnival Puppet Theatre*, Cambridge, 1990, pp. 26–7.

37 Reviewed thoroughly in Jeffrey Brooks, *When Russia Learnt to Read. Literacy and Popular Literature, 1861–1917*, Princeton, NJ, 1985. See also chapter 4.

38 N. F. Shcherbina, *Polnoe sobranie sochinenii*, St Petersburg, 1873, pp. 325–36. I am grateful to Paul Foote of Queen's College, Oxford, for this reference.

39 V. G. Belinskii, *Polnoe sobranie sochinenii,* vol. 3, Moscow, 1953, pp. 199–201.

40 A. V. Tereshchenko, *Byt russkogo naroda,* St Petersburg, 1848, pt 7, p. 275.

41 Vol. 1, Moscow, 1865, reprinted Moscow 1994, p. 33.

42 A. M. Skabichevskii, *Ocherki istorii russkoi tsenzury: 1700–1863,* St Petersburg, 1892, pp. 357–8.

43 *Rasskazy o temnykh predmetakh,* St Petersburg, 1861, pp. 19–20.

44 Skabichevskii, *Ocherki,* pp. 357–8, mistakenly assumed that the offending volume was a Petersburg rather than Moscow production.

45 The cartomantic guide was *An Instruction for Fortune Telling with the Fortune-Telling Cards of the Famous Clairvoyant Mlle Lenormand.* The only book to escape the ban in the following years was a dreambook published in 1858. A guide to Yuletide divination, which also appeared in that year, could slip pass the censors more easily, because of its folk origin and rôle in the seasonal festivities among all social groups.

46 V. N. Marakuev, *Chto chital i chitaet russkii narod,* speech delivered on 9 March in the Polytechnical Museum, Moscow, 1886, p. 34. He specifically mentions dreambooks and *Solomon.* Rovinskii, too, named these two as essential prerequisites of peasant, merchant and lower-class urban life (D. A. Rovinskii, *Russkie narodnye kartinki,* 5 vols., St Petersburg, 1881, vol. 5, p. 95).

47 Nekrasova, 'Narodnye knigi', p. 132, noted the enormous popularity of *Solomon* in 1861.

48 N. Bukhalov, *Snovideniia i privideniia,* Moscow, n.d., p. 4.

49 Brooks, *When Russia,* pp. 246–54.

50 N. A. Rubakin, 'K kharakteristike chitatelia i pisatelia iz naroda', *Severnyi vestnik,* no. 4, 1891, pt 1, pp. 130–1.

51 *Ezhegodnik,* p. 157.

52 Brooks, *When Russia,* pp. 31–2.

53 'Usloviia rasprostraneniia obrazovaniia v narode', I. I. Ianzhul et al., *Ekonomicheskaia otsenka narodnogo obrazovaniia,* 2nd edn, St Petersburg, 1899, p. 113.

54 Nekrasova, 'Narodnye knigi', pp. 12–13. Sytin's career is discussed in chapter 4.

55 Kh. D. Alchevskaia et al., *Chto chitat' narodu,* vol. II, 1889, pp. 681–2. The offending story was *The Reader of Coffee Grounds,* St Petersburg, 1885, price 5 kopecks.

56 N. G. Pomialovskii, *Seminary Sketches,* 1862–3, trans. Alfred P. Kuhn, Ithaca–London, 1973, p. 80.

57 *O vere v snovideniia* (Izd. russkogo Sviato-Il'inskogo skita na Afone, no. 41), St Petersburg, 1896.

58 Ibid., p. 8.

59 Brooks, *When Russia,* p. 295.

4 PRINTERS AND PUBLISHERS

1 Bernard Capp, *Astrology and the Popular Press: English Almanacs 1500–1800*, London and Boston, 1979, p. 37.
2 Gary Marker, *Publishing, Printing and the Origins of Intellectual Life in Russia, 1700–1800*, Princeton, 1985, pp. 77–83.
3 Ibid., pp. 77–9.
4 Max J. Okenfuss, *The Rise and Fall of Latin Humanism in Early-Modern Russia: Pagan Authors, Ukrainians, and the Resiliency of Moscovy*, Leiden–New York–Cologne, 1995, pp. 141–2.
5 Marker, *Publishing*, p. 82.
6 SK3378, 3379, 3380 (physiognomy and chiromancy); 2865, 2866 (dreams); 4683, 4684, 4685 (geomantic oracle); add.446 and n-e399 (wheel of fortune).
7 Marker, *Publishing*, p. 79.
8 Hippius: SK3381; Okurokov: SK619, 2734 and 7626. This last book, well produced but relatively short, was not expensive: it could be had for forty-five kopecks at Kotel'nikov's shop in Kaluga in 1795, but rather later, in 1815, when it had presumably acquired a certain additional charm, it cost eighty kopecks in Plavil'shchikov's shop (see *Reestr rossiiskim knigam prodaiushchimsia v Sanktpeterburge u Vasil'ia Plavil'shchikova*, St Petersburg, 1815).
9 SK3382 (1786) and 4552 (1787).
10 Marker, *Publishing*, p. 105.
11 Popov rented Moscow University Press from 1802–6. Beketov published about 120 books between 1801 and 1811.
12 SK1734. Bogdanovich also produced a dreambook, *A Dreambook or the Interpretation of Dreams* (add.98) the same year, but evidently nervous of the threat to his reputation, omitted his name.
13 SK add.10, and n-e400. The publisher of the latter is unknown, but, as another edition of the book, *An Innocent and Entertaining Pastime for Idle Hours . . .* (from the editions of 1770 and 1779) had been published by Claudia the year before, it is quite possible that this came from the same source.
14 SK5075, 620, 334 (the last under commission from Matvei Glazunov, the bookseller, who subsequently founded a publishing house with his brother Ivan).
15 SK2843.
16 SK6700, add.163.
17 SK3491.
18 SK5567.
19 SK333, 8840.
20 SK4686.
21 SK6701.
22 At Moscow University Press, SK619, 2734.

23 For example, *The Astrologer or New Oracle, Revealing the Fate . . .*, St Petersburg, 1822, contained sections on cartomancy, fortune-telling with beans and coffee grounds, geomancy as well as Yuletide divination and riddles. It cost five rubles in Glazunov's book catalogue of 1829.

24 R. N. Kleimenova, *Knizhnaia Moskva pervoi poloviny XIX veka,* Moscow, 1991, p. 105.

25 Reshetnikov's press operated 1789–97. In 1788 he had Annenkov print a fortune-telling book for him.

26 Kleimenova, *Knizhnaia Moskva,* pp. 106–7.

27 On censorship in the early years of the reign of Nicholas I, see Charles A. Ruud, *Fighting Words: Imperial Censorship and the Russian Press, 1804–1906,* Toronto–Buffalo–London, 1982, pp. 52–61.

28 M. Beaven Remnek in Miranda Beaven Remnek ed., *Books in Russia and the Soviet Union Past and Present,* Wiesbaden, 1991, p. 31.

29 Ibid.

30 An exception is the dreambook produced in Kaluga in 1787.

31 *The Key to the Elucidation of Dreams . . .*, a twenty-one-page book with 103 lithograph portraits published by Konrad Vingeber, and *The Art of Interpreting Dreams,* published by Zhernakov in 1846.

32 Jeffrey Brooks, *When Russia Learned to Read. Literacy and Popular Literature, 1861–1917,* Princeton, NJ, 1985, p. 92, suggests, by contrast, that as far as cheap fiction was concerned, St Petersburg publishers predominated in the pre-emancipation period.

33 Book totals are taken from Kleimenova, *Knizhnaia Moskva.*

34 Kleimenova, *Knizhnaia Moskva,* pp. 123–4.

35 I have not seen this book myself, but there is no particular reason to disbelieve the source, M. D. Ol'khin, *Sistematicheskii reestr russkim knigam s 1831 po 1846 god,* St Petersburg, 1846 (hereafter Ol'khin, *Sistematicheskii reestr*), no. 3748.

36 An exception was V. V. L'vov who ran the press of the First Cadet Corps in Moscow in the 1830s and 1840s.

37 *A Mysterious Prediction, or Solitaire with Cards,* 1833; *The Shop of All Delights* (2), 1836; *The Fortune-Teller or A New Method of Reading the Cards,* 1838.

38 Kleimenova, *Knizhnaia Moskva,* pp. 91–3, describes the serious range of books published by the Institute. Nothing more frivolous than a song-book comes into her list of book categories.

39 For more details of the Kirillov press, see Kleimenova, *Knizhnaia Moskva,* p. 111.

40 V. G. Belinskii, *Polnoe sobranie sochinenii,* vol. 3, Moscow, 1953, pp. 199–201.

41 Kleimenova, *Knizhnaia Moskva,* p. 111.

42 Ibid., p. 112.

43 *A New and Most Complete Divinatory Oracle . . .*, in thirteen books and

three parts, 1833, 1837, 1838. Listed by Ol'khin, *Sistematicheskii reestr*, no. 3761, who gives the price for the 1833 edition. *The Newest and Most Complete Astronomical Telescope* . . . had more than 500 pages and could not have been cheap.

44 Kleimenova, *Knizhnaia Moskva*, pp. 112–13.

45 Novels and tales by the prolific Kuzmichev were frequently published in the 1830s and 1840s. He was also the author of another divinatory book *The Mysterious Gypsy* . . ., which ran to several editions.

46 A. V. Blium, 'Russkaia lubochnaia kniga vtoroi poloviny xix veka', *Kniga. Issledovaniia i materialy*, vol. 42, Moscow, 1981, p. 97.

47 Ibid., p. 109.

48 Bibliographical guides are even fewer for the second half of the nineteenth century. For the eighties and early nineties, useful information is to be found in *Ezhegodnik ili Obzor knig dlia narodnogo chteniia i narodnykh kartin 1891, 1892 gg.*, Literacy Committee of the Imperial Agricultural Society in Moscow, 1893 and *Obzor knig 1893*, Moscow, 1894, and V. I. Mezhov, *Piatoe pribavlennie k sistematicheskoi rospisi knigam, prodaiushchimsia v knizhnykh lavkakh Ivana Il'icha Glazunova. Sostavleno za 1883–1887 vkl.*, St Petersburg, 1889.

49 Brooks, *When Russia*, examines this subject in depth.

50 Blium, 'Lubochnaia kniga', p. 109.

51 *Ezhegodnik 1892*, pp. 30–1.

52 A. Bakhtiarov, *Briukho Peterburga*, St Petersburg, 1888, pp. 264–5. Distribution was in the hands of people who traded fish in the spring, game in the winter and, in the autumn, cheap books, purchased at the Apraksin market. More specifically, they were peddled during the popular autumn festivities on the Field of Mars by colporteurs, who tried to entice passers-by into purchasing their books, which lay spread out on bast matting.

53 Brooks, *When Russia*, p. 93.

54 Kholmushin also put out eight editions of *The Newest Dreambook and Rules of Chiromancy* . . . between 1891 and 1907.

55 On this book and its author, see p. 27 and chapter 7.

56 Brooks, *When Russia*, pp. 94–5.

57 In 1884 Ioganson published a similarly entitled book, priced at one ruble, in a print run of 4,800.

58 Blium, 'Lubochnaia kniga', p. 98.

59 A further edition came out in 1903, but there were inevitably some in between.

60 Several other publishers put out rival Zadekas: Manukhin (tenth reprint, 1880), Abramov' (eighth, 1881), Zhivarev (third, 1865, and ninth, 1897 – a variant that included Yuletide divination), Vil'de (various editions 1900–17).

61 Brooks, *When Russia*, p. 99.

62 M. N. Kufaev, *Istoriia knigi v XIX veke*, Leningrad, 1927, p. 202.

63 Brooks, *When Russia*, p. 96.
64 Ibid., pp. 96–7.
65 Charles A. Ruud, *Russian Entrepreneur. Publisher Ivan Sytin of Moscow, 1851–1934*, Montreal–Kingston–London–Buffalo, 1990, offers a full discussion of Sytin's career, though his discussion of Sytin's early efforts as a publisher of cheap commercial books (pp. 22–5) tends to suggest that Sytin was alone in making changes to shorter, more accessible editions. He simply performed much better in the areas of production and distribution. For a somewhat different view of Sytin see E. A. Dinershtein, *I. D. Sytin*, Moscow, 1983.
66 V. N. Marakuev, *Chto chital i chitaet russkii narod* (Publichnoe chtenie 9 marta 1884 g., v Politekhnicheskom muzee), Moscow, 1886, pp. 31–2.
67 Ruud, *Russian Entrepreneur*, e.g. p. 22.
68 Ibid., pp. 99–100.
69 *Illiustrirovannyi katalog knig knigoizdatel'stva T-va I.D. Sytina*, Moscow, 1910.
70 *Ocherk izdatel'skoi deiatel'nosti T-va I.D. Sytina*, Moscow, 1910.
71 *Katalog knigoizdatel'stva T-va I.D. Sytina v Moskve 1914*, Moscow, 1914.
72 Undoubtedly, other provincial publishers (and editions) existed, but the examples here indicate how widely fortune-telling books were viewed as a commercial proposition.

5 WOMEN, MEN AND DOMESTIC FORTUNE-TELLING

1 Mary Wollstonecraft, *A Vindication of the Rights of Women*, ed. with an intro. by Miriam Brody, London–New York–Auckland–Victoria, 1992, p. 307.
2 'Life at the margins: women, culture and narodnost' 1880–1920', ed. Marianne Liljeström, Eila Mäntysaari, and Arja Rosenholm, *Gender Restructuring in Russian Studies: Conference Papers – Helsinki, August, 1992* (Slavica Tamperensia, 2), Tampere, p. 147, hereafter, Kelly, 'Life'.
3 N. S. Sokhanskaia (Kokhanovskaia), 'Avtobiografiia', *Russkoe obozrenie*, no. 40, 1896, p. 466.
4 M. S. Tsebrikova, 'Kotoryi luchshe', *Svidanie. Proza russkikh pisatel'nits 60–80–x godov XIX veka*, Moscow, 1987, pp. 258–9. Fortunately, a few less self-conscious aristocratic women mention involvement in fortune-telling in their memoirs and I have drawn on these (e.g. the poet Fet's daughter, 'Missie' Vassiltchikov etc.).
5 E. V. Minyonok, writing on the basis of research in the Kaluga region in the 1980s and 1990s, notes that female healers are the only ones to deal with children's illness; see 'The role of women in traditions of exorcism' (Paper given at the Woman and Freedom Options in the World of Traditions and Changes Materials of 1993. International Conference on Ethnology and Anthropology Institute, RAN), p. [2].

6 Witness the long list of misogynistic proverbs, including those concerned with kin-work, in Dal''s collection of Russian proverbs.

7 Judith Devlin, *The Superstitious Mind: French Peasants and the Supernatural in the Nineteenth Century*, New Haven–London, 1987, p. 218.

8 Patrick Curry, *A Confusion of Prophets: Victorian and Edwardian Astrology*, London, 1992, pp. 78–9, quotes a review in *The Times* of 1862 which designates the supporters of astrology as 'silly women and worn-out fashionables'.

9 The book, *Liubopytnoi, zagadchivoi i predskazchivoi mesiatseslov na 1796 god i na sleduiushchiia. Dlia molodykh krasavits*, St Petersburg, 1796 (SK3866), despite appearances, was not a fortune-telling book, but a collection of moral advice to young girls. Only the foreword can be attributed to Osipov himself.

10 In the 1816 edition held by the Russian State Library in Moscow.

11 The two main exceptions, Catherine the Great and Princess Dashkova, were both wealthy educated women who were essentially only interested in publishing their own works. Neither was involved in commercial publishing.

12 N. Chechulin, *Russkoe provintsial'noe obshchestvo vo vtoroi polovine XVIII veka*, St Petersburg, 1889, p. 37; Paul Dukes, *Catherine the Great and the Russian Nobility*, Cambridge, 1967, pp. 195–210, shows that the nobility's prime interest in education was to ensure that their children (here read 'boys') could enter government service. Education was less important for girls who were mainly educated at home in the social arts, which did not offer the intellectual grounding that might allow a young lady to combat a belief in fortune-telling. In the eighteenth and early nineteenth centuries, girls from other social groups were rarely literate.

13 The front cover of the journal, *Novosel'e*, 2, reproduced in T. Grits, V. Trenin and M. Nikitin, *Slovesnost' i kommertsiia. (Knizhnaia lavka A.F. Smirdina)*, Moscow, 1929.

14 Wendy Rosslyn, 'Anna Bunina's "Unchaste relationship with the Muses": patronage, the market and the woman writer in early-nineteenth-century Russia', *Slavonic and East European Review*, vol. 74, 1996, pp. 234–7.

15 Gary Marker, *Publishing, Printing and the Origins of Intellectual Life in Russia, 1700–1800*, Princeton, NJ, 1985, pp. 209–10.

16 G. Guroff and S. Frederick Starr, 'A note on urban literacy in Russia, 1890–1914', *Jahrbuch für Geschichte Osteuropas*, vol. 19, 1977, pp. 510–31.

17 D. A. Rovinskii, *Russkie narodnye kartinki*, vol. 2, St Petersburg, 1881, pp. 471–82, lists three versions dating between 1800 and 1830. More certainly existed.

18 *O vere v snovideniia* (Izd. russkogo Sviato-Il'inskogo skita na Afone, no. 41), St Petersburg, 1896.

19 See chapter 8.

20 On the role of leisure in the social routine in pre-industrial and modern societies (with special reference to Britain and the United States), see Gary Cross, *A Social History of Leisure since 1600*, State College, PA, 1990.

21 See Judith Vowles, 'The "feminization" of Russian literature: woman, language and literature in eighteenth-century Russia', *Women Writers in Russian Literature*, ed. Toby W. Clyman and Diana Greene, Westport, CT, 1994, pp. 35–60; Gitta Hammarberg, 'Flirting with words: domestic albums, 1770–1840', *Russia – Women – Culture*, ed. Helena Goscilo and Beth Holmgren, Bloomington–Indianapolis, 1996, pp. 297–320.

22 Lavater, discussed in chapter 3, had royal patrons of both genders, as did mesmerism, indicating that the appeal of the protosciences was not exclusively to men.

23 The detail in *The Captain's Daughter* is anachronistic, since the book is set in 1773, when cartomancy is very unlikely to have reached the Bashkir steppe. However, judging by his description of cartomancy as part of Tat'iana's attachment to 'old-time folkways', Pushkin evidently thought it had a longer history in Russia than it had. For Pushkin, therefore, cartomancy was a long-established women's pastime.

24 Editions also in 1833 and 1843.

25 *Zhurnaly Kamer-fur'erskie*, St Petersburg, 1883–5.

26 For example, in 1847 A. Gol[itsynskii] published a humorous but critical account of the contemporary craze for playing préférence (M. M. Minasian, *Preferans ili kartiny domashnei zhizni*, Moscow, 1993, pp. 14–174). It is highly unlikely that his strictures had any impact on the game's popularity.

27 Iu.M. Lotman, *Besedy o russkoi kul'ture. Byt i traditsii russkogo dvorianstva (XVIII-nachalo XIX veka)*, St Petersburg, 1994, pp. 141–5.

28 'Nevinnyi' with one 'n', 'oracle' phonetically spelt to begin with 'a' etc.

29 I. P. Sakharov, *Skazaniia russkogo naroda: sobrannye I. P. Sakharovym* (from the edition of 1885), Moscow, 1990, pp. 115–16.

30 *Sochineniia Imperatritsy Ekateriny II. Proizvedeniia literaturnye*, ed. A. I. Vvedenskii, St Petersburg, 1893, p. 420.

31 A. F. Tiutcheva, *Pri dvore dvukh imperatorov. Vspominaniia, dnevnik 1853–55*, trans. E. V. Ger'e, ed. S. V. Bakrushin, Moscow, 1929 (reprinted Cambridge 1975), vol. 1, pp. 125, 128, 132; vol. 2, pp. 53, 74–5.

32 As Leea Virtanen notes, 'Dream-telling today', *Studies in Oral Narrative*, ed. A–L. Siikala (Studia Fennica 33), Helsinki, 1990, p. 138, the practice is widespread also in Scandinavia.

33 Sakharov, *Skazaniia*, p. 130; *O vere*, p. 1.

34 T. Luckman, *The Invisible Religion*, London, 1967.

35 Except for professional fortune-tellers who are discussed in chapter 6.

6 FORTUNE-TELLERS AND THEIR CLIENTÈLE

1 This chapter appeared in slightly adapted form as 'Zarisovki rossiiskogo byta XVIII-XIX vekov: gadalki i ikh klienty', *Otechestvennaia istoriia*, no.1, 1997, pp. 158–67.
2 Scapulomancy was well known in the ancient world, medieval Europe and Byzantium.
3 For example, in 1740 a certain Iakov Iarov was accused of witchcraft and telling fortunes with dice and a Psalter.
4 M. D. Chulkov, *Abevega russkikh sueverii*, Moscow, 1786 (hereafter Chulkov, *Abevega*), pp. 70, 72–6.
5 I. P. Sakharov, *Skazaniia russkogo naroda: sobrannye I.P. Sakharovym*, (from the edition of 1885), Moscow, 1990, pp. 130–1 (hereafter Sakharov, *Skazaniia*).
6 A. V. Tereshchenko, *Byt russkogo naroda*, St Petersburg, 1848, pt 7, p. 275. Tereshchenko obviously used Sakharov as a source, and he may simply have misread him at this point. Since, however, he adds to Sakharov's discussion of oneiromancers, I am inclined to accept his statement. The confusion may result from differing practice in the areas where they collected their material.
7 Tereshchenko, *Byt*, pp. 275–6; Sakharov, *Skazaniia*, p. 130.
8 *Polnoe sobranie russkikh zakonov*, XXI, no. 15379.
9 Chulkov, *Abevega*, pp. 72, 307.
10 Under the heading 'vorog', sub-heading 'vorozhit''.
11 *Svidanie. Proza russkikh pisatel'nits 60–80–kh godov XIX veka*, Moscow, 1987, pp. 258–9. One may also note that in Il'in's play, *The Physiognomer and Chiromancer* (Moscow, 1816), the Princess, who is hoping to dissuade her friend's husband from advertising his palm-reading and other skills, disguises herself as a gypsy and complains that he is ruining their trade.
12 D. Fearon de l'Hoste Ranking, 'The gypsies of Central Russia', *Journal of the Gypsy Lore Society*, vol. 6, pp. 94–6.
13 David M. Crowe, *A History of the Gypsies of Eastern Europe and Russia*, London–New York, 1995, pp. 153–4, 170.
14 *Liubopytnoi, zagadchivoi, ugadchivoi i predskazchivoi mesiatseslov na 1796 god i na sleduiushchiia. Dlia molodykh krasavits*, St Petersburg, 1796 (SK3866).
15 E.g. *The Gypsy Woman, Interpreting Dreams . . .*, Moscow, 1789 (SK8128), though this was probably translated; F. Kuzmichev, *The Mysterious Gypsy Woman, Foretelling the Fate of Young Men and Women*, Moscow, 4 edns, 1836–9. A set of special fortune-telling cards published in San Francisco in 1992 (Svetlana Aleksandrovna Touchkoff,

Russian Gypsy Fortune-Telling Cards) claims to be a system learnt by the author's mother in Russia from a gypsy. These are relatively isolated examples.

16 *Zhivopisets*, pt 1, 1772, p. 348, in *Satiricheskie zhurnaly N. I. Novikova*, ed. P. N. Berkov, Moscow–Leningrad, 1950.

17 Ibid., p. 348. He remarks that so great and so regular was the expenditure on the fortune-teller that it ought to be written into the household budget.

18 Otshel'nik, *Peterburgskie gadalki, znakhari, iurodivye i pr. (Ocherki peterburgskoi zhizni)*, St Petersburg, 1894.

19 Ibid., p. 15.

20 Ibid., pp. 36–40.

21 Foreigners had set themselves up as fortune-tellers in Petersburg by the 1820s, since the clairvoyant visited by Pushkin is known to have been German. Despite the reputation of Finns (Chukhontsy) as possessing prophetic powers, I have no evidence that they earned their living in Russian towns in this way.

22 Otshel'nik, *Peterburgskie gadalki*, pp. 19–27, 100–8.

23 Tereshchenko, *Byt*, p. 260.

24 Novikov, *Zhivopisets*, p. 348.

25 Ibid., pp. 349–50. It was not unique to Russia, as Keith Thomas indicates (*Religion and the Decline of Magic*, London, 1971, pp. 252–64). The custom survived into the nineteenth century; witness Washington Irving's remark made on a stay in London that 'an old woman that lives in Bull-and-Mouth Street makes a tolerable subsistence by detecting stolen goods' (quoted by Patrick Curry, *A Confusion of Prophets: Victorian and Edwardian Astrology*, London, 1992, p. 9).

26 African methods of divination operate on this principle (E. E. Evans-Pritchard, *Witchcraft, Oracles and Magic among the Azande*, Oxford, 1937, p. 173). Magical thief-detection is discussed in Thomas, *Religion*, pp. 257–64.

27 The description is from Sakharov (*Skazaniia*, p. 119), but the technique was well-known elsewhere (see Thomas, *Religion*, pp. 253–4).

28 R. E. F. Smith and David Christian, *Bread and Salt: A Social and Economic History of Food and Drink in Russia*, Cambridge, 1984, p. 179. Reading the coffee cups is attested in Britain from 1754 (see Thomas, *Religion*, p. 285).

29 M. Zabylin (*Russkii narod. Ego obychai, obriady, predaniia, sueveriia i poeziia*, Moscow, 1880, reprinted Moscow, 1992, pp. 22–3), mentions the use of this technique for thief detection only as an afterthought, and says that any book could be used. By the late nineteenth century, therefore, it had lost its function of frightening the guilty and was used primarily for divining marital prospects. He also lists another type in which the psalter is opened at random, sometimes with the number of the prophetic line selected in advance.

30 Sakharov, *Skazaniia*, pp. 117–18; Tereshchenko, *Byt*, pp. 258–9.
31 Zabylin, *Russkii narod*, pp. 21–2.
32 Attested by V. F. Shcherbakov and M. P. Pogodin. See V. V. Veresaev, *Pushkin v zhizni*, pts 1–4, Moscow, 1926–7, pp. 55–6.
33 *Polnoe sobranie zakonov*, xx, no. 14392; xxi, no. 1539.
34 Sakharov, *Skazaniia*, pp. 115–17; Tereshchenko, *Byt*, p. 260.
35 He also casually remarks that there are those who tell fortunes from the shapes made by melted wax, a method adopted from Yuletide practice (p. 6).
36 *Zhivopisets*, pt 1; Chulkov, *Abevega*, p. 76.
37 Ewa M. Thompson, *Understanding Russia. The Holy Fool in Russian Culture*, Lanham–New York–London, 1987, pp. 31–46.
38 I. M. Lewis, *Ecstatic Religion*, 2nd edn, London–New York, 1989, chs. 1–4.
39 Thompson, *Understanding Russia*, p. 39.
40 This is not the case everywhere. For example, in contemporary Portugal, urban professional white witches are usually men. The refusal of priests nowadays to undertake exorcism and healing by prayer may explain this phenomenon. Male urban white witches have taken on the prestige and influence of the priest at the expense of rural white witches who are mainly women (João de Pina-Cabral, *Sons of Adam, Daughters of Eve*, Oxford, 1986, pp. 191–5).
41 A. F. Tiutcheva, *Pri dvore dvukh imperatorov. Vospominaniia, dnevnik 1853–55*, trans. E. V. Ger'e, ed. S. V. Bakrushin, Moscow, 1929 (reprinted Cambridge 1975), vol. 2, p. 53.
42 Sakharov, *Skazaniia*, p. 117.
43 Novikov, *Zhivopisets*, p. 348.
44 M. I. Lekomtseva and B. A. Uspenskii, 'Opisanie odnoi semioticheskoi sistemy s prostym sintaksisom' (p.100), and B. F. Egorov, 'Prosteishie semioticheskie sistemy i tipologiia siuzhetov' (p.106), both in *Trudy po znakovym sistemam*, vol. 2, Tartu, 1965.
45 Chulkov, *Abevega*, p. 76.
46 Novikov, *Zhivopisets*, p. 350.
47 Sakharov, *Skazaniia*, p. 115. Tereshchenko largely repeats Sakharov.
48 Novikov, *Zhivopisets*, p. 351.
49 V. I. Maslov, *Literaturnaia deiatel'nost' K.F. Ryleeva*, Kiev, 1912, p. 65; N. Ya. Edelman, *Lunin*, Moscow, 1970, p. 40. They visited Mlle le Normand at different times to have their palms read. She made each the same prediction, of an unnatural death worse than death on the battlefield or in a duel.
50 Otshel'nik, *Petersburgskie gadalki*, p. 51.
51 Ibid., pp. 19–27.
52 Ibid., pp. 8–15.
53 Novikov, *Zhivopisets*, p. 350.
54 'Vorozheia', *Sobranie sochinenii*, vol. 4, St Petersburg–Moscow, 1897, pp. 218–19.

55 Tereshchenko, *Byt*, p. 261.
56 Ibid., pp. 261–2; Otshel'nik, *Petersburgskie gadalki*, p. 51.
57 Michael MacDonald, *Mystical Bedlam: Madness, Anxiety and Healing in Seventeenth-Century England*, Cambridge, 1981, p. 39.
58 Ibid., p. 35.
59 Professor John Widdowson of Sheffield University tells me that when he conducted a small survey in the late eighties into fortune-telling on council estates in the city, he discovered large numbers of semi-professional fortune-tellers.

7 SAGES AND PROPHETS

1 For example, *De somnio et vigilia*, in which Albertus Magnus discusses dreams and dream interpretation, and Aristotle, *De insomniis et de divinatione per somnium.*
2 The physiognomy text, a translation from German (*Albertus Magnus' Science of Understanding People . . .*, Moscow, 1811) also listed other physiognomers, but in a group at the end of the title; the dreambook is *A Pocket Dreambook, Revealing the Secrets of Albertus Magnus*, Moscow.
3 *Entertaining Magic or The Revelation of Miraculous and Amazing Mysterious Experiments Known as Focus Pocus.*
4 A. A. Vadimov and M. A. Trivas, *Ot magov drevnosti do illuzionistov nashikh dnei*, Moscow, 1966, pp. 77–83.
5 For example, *Caliostro or Fortune-Telling with Cards. A New and Hitherto Totally Unknown Method of Divination, Fully Satisfying All Desires of Those Participating, Verified by the Famous Lenormand and Swedenborg*, Moscow, 1843.
6 'Gadal'nye karty', *Rossia v pis'menakh*, vol. 1, Moscow-Berlin, 1922, pp. 111–21.
7 For example, *The Ancient and Modern Oracle of Famed Egyptian Sages and Astronomers . . .*, Moscow, 1848, or the dream section in a Sytin compendium, *The New and Complete Oracle and Magician . . .* (editions 1890s–1917).
8 For example, *The Magic Mirror, Revealing the Secrets of Albertus Magnus and Other Renowned Egyptian Sages and Astronomers . . .*, 7 editions 1794–1818. Some gave long lists of foreign sages, Indian, Chinese, Persian, Arabic, Jewish, Greek, African, but these did not catch on. In the case of Jewish cabbalists, the reason is obvious; the average lower-class Russian reader was not likely to regard anything Jewish as a plus.
9 So called because this was one of the American dreambooks which claimed to help work out lucky numbers for use in the gambling system known as policy by assigning numerical value to dreams. This type of dreambook is always attributed to, or authored by men in recognition of the male involvement in gambling.
10 Indeed, in the sixteenth and seventeenth centuries, it played a sig-

nificant rôle in validating change by suggesting that political and social turbulence had been predicted by the ancients. For a discussion of the types of prophecy and their rôle in England, see Keith Thomas, *Religion and the Decline of Magic*, London, 1971, ch. 13; on political prophecy and almanacs, see Bernard Capp, *Astrology and the Popular Press: English Almanacs 1500–1800*, London–Boston, 1979, pp. 35–36 and ch. 3.

11 *Leseges, Brosch* no. 17, where it is bound together with other pamphlets. It was Vladimir Nabokov (*Eugene Onegin*, New York, 1964, vol. 2, p. 515) who first researched the pamphlet at the Swiss end, declaring, without offering any supporting evidence, 'that the pamphlet was widely distributed; versions of it were included in various divinatory compilations, German and Russian'. Quite the contrary, it seems not to have been widely known in German-speaking areas, as M. Iskrin ('Kto takoi Martyn Zadeka?', *Almanakh bibliofila*, Moscow, 1975, p. 174) indicates when recounting his vain efforts to trace the work in Leipzig and Berlin (where it had been lost).

12 See Iskrin, 'Kto', pp. 171–4, who makes a cogent case for Kurganov as author.

13 As Iskrin points out (p. 171), two other prophecies were popular though they did not rival Zadek: Mustaph-Eddin's about the fall of Turkey ran to two editions in the eighteenth century with another in 1828, and the predictions of Tommaso Guiseppe Moult, which were medieval in origin, appeared in 1778 and 1806 as well as in divinatory compilations such as the *The Ancient Astrologer*. . ., Moscow 1814.

14 For example, in 1839 N. Stepanov reprinted his 1829 edition of *The Newest and Most Complete Astronomical Telescope* . . ., a pseudo-scientific work, in which the prophecy was in part 7, while in 1862, N. Ernst reprinted *The Magician or A New and Complete Omnipurpose Oracle* . . ., taken probably from the 1822 edition. Finally, Sytin's *New and Complete Oracle and Magician* . . ., 1891–1917, based on a compendium of the period 1800–30, also contained the Zadek text, though one wonders what early twentieth-century readers made of it.

15 *Obstoiatel'noe i vernoe opisanie dobrykh i zlykh del rossiiskogo moshennika, vora, razboinika i byvshego moskovskogo syshchika Van'ki Kaina*, St Petersburg, 1779, reprinted in *Povesti razumnye i zamyslovatye*, ed. S. Iu. Baranov, Moscow, 1988, p. 331.

16 Iu. M. Lotman, *Roman A. S. Pushkina 'Evgenii Onegin'. Kommentarii*, Leningrad, 1980, p. 277.

17 For further discussion of Tat'iana's Martyn Zadeka, see W. F. Ryan and Faith Wigzell, 'Gullible girls and dreadful dreams: Zhukovskii, Pushkin and popular divination', *Slavonic and East European Review*, vol. 70, 1992, pp. 647–69. The term Chaldean is not taken from fortune-telling books, but relies on a whole set of perceptions elaborated by Irina Reyfman, *Vasilii Trediakovskii: The Fool of the 'New'*

Russian Literature, Stanford, 1990, pp. 105, 123, 142–3, 148–9. Relevant points here are the association of Chaldeans with magic and astrology, as well as, perhaps, their connection with Yuletide festivities, given that this chapter of *Eugene Onegin* is set at that time of year.

18 Iskrin, 'Kto', pp. 169–70.

19 Ibid., pp. 174–5. Iskrin also notes that, in the 1770s, Voltaire was living at Ferney, far from Paris society, going on to imply a link between Zadek and the person of Voltaire. This suggestion should be rejected; Ferney and Solothurn are some distance apart, and if the link with Voltaire, as opposed to his work, was intended, it is likely that there would have been less insistence in the pamphlet on the precise geographical details of Zadeck's place of residence and way of life (his diet of herbs for example).

20 Nabokov, *Onegin*, vol. 2, p. 514, suggests a further, if remote, possibility: Zedechias, an eighth-century cabbalist.

21 In 1817 Vel'tman was posted to Bessarabia where he remained for some years.

22 Iskrin, 'Kto', p. 175.

23 Fedorov, too, was of a much humbler background than Pushkin.

24 Iskrin, 'Kto', p. 170, wrongly states that the dream guide forms the major part of the book. He further suggests that it comes from an earlier compendium in which Komissarov was involved, *The Magic Mirror*. . ., Moscow, 1794, where the dream section does occupy pride of place. However, the texts, though similar, are not identical.

25 See R. N. Kleimenova, *Knizhnaia Moskva pervoi poloviny XIX veka*, Moscow, 1991, p. 106.

26 *Interpretation of Dreams According to Astronomy* . . ., 1768, 1772, 1788.

27 The date on the cover is 1849.

28 For more details, see chapter 4.

29 I have been unable to establish the identity of this writer. The others are drawn from I. F. Masanov, *Dictionary of the Pseudonyms of Russian Writers, Scholars and Public Figures*, vols. 1–4, Moscow, 1956–66.

30 I. M. Lewis, *Ecstatic Religion*, 2nd edn., London–New York, 1989, p. 65; J. Dubisch, 'Gender, kinship and religion: "reconstructing" the anthropology of Greece', Peter Loizos and Evthymios Papataxiarchis, *Gender and Kinship in Modern Greece*, Princeton, 1991, p. 42.

31 Alfred Marquiset, *La célèbre Mlle Lenormand*, Paris, 1911, p. 31; Charles Neilson Gattey, *Visionaries and Seers*, Bridport, 1988, pp. 157–83.

32 V. I. Maslov, *Literaturnaia deiatel'nost' K. F. Ryleeva*, Kiev, 1912, p. 65; N. Ya. Edelman, *Lunin*, Moscow, 1970, p. 40.

33 K. Frank Jensen, *The Prophetic Cards – A Catalog of Fortune-Telling Cards*, Roskilde, 1985, section 2, introduction.

34 The use of names of people (here Cagliostro) as the name of the book rather than of its supposed author is not uncommon. Its confused use here in a book ascribed to two other sages suggests that the

name of Cagliostro had also lost its specific connotations in Russia by this time.

35 For example, *An Instruction for Fortune-Telling with the Fortune-Telling Cards of the Famous Clairvoyant Mlle Lenormand* . . ., Moscow, 1850.

36 *The Interpreter of Dreams by the Well-Known French Dream Interpreter, Mlle Lenormand* . . ., Moscow, 1862. She is also the 'author' of several American dreambooks.

37 Harry B. Weiss, *Oneirocritica Americana: The Story of American Dream Books*, New York, 1944, pp. 26–37.

38 For example, *The Key to the Elucidation of Dreams* . . ., St Petersburg, 1838, an enlarged edition of the Paris edition of Michel de la Porte.

39 *The Ancient and Modern Astrologer* . . ., Moscow.

40 For a discussion of the rôle of gypsies and fortune-telling in Russia, see chapter 6.

41 *3000 Dreams. A Detailed Elucidation of All Manner of Dreams* . . ., St Petersburg, 1870.

42 *Moskovskie legendy, zapisannye Evgeniem Baranovym*, ed. Vera Bokova, Moscow, 1993.

43 The censors disliked derogatory references to well-known people and their families. Thus the ballad *Prince Volkonskii and Vania the Steward* was seen in the nineteenth century as disparaging to the Volkonskii family and banned.

44 For example, the dreambook regularly published in the 1890s: *One Million 200,000 Dreams.*

8 DISAPPEARANCE AND REVIVAL

1 The latest date of publication by houses based in Moscow is, as far as I know, 1918, when, for example, Sytin and Co. produced another edition of a long 258-page work, *The New and Most Complete Dreambook and Interpreter of Prophetic Dreams* and the Bel'tsov Press a 95–page *Complete and Best Dreambook.*

2 Of the terms employed, in fact only *charodei* refers to the oral magic tradition. *Mag* is an imported word (related to the word *magiia*, magic), and *kudesnik* belongs to Old Russian literary tradition.

3 L. G. Graham, *Science in Russia and the Soviet Union*, Cambridge, 1993, pp. 123–34.

4 L. Trotsky, *Literature and Revolution*, 1924, Ann Arbor, Michigan, 1968, pp. 252–3, quoted by Katerina Clark, 'The changing image of science and technology in Soviet literature', *Science and the Soviet Social Order*, ed. Loren R. Graham, Cambridge, MA–London, 1990, p. 260.

5 Clark, 'Changing image', p. 262.

6 See Harvey Balzer, 'Engineers: the rise and decline of a Soviet myth', Graham, *Science*, pp. 141–67, and Paul R. Josephson, 'Rockets, reactors and Soviet culture', Graham, *Science*, pp. 168–91.

7 For a general discussion, see Judith Devlin, *The Superstitious Mind: French Peasants and the Supernatural in the Nineteenth Century*, New Haven–London, 1987, pp. 215–17.

8 See Sheila Ostrander and Lynn Schroder, *Psi: Psychic Discoveries behind the Iron Curtain*, London, 1973; Henry Gris and William Dick, *The New Soviet Psychic Discoveries*, London, 1988.

9 I am extremely grateful to Vladimir Druk for permission to use a selection of this material.

10 For example, in 1995 A. V. Pigin collected some interesting traditional dream symbols from two women aged seventy and eighty-two from villages in the Kargopol' region of Arkhangel district.

11 Based on a discussion in 1991 with an informant.

12 See A. I. Lekomtseva and B. A. Uspenskii, 'Opisanie odnoi semioticheskoi sistemy s prostym sintaksisom', *Trudy po znakovym sistemam*, vol. 2, Tartu, 1965, pp. 94–105.

13 K. Chukovskii, *Dnevnik 1901–1929*, Moscow, 1991, vol. 1, pp. 201–2. Chukovskii himself used Thomas Moore (p. 379).

14 A. I. Min'ko, *Znakharstvo. Istoki, sushchnost', prichiny bytovaniia*, Minsk, was still arguing against folk healing in 1971, while O. F. Fishman ('Sotsiokul'turnyi status i ritual'noe povedenie "znaiushchikh" v Tikhvinskom krae', *Zhivaia starina*, no. 4, 1994, pp. 24–5), makes it clear that in the Tikhvin area the *znakharka* (he only refers to women) is still a common figure, a fact corroborated by the women I spoke to in Karelia. The role of folk healers, midwives, and sorcerers in the present-day Russian village is discussed by Iu. I. Smirnov and V. N. Il'inskaia, *Vstanu ia blagoslovias' . . . Lechebnye i liubovnye zagovory, zapisannye v chasti Arkhangel'skoi oblasti*, Moscow, 1992, pp. 6–7. Finally, for a more sensationalist account of a supposed witch's curse and the rôle of the folk healer in a south Russian village, see *The Times* of 4 April 1997.

15 Interviewed in the Russian version of the magazine *Elle*, April/May 1996, pp. 56–60. Despite her Western psychic vocabulary, Tamara is described in the article in Russian as *vedun'ia* or *koldun'ia*, both words with a long history in Russia.

16 S. Parkhomenko, 'Merlin's Tower', *Moscow News*, no. 29, 1995, pp. 8–9.

17 Reported in *The Independent*, 29 June 1996.

18 *A Million Dreams (3)*, Moscow, 1990; *Sleep and Dreams. A Scientifically Based Interpretation of Dreams . . .*, Moscow.

19 E.g. a rival translation of the Hindman book, published by Fair, Moscow, 1995, or *A Dreambook. The Interpretation of Dreams from Artemidorus to Miller*, Moscow, 1996.

20 The exception here is *A New and Complete Dreambook*, Moscow, 1994, a compilation from three pre-Revolutionary books. Not only is it a

more than averagely scrupulous work, but it reproduces a number of texts that Sytin and some other publishers had revived at the end of the nineteenth century, such as the 'Fortune-Teller, Divining Names' (from a late eighteenth- or early nineteenth-century original), *Solomon*, and the Arabic cabbalistic numerological text found mainly in the eighteenth century. The volume is also exceptional in that profits from it go not into private hands, but to support football for the disabled.

21 For example, *A Million Dreams. A New and Complete Dreambook*, Moscow, 1990, was a straight reprint of a Sytin edition of 1901, while I. S. Semenova, the compiler of *Horoscope, Divination, Dreambook*, Moscow, 1990, used material from *How to Recognise a Person's Character* of 1897. *A New and Complete Dreambook*, Moscow, 1994, used a couple of Sytin compendia as well as Vil'de's *A Million 200,000 Dreams* of 1897; Miss Hussey's dreambook was not only republished in 1990 in a print run of 500,000, but was also included in a compendium *Stars and Fates*, Ekaterinburg, 1994.

22 For example, *A New and Complete Dreambook*, Moscow, 1994.

23 From *The Interpretation of Dreams (A Dreambook)*, New York, 1985.

24 *A Dreambook or The Interpretation of Dreams*, translated from the German of Gustavus Hindman Miller, Moscow, 1995; *The New Dreambook*, Minsk, 1995, from the revised edition of 1994 of the 'well-known Western dreambook by Tony Crisp'; *A Dreambook. Interpretations of Dreams from Artemidorus to Miller*, Moscow, 1996. For a discussion of Zadkiel, see Patrick Curry, *A Confusion of Prophets: Victorian and Edwardian Astrology*, London, 1992, pp. 61–108.

25 For example, Evgenii Tsvetkov, *In the Realm of Sleep and Death*, Moscow, 1991, or *A Dreambook*, compiled by A. T. Temiraeva, Moscow, 1993, which, though not alphabetical, does include well-known interpretations such as that dreaming of bears means marriage (cf. Tat'iana's dream).

26 For example in the 1990 Kniga Printshop reprint of *A Million Dreams* (3) of 1901, in *A New and Complete Dreambook*, Moscow, 1994, or *Omens, Spells and Fortune-Telling*, Kharkov, Mitets', 1995.

27 In *Omens, Spells and Fortune-Telling*, pp. 225–9.

28 For example, V. Kirnosov, *Talking Stars. Practical Astrology*, Moscow, 1992; *Horoscope, Divination, Dreambook*, Moscow, 1990.

29 Parkhomenko, 'Merlin', and a commentary by Vladimir Fedorovskii on Rogozin and his activities in *Le Nouvel Observateur*, 11–17 April 1996.

30 See, for example, *Stars and Fates*, Ekaterinburg, 1994.

31 *Torot. The Secret Gypsy Art of Fortune-telling with 52 Cards*, c. 1990.

32 Female author/compilers include S. S. Skol'zhnikova (*The Mysterious World of Fortune-Telling*, Moscow, 1989); A. T. Temiraeva (*Dreambook*,

Moscow, 1993), and A. A. Shtirbu and R. G. Polenova, who put out a reprint of a dreambook text taken from Sytin editions of 1901 and 1911 (*Dreambook*, Tiraspol′, 1991). Most contemporary fortune-telling books are either anonymous or compiled by men.

CONCLUSION

1 Quoted by the film-maker Nikita Mikhalkov in an interview published in *Argumenty i fakty*, no. 35, 1993, p. 9.
2 See *The Independent on Sunday*, 8 September 1996.
3 Gérard Miller, quoted in *The Times*, 3 May 1996.
4 *The Superstitious Mind: French Peasants and the Supernatural in the Nineteenth Century*, New Haven–London, 1987, especially ch. 2.
5 See Keith Thomas, *Religion and the Decline of Magic*, London, 1971, especially ch. 22.
6 Jeffrey Brooks, *When Russia Learnt to Read: Literacy and Popular Literature, 1861–1917*, Princeton, 1985, p. 353.
7 Burke, *Popular Culture in Early Modern Europe*, London, 1978.
8 Stites, *Russian Popular Culture: Entertainment and Society since 1900*, Cambridge, 1992, p. 1.

Select bibliography

NB The following abbreviations are used for place names: Moscow – Mw; Leningrad – Ld; St Petersburg – St P. All other place names are given in full.

A. FORTUNE-TELLING BOOKS

The bibliography contains details of all fortune-telling books mentioned in the text. These are only a portion of the total number of titles published. I have included mention of all editions of a given volume of which I am aware, using 'e.g.' to indicate that others exist, but the precise years in which they appeared are not known. Books are listed alphabetically rather than by the name of the compiler, since attributions are so frequently spurious or inconsistently used from one edition to another. The name of any supposed compiler then follows. Titles are listed according to my English renderings, followed by Russian titles, with place of publication and catalogue number for eighteenth-century books according to the *Svodnyi katalog russkoi knigi grazhdanskoi pechati XVIII veka, 1725–1800*, 6 vols., Moscow, 1962–75 (SK plus number, with 'add.' for those in the supplementary catalogue and 'n-e' for those not extant). A question mark replacing any of the publication details indicates incomplete information as opposed to the absence of these details, which are shown by the abbreviations 'n.d.' (no date), 'n.p.' (no place) or 'n. publ.' (no publisher given). When the same information is given in square brackets, it indicates that it has been drawn from other sources (e.g. the *Svodnyi katalog* or library catalogues).

1,000,000 dreams

(1) *A Million Dreams, Selected from the Works* . . . [*Million snov, vybrannykh iz sochinenii* . . .], Mw: Manukhin, e.g. 1875

(2) *A Million Dreams. A Manual, Compiled from the Works* . . . [*Million snov. Rukovodstvo, sostavlennoe* . . .], sometimes attr. Mlle Lenormand, Mw: Gubanov e.g. 1892, 1896; Kiev: Gubanov, e.g. 1893, 1896, 1909

(3) *A Million Dreams. A New and Complete Dreambook* . . . [*Million snov.*

Novyi i polnyi sonnik . . .], Mw: Sytin, e.g. 1891, 1893, 1898, 1901, 1902, 1906, 1911, 1918; Mw: Sovaminko, 1990 (reprinted from the Sytin edn. of 1902); Mw: Kniga Printshop, 1990; as *Dreambook (The Interpretation of Dreams)* [*Sonnik (Tolkovanie snov)*], comp. A. A. Stirbu and R. G. Polenova, Tiraspol': Tiraspol'skaia fabrika ofsetnoi pechati 1991 (from the Sytin edns of 1901, 1911)

Over 1,000,000 dreams

(1) *Over One Million Dreams . . .* [*Million snov – s lishkom . . .*], Mw: [?], 1879

1,200,000 dreams

(1) *A Million 200,000 Dreams. The Interpretation of Dreams . . .* [*Million 200,000 snov. Tolkovanie snov . . .*], Mw: Presnov, e.g. 1891

(2) *A Million 200,000 Dreams. A Manual, Compiled from the Works . . .* [*Million 200,000 snov. Rukovodstvo, sostavlennoe . . .*], Mw: Gubanov, e.g. 1892, 1899; Mw: Vil'de, e.g. 1897, 1899

1,500,000 dreams

(1) *One Million 500,000 Dreams. The Interpretation of Dreams . . .* [*Odin Million 500,000 snov. Tolkovanie snov . . .*], Mw: Ermakov, e.g. 1896 (reprinted Mw: Vneshtorgizdat, 1989)

3000 Dreams, A Detailed Elucidation of All Manner of Dreams, in All their Manifestations. Presented in Alphabetical Order [*3000 snov. Podrobnoe ob"iasnenie vsiakogo roda snovidenii, vo vsekh ikh proiavleniiakh. Izlozhennoe v alfavitnom poriadke*], St P.: Strauf, 1870

Albertus Magnus' Science of Understanding People, Selected from Ancient Manuscripts . . . [*Velikago Alberta nauka razpoznavat' liudei, izbranaia iz drevnikh rukopisei . . .*], Mw: [?], 1811

The Ancient and Modern Astrologer or A Complete Divinatory Oracle . . . [*Astrolog drevnii i novyi ili Orakul gadatel'nyi polnyi . . .*], Mw: [?], 1814; Mw: Semen, 1824–5

The Ancient and Modern Astronomical Telescope or The Complete Collection of Information about Astronomy, Chronology, Astrology and Chiromancy. With a Predictive Calendar for 336 Years [*Drevnii i novyi astronomicheskii teleskop ili Polnoe sobranie svedenii, otnosiashchikhsia do Astronomii, Khronologii, Astrologii i Khiromantii. S predskazatel'nym kalendarem na 336 let*], St P.: Glazunov, 1821

The Ancient and Modern Oracle of Famed Egyptian Sages and Astronomers . . . [*Drevnii i novyi orakul slavnykh egipetskikh mudretsov i astronomov . . .*], Mw: Smirnov, 1848

The Ancient and Modern Permanent Divinatory Oracle, Discovered After the Death of a Certain One-Hundred-and-Six-Year-Old Man Martin Zadek . . . [*Drevnii i novyi vsegdashnii gadatel'nyi orakul, naidennyi posle smerti odnogo stoshestiletniago startsa Martina Zadeka . . .*], comp. S. Komisarov, Mw: Rüdiger and Claudia at the University Press, 1800 (SK 3077); Mw: Reshetnikov, 1814, 1821

The Ancient Astrologer or Oracle of Those Most Skilled in Divination: Martin

Zadek, Guiseppe Moult, Tycho Brahe and the Physiognomer Lavater and Others . . . [Drevnii astrolog ili Orakul iskusneishikh vo gadanii Martyna Zadeka, Iosifa Mutta, Tikhobraga i Fiziognomista Lavatera i drugikh], Mw: Reshetnikov, 1814, 1820

The Art of Interpreting Dreams: A Detailed Explanation of All Dreams and Visions . . . [Iskustvo (sic!) tolkovat' sny, podrobnoe iz"iasnenie vsekh snov, videnii . . .], St P.: Zhernakov, 1846

The Astrologer or New Oracle, Revealing the Fate of Human Happiness and Unhappiness in the Mirror of Albertus Magnus . . . [Astrolog ili Novoi orakul, otkryvaiushchii sud'bu shchastiia i neshchastiia chelovecheskago, v zertsale velikago Alberta . . .], comp. L. Prokhorov, Mw: [?] 1794 (SK n-e 680; Mw: Rüdiger and Claudia on commission from Glazunov, 1798; Mw: [?] 1805, 1810; St P.: Glazunov, 1817, 1822; Mw: Reshetnikov, 1819; Mw: Semen, 1826

Astrological Horoscopes and Their Significance in the Life of Man [Astrologicheskie goroskopy i ikh znachenie v zhizni cheloveka], Mw: Bykov, 1912

The Astronomical Telescope, or A General Astronomical, Physical and Economic Calendar for 200 Years [Astronomicheskii teleskop, ili obshchii Astronomicheskii, Fizicheskii, Ekonomicheskii Kalendar' na 200 let], Mw: Kriazhev and Mei, 1804; (with varying sub-titles) Mw: Reshetnikov, 1814, 1815, 1818; Mw: Abramov, 1874

The Book of Fate or The Fortune-Teller of the Drawing Room [Kniga sud'by, ili Vorozhei gostinnykh], St P.: Frants, 1843

The Book of Fate. The Pages of Sambeta, the Persian Sibyl [Kniga sud'by. Listy Sambety sivilly persidskoi], Mw: Lazarev Institute of Oriental Languages, 1838

Bruce's Pocket Oracle, or A New Fortune-Telling Book (in Verse) [Karmannyi orakul Briusa: Novaia gadatel'naia kniga],]Mw: [?], 1846

Caliostro or Fortune-Telling with Cards. A New and Hitherto Totally Unknown Method of Divination, Fully Satisfying All the Desires of Those Persons Participating, and Approved by the Famous Fortune-Tellers Lenormand and Swedenborg [Kaliostro ili gadanie po kartam. Novyi i sovershenno dosele neizvestnyi sposob gadaniia vpolne udovletvoriaiushchii vse zhelaniia zagadyvaiushchikh osob, odobrennyi znamenitymi gadateliami Lenormanom i Svedenborgom], Mw: Kirillov, 1843

The Characteristics of Man or The Simplest Means of Determining Character [Kharakteristika cheloveka ili samyi legkii sposob uznavat' kharakter cheloveka], St P.: Acad. Press, 1839

The Complete Dreambook [Polnyi sonnik], Tallinn: 'Marina' cooperative, 1990

A Complete Entirely New Dream Interpreter with a Scientific Explanation of the Theory of Dreams, Hallucinations and Sonambulism . . . [Polnyi noveishii snotolkovatel' s nauchnym ob"iasneniem teorii snov, galliutsinatsii i sonambulizma . . .], Mw: Bakhmetev, 1869

The Complete Fortune-Telling Cards or A New Revelation of the Secrets of

Cartomancy [*Polnye gadatel'nye karty ili novoe otkrytie tainstv kartomanii*], St P.: [?], 1830

A Curious and Brief Elucidation of the Worthwhile Sciences of Physiognomy and Chiromancy [*Kurioznoe i kratkoe iz"iasnenie liubopytstva dostoinykh nauk fiziognomii i khiromantii*], Mw: Moscow University Press, 1765, 1768, 1773; Mw: Senate Press, 1781; Mw: Gippius, 1786, Mw: Reshetnikov, 1789, 1791, 1793, 1793 (SK 3378–85), 1807

The Curious Prediction of the Venerable One-Hundred-and-Six-Year-Old Renowned Swiss Man Martyn Zadek about Future Events and His Interpretation of Dreams . . . [*Martyna Zadeka sto-shestiletniago slavnago shveitsarskago startsa liubopytnoe predskazanie na budushchiia vremena i tolkovanie im snov*], Mw: Glazunov, 1807

A Diversion in Times of Tedium or A New Entertaining Method of Reading the Cards [*Zabava v skuke, ili Novoi uveselitel'noi sposob gadat' na kartakh*], Mw: Annenkov Press on commission from Reshetnikov, 1788; Mw: Reshetnikov, 1791 (SK 2286–7)

The Domestic Magic Book of Akhnazarus Tovius of Moldavia [*Domashnaia volshebnaia knizhka Akhnazara Toviia Moldavanina*], St P.: Ioganson, 1884; Mw: Zemskii [?]

The Drawing Room Soothsayer and Diviner. A Fortune-telling Book for the Inquisitive . . . A New Method of Divination by the Famous Mademoiselle Lenormand [*Komatnyi veshchun i proritsatel'. Gadatel'naia kniga dlia liuboznatel'nykh liudei . . . Novaia metoda gadaniia znamenitoi devitsy Lenorman . . .*], Mw: Presnov, 1874

The Dreambook [*Sonnik*], comp. A. T. Temiraeva, Mw: Izyskatel', 1993

A Dreambook, Ascribed by Muslims to the Old Testament Patriarch Joseph, Son of Jacob [*Snotolkovatel' pripisyvaemyi musul'manami vetkhozavetnomu patriarkhu Iosifu, synu Iakova*], ed. P. A. Poliakov, Kazan': Kazan' University Press, 1901

A Dreambook. Interpretations of Dreams from Artemidorus to Miller [*Sonnik ili tolkovaniia snov ot Artemidora do Millera*], Mw: Zolotoi telenok, 1996

A Dreambook of 215 dreams, or The Interpretation of Dreams by Various Egyptian and Indian Sages and Astronomers [*Sonnik 215 snov, ili tolkovanie snovidenii raznykh egipetskikh i indeiskikh mudretsov i astronomov*], Mstera: Golyshev, e.g. 1865, 1867, 1868, 1871, 1874, 1879, 1883

A Dreambook or Guide to the Elucidation and Interpretation of Dreams, Compiled According to the Guidance of the Famous Seers Lenormand, Swedenborg, Briuss (sic!) and Others [*Sonnik ili rukovodstvo k ob"iasneniu i istolkovaniu vidennykh snov, sostavlennyi po rukovodstvam znamenitykh predskazatelei Lenorman, Swedenborg, Briussa i drugikh*], St P.: Spiridonov, 1865

A Dreambook, or The Interpretation of Dreams [*Sonnik ili tolkovanie snov*], G. H. Miller, St P.: Spiks, 1995; Mw: Fair, 1995

A Dreambook, or The Interpretation of Dreams Arranged in Alphabetical Order, with Essential Commentaries . . . [Sonnik ili istolkovanie snov po alfavitu raspolozhennoe, s nuzhnymi primechaniiami . . .], St P.: Bogdanovich, 1791 (SK add.198); St P.: [?], [1820]

A Dreambook, or The Interpretation of Dreams Occurring to Sleeping People, with Essential Commentaries, and the Opinion of Two Famous Writers on Dreams . . . [Sonnik ili istolkovanie snov prikliuchashchikhsia spiashchim liudiam, s nuzhnymi primechaniiami, mneniem dvukh znamenitykh pisatelei . . .], St P.: [?], 1784 (SK n-e 775)

A Dreambook, or The Interpretation of Dreams Selected from Astronomical and Physical Observations and Arranged in Alphabetical Order . . . [Sonnik ili istolkovanie snov vybrannoe iz nabliudenii astronomicheskikh i fizicheskikh i po alfavitu raspolozhennoe . . .], St P.: Henning, 1784; Kaluga: Baturin, 1787 (SK 6700–1); Mw: Smirnov, 1838, 1843, 1846; Mw: Sharapov, e.g. 1868, 1872, 1876, 1877

A Dreambook or The Interpreter of Dreams. A Merry Tale-Teller for Old and Young [Sonnik ili tolkovatel' snov. Veselyi skazochnik dlia starogo i malogo], St P.: Trusov, 1858

A Dreambook or What Happens in Sleep [Sonnik ili chto proiskhodit vo sne], Ekaterinburg: Lekton, 1994

A Dreambook, Telling Mother Truth [Sonnik, skazuiushchii matku pravdu], comp. S.A., St P.: Provincial Administration Press (SK 6702), 1799; Smolensk: Provincial Administration Press, 1801; Mw: [? Khavskii], 1831; Mw: Khavskii, 1839

A Dreambook. The Interpetation of Dreams [Sonnik. Tolkovanie snov], comp. E. Tsvetkov, Mw: Prometei, 1990

Eastern Planetary Oracle, or a New, Most Accurate Means of Finding Out about the Past, Present and Future by Means of Secret Circles . . . [Vostochnyi planetnyi orakul, ili novyi, verneishii sposob uznavat' proshedshee, nastoishchee i budushchee posredstvom tainstvennykh krugov], St P.: Trei, 1851

An Egyptian Oracle, or the General, Complete and Newest Divinatory Means, Providing People of Both Sexes with Innocent Amusement . . . [Ekipetskii orakul, ili Vseobshchii polnyi noveishii gadatel'nyi sposob, sluzhashchii k nevinnomu uveseleniiu liudei oboego pola . . .], Mw: [n. publ.], 1796 (SK 2121); Mw: Stepanov, 1841

Entertaining Magic, or The Revelation of Miraculous and Amazing Mysterious Experiments, Known as Focus Pocus . . . [Uveselitel'noe volshebstvo, ili Otkrytie chudesnykh i udivitel'nykh tainstvennykh opytov, izvestnykh pod nazvaniem Fokus Pokus . . .], H. Decremps, St P.: [Sytin], 1791 (SK 1745)

Folk Healing or Russian Folk Charms and a Complete Collection of All Manner of Beliefs, Superstitions and Sorcery for All Occasions in Life . . . [Znakharstvo ili russkie narodnye zagovory i polnoe sobranie vsevozmozhnykh poverii, sueverii, predrassudkov i koldovstva na vse sluchai zhizni . . .], Mw: Aviator, 1911

The Fortune-Teller or A New Method of Reading the Cards [*Vorozheia ili novyi sposob gadat' na kartakh*], Mw: Moscow University Press, 1838

The Genuine Fortune-Teller, or A True and Complete Method of Guessing Names . . . [*Nelozhnoi vorozheia ili Vernoi i polnoi sposob kak otgadyvat' imena . . .*], Mw: Gippius, 1787; St P.: Sytin, 1792; Mw: [n. publ.], 1793

A Girlish Trinket, With Which Men Too May be Diverted, or A Bouquet of Flowers not for the Corsage but the Heart [*Devich'ia igrushka, kotoroiu mogut zanimat'sia i mushchiny, ili Puket tsvetov ne dlia grudei, a dlia serdtsa*], St P.: Bogdanovich, 1791 [SK 1734)

The Gypsy Woman, Interpreting Dreams, Predicting to Each Person, What May Happen on Any Day . . . [*Tsyganka, tolkuiushchaia sny, predskazyvaiushchaia kazhdomu, chto v kakoi den' s nim prikliuchit'sia mozhet . . .*], Mw: Claudia, 1789 (SK 8128)

A Horoscope, Divination, Dreambook [*Goroskop, gadaniia, sonnik*], comp. I. S. Semenova, Mw: RIO Uprpolitgrafizdat Mosoblispolkoma

How to Recognize a Person's Character [*Kak uznavat' kharakter cheloveka*], St P.: supplement to the journal *Nature* (series *The Useful Library*),1897

An Innocent and Entertaining Pastime for Idle Hours . . . [*Bezvinnoe i uveselitel'noe preprovozhdenie prazdnago vremeni . . .*], Mw: Moscow University Press, 1770 (SK 446)

An Instruction for Fortune-Telling with the Fortune-Telling Cards of the Famous Clairvoyant Mlle Lenormand . . . [*Nastavlenie dlia gadaniia gadatel'nymi kartami znamenitoi predskazatel'nitsy devitsy Lenorman . . .*], trans. A. Semenkovich, Mw: Semen, 1850, 1852

The Interpretation of Dreams: A Complete Collection of Yuletide Pleasures [*Tolkovanie snovidenii: polnoe sobranie sviatochnykh uveselenii*], attr. Martyn Zadeka, Mw: Zhivarev, e.g. 1865 (3rd edn.), 1897 (9th edn.)

The Interpretation of Dreams (A Dreambook) [*Tolkovanie snov (Sonnik)*], New York: [n. publ.], 1985

The Interpretation of Dreams by the Venerable 106-Year-Old Man, Martin Zadek later *Zadeka* and with slight variants in the spelling of the title [*Tolkovanie snovidenii sta-shestiletniago startsa Martyna Zadeka/i*]:

(1) Mw: Smirnov/a, e.g. 1848 or 1849, 1860, 1865, 1870, 1877 (8th edn.), 1903

(2) Mw: Abramov, e.g. 1869, 1871, 1872, 1875 (6th edn.), 1881 (8th edn.)

(3) Mw: Presnov, e.g. 1873 (5th edn.), 1874, 1877 (8th edn.), 1879, 1880 (both 9th edns!), 1885 (10th edn.)

(4) Mw: Sytin, e.g.1886, 1893, 1894, 1895, 1898, 1900, 1901, 1903, 1907, 1909, 1912, 1914, 1915

(5) Mw: Vil'de, e.g. 1897, 1904, 1911

The Interpretation of Dreams, According to Astronomy, Occurring According to the Movements of the Moon, Translated from Polish [*Istolkovanie snov po astronomii proiskhodiashchikh po techeniiu Luny. Perevedeno s pol'skago A.V.*], Mw: Moscow University Press, 1768, 1772, 1788 (SK 2685–7)

The Interpreter of Dreams by the Well-Known French Dream Interpreter, Mlle Lenormand . . . [*Istolkovatel' snov izvestnoi frantsuzskoi snogadatel'nitsy, gospozhi Lenorman . . .*], Mw: Weimar, 1862

An Interpretive Dreambook, a Collection of Interpetations of Various Dreams from the Experience of My Hundred-Year-Old Relatives [*Tolkovyi sonnik ili sobranie tolkovanii razlichnykh snov, po opytam stoletnikh moikh rodstvennikov*], Mw: Manukhin 1869; (later as *A New Interpetive Dreambook . . .*) Mw: Manukhin, 1882; Mw: Ioganson, 1873, 1876, 1882; Mw: Poliakov, 1892

In the Realm of Dreams and Death [*V tsarstve sna i smerti*], comp. E. Tsvetkov, Mw: RIMEKS, 1991

The Key to the Elucidation of Dreams, Compiled from the Works of the Most Illustrious Dream Interpreters: Cagliastro (sic!), Albertus Magnus, Martyn Zadek, Indian, Gypsy, Chinese and African Sages, and Verified by the Explanations of the Famous Finnish Fortune-Teller [*Kliuch k iz"iasneniu snov, sostavlennyi po sochineniiam slavneishikh snotolkovatelei: Kaliastro, velikago Alberta, Martyna Zadeka, indeiskikh, tsyganskikh, kitaiskikh i afrikanskikh mudretsov, i poverennyi s iz"iasneniiami znamenitoi chukhonskoi vorozhei*], St P.: Vingeber, 1838

King Solomon's Divinatory Circle [*Gadatel'nyi krug tsaria Solomona*] also known as *A Little Divinatory Book* [*Gadatel'naia knizhka*], *lubok* editions from the end of the eighteenth century; Mw: Selivanovskii, 1829; Mw: Stepanov, 1831; St P.: Ministry of Education Press, 1833; St P.: Krai, 1834; Mw: Evreinov, 1839; Mw: Kirillov, 1839, 1841 (2 edns), 1845; Mw: Lazarev Institute of Oriental Languages Press, 1840; Mw: Stepanov, 1843, 1844 plus constant republication by most publishers operating in this market before 1917

A Lady's Album, or A Fortune-Telling Book for Entertainment or Pleasure [*Damskii al'bom, ili gadatel'naia knizhka dlia uveseleniia i zabavy*], Mw: [?], 1816; Mw: Theatre Press, 1820

A Little Divinatory Book [*Gadatel'naia knizhka*]: see under *King Solomon's Divinatory Circle*

A Little Divinatory Book about Love [*Liubovnaia gadatel'naia knizhka*], A. Sumarokov, St P.: Academy Press, 1781, [n.p, n. publ., n.d.]; St P.: [n. publ., n.d] (SK 6964–6); vol. IV of collected works, Mw: Novikov at Moscow University Press, 1781 (SK 6940)

The Little Divinatory Book Known as a Geomantic Oracle . . . [Gadatel'naia knizhka nazyvaemaia orakul . . .], comp. K. Meier, St P.: Artillery and Engineering Cadet Corpus [1789] (SK n-e 440)

The Magician or A New and Complete Omnipurpose Oracle, Garnered from Ancient and Most Recent Sages and Astronomers . . . [*Charodei ili novyi i polnyi vseobshchii orakul, sobrannyi iz drevnikh i noveishikh mudretsov i astronomov . . .*], Mw: Cadet Corpus Press, 1816, 1822; Mw: [?], 1829; Mw: Ernst, 1862

The Magic Fortune-Telling Cards. The Secrets of Life and Death, Based on

Predictions [*Volshebnye gadatel'nye karty. Tainy zhizni i smerti, osnovannye na predskazaniiakh*], Mw: Orlov, 1885

The Magic Indicator. Fortune-Telling in the Cards [*Magicheskaia strelka. Gadanie po kartam*], Mw: Stepanov, 1843; Mw: Kudravtsev, 1860

The Magic Mirror, Revealing the Secrets of Albertus Magnus and Other Renowned Egyptian Sages and Astronomers . . . [*Volshebnoe zerkalo, otkryvaiushchee sekrety velikago Al'berta i drugikh znamenitykh egipetskikh mudretsov i astronomov . . .*], Mw: S. Komisarov at the Zelennikov Press, 1794 (SK 8840); Mw: Glazunov at the Reshetnikov Press, 1799 (SK n-e 681); [? Mw: Reshetnikov], 1801; Mw: Reshetnikov, 1808; [?Mw: ?, 1814]; Mw: Vsevolozhskii, 1816; Mw: Reshetnikov, 1818

The Miraculous Diviner Reveals Your Thoughts [*Chudesnyi gadatel' uznaet zadumannye pomyshleniia*], comp. F. Kuzmichev, Mw: Kirillov, 1838; Mw: Smirnov, 1839

A Morning Pastime over Tea, or A New, Complete and as Far as Possible Accurate Interpretation of Dreams According to Astronomy and in Verse [*Utrennee vremiapreprovozhdenie za chaem ili v stikhakh novoe, polnoe i po vozmozhnosti dostovernoe istolkovanie snov po Astronomii*], St P.: Okurokov at St. Petersburg University Press, 1799 (SK 7626)

Morpheus – The Interpreter of Dreams in Alphabetical Order [*Morfei – istolkovatel' snovidenii v alfavitnom poriadke*], Pskov: Neiman, 1876

The Most Complete Dreambook and Interpreter of Various Portents [*Polneishii sonnik i istolkovatel' razlichnykh primet*], St P.: Shataev, 1872, 1878, 1881

A Muslim Dreambook [*Musul'manskii sonnik*], N. G. Mallitskii, Kazan': Kazan' University Press, 1902; Tashkent: Iosh gvardiia, 1990

The Mysterious Gypsy Woman Foretelling the Fate of Young Men and Women [*Tainstvennaia tsyganka, predskazyvaiushchaia sud'bu zhenikham i nevestam*], comp. F. Kuzmichev, Mw: Kirillov, 1836; Mw: Smirnov, 1837, 1838, 1839

A Mysterious Prediction or Solitaire with Cards [*Tainstvennoe predskazanie ili Kartochnyi seliter*], Mw: Moscow University Press, 1833 (from an earlier edn. before 1825)

The Mysterious World of Fortune-Telling [*Tainstvennyi mir gadaniia*], comp. S. S. Skol'znikova, Mw: Soviet Patriot, 1989

The New and Complete Astronomical Telescope or An Astronomical, Astrological, Physical, Economic Calendar for 200 years [*Novyi i polnyi Astronomicheskii teleskop ili astronomicheskii, astrologicheskii, fizicheskii, ekonomicheskii kalendar' na 200 let . . .*], attr. S. Petrov, Mw: [?], 1819; Mw: Glazunov, 1823

A New and Complete Dreambook. The Prediction of Dreams . . . [*Novyi polnyi sonnik. Predskazanie snov . . .*], comp. V. Chubatyi, Mw: Arfa, 1994

A New and Most Complete Divinatory Oracle or The Miraculous Secret of Predictions, Wizardry and Magic . . . [*Novyi i polneishii gadatel'nyi orakul ili Chudesnoe tainstvo predskazanii, koldovstva i charodeistva . . .*], comp. I. Danilevskii, Mw: Stepanov, 1833, 1837, 1838

A New and Most Reliable Means of Fortune-Telling, or The Prophet at New Year [*Novyi i verneishii sposob otgadyvat', ili Veshchun na novyi god*], St P.: [Academy of Sciences], 1787 (SK 4690)

A New Book. Household Remedies. The Bruce Calendar for 200 years. A Course in Folk Healing, Magic, Sorcery and A Complete Collection of Russian Folk Spells [*Novaia kniga. Domashnii lechebnik. Kalendar' na 200 let Briusa. Kurs znakharstva. Charodeistvo, volshebstvo i vse russkie narodnye zagovory*], Mw: Starye zavety, e.g. 1916 (3rd edn) 1917 (4th and 5th edns)

A New, Complete and Detailed Dreambook, Signifying the Amplified Interpretation and Elucidation of Every Dream . . . [*Novyi polnyi i podrobnyi sonnik, oznachaiushchii prostrannoe istolkovanie i ob"iasnenie kazhdago sna . . .*], St P.: [?], 1802; St P.: at the Imperial Press, 1811; St P.: on the Department of Foreign Trade Press, 1818; St P.: Kholmushin, 1912

The New Complete Oracle and Magician, Foretelling the Future from Questions Posed . . . [Novyi polnyi orakul i charodei, predskazyvaiushchii budushchee po predlozhennym voprosam . . .], Mw: Sharapov, e.g. 1883, 1889; Mw: Sazonov, e.g. 1883, 1899; Mw: Sytin, e.g. 1891, 1892, 1912, 1917

A New Dreambook: Guide to the Interpretation of Dreams and Experiences of the Sleeping [*Novyi sonnik: Rukovodstvo po istolkovaniiu snov i perezhivanii spiashchikh*], Tony Crisp, trans. S. A. Ananin, Minsk: Potpourri, 1995

A New Dreambook, or The Interpretation of Dreams in Alphabetical Order; With a Section by Wise Old Women; Selected from the Works of Famous Men . . . [*Novyi Sonnik, ili tolkovanie snov po alfavitu; s prisovokupleniem starykh predskazatel'nits; Vybrannyi iz sochinenii znamenitykh muzhei . . .*], Mw: Kuznetsov, 1831

A New Explanitory (sic!) Dreambook [*Novyi talkovyi sonnik*], Mw: Manukhin, 1882

A New Fortune-Telling Method Translated from Arabic [*Novoi gadatel'nyi sposob pereveden s arabskago iazyka*], Mw: Moscow University Press, 1765, 1768, 1774 (SK 4683–5)

A New Fortune-Telling Method with An Addition Translated from Arabic [*Novoi gadatel'nyi sposob s pribavleniem pereveden s arabskago iazyka*], Mw: Ponomarev, 1788; St P.: Sytin, 1793 (SK 4686–7)

A New Means of Learning the Characteristics of Each Man from his Physical Appearance: The Work of Michael Scot . . . [*Novoi sposob, kak uznavat' mozhno kazhdago cheloveka svoistva po ego slozheniiam: soch. Mikhaila Skota . . .*], Mw: Senate Press, 1781 (SK 6533)

The New Oracle or an Innocent Sibylline Divination Based on a Random Series of Dots . . . [*Novyi orakul ili nevinnoe Sivillino gadanie po sdelannym na udachu tochkam . . .*], Mw: Kirillov, 1844

The New Predictor, The Sorcerer or Fortune-Teller . . . [*Novoi predskazatel' i koldun ili vorozhaika . . .*], St P.: Sytin, 1795

The Newest and Most Complete Astronomical Telescope or The Truest, General and Detailed Astronomical, Astrological, Political, Physical, Dietetic and Economic Guide for Town and City Dwellers With a Predictive Calendar for

336 Years [*Noveishii i samyi polnyi Astronomicheskii teleskop ili samoverneishii, obshchii i podrobnyi astronomicheskii, astrologicheskii, politicheskii, fizicheskii, dieticheskii i ekonomicheskii nastavnik na gorodskikh i sel'skikh zhitelei, s predskazatel'nym kalendarem na 336 let*], Mw: Stepanov, 1829, 1839

The Newest Complete Oracle, Divining and Predicting with Clear Answers the Fate of Young Lads and Lassies, the Unwed and the Wed . . . [*Noveishii polnyi orakul, ugadyvaiushchii i predskazyvaiushchii v iasnykh otvetakh sud'bu zhenikham i nevestam, kholostym i zhenatym . . .*], Mw: Smirnov, 1839, 1843, 1846, 1868; Mw: Sharapov, 1875, 1877, 1877

The Newest Dreambook and Rules of Chiromancy or The Secrets of the Palm . . . [*Noveishii sonnik i pravila khiromantii ili tainy ruki . . .*], Mw: Kholmushin, 1891, 1898, 1899, 1901, 1902, 1903, 1904, 1907 (also called 7th edn)

The Newest Dream Interpreter Compiled from the Manuals of Foreign Men Skilled in the Science of Dream Divination . . . [*Noveishii snotolkovatel' sostavlennyi iz rukovodstva inostrannykh i v snogadatel'noi nauke iskusnykh muzhei . . .*], Mw: Stepanov, 1829

The Newest Dream Interpreter, Telling Mother Truth [*Noveishii snotolkovatel', skazuiushchii matku pravdu*], Mw: Selivanovskii, 1829

The Newest Fortune-Telling Cards Replacing All Oracles, Astrologers, Caballistics, Coffee-Cup Readers and Card and Bean Diviners . . . [*Noveishie gadatel'nye karty, zameniaiushchie soboiu vse orakuly, astrologi, kabalistiki, kofeinitsy, vorozhei na kartakh i bobakh . . .*], Mw: Vsevolozhskii, 1814; Mw: Moscow University Press, 1816

The Newly Appeared Wizard Recounting the Divination of the Spirits. An Innocent Distraction in Hours of Boredom for Those Not Wishing to Engage upon Anything Better . . . [*Novoiavlennyi vedun povedaiushchii gadaniia dukhov. Nevinnoe uprazhnenie vo vremia skuki dlia liudei ne khotiashchikh luchshim zanimat'sia . . .*], comp. F. Karzhavin, St P.: Schnorr, 1795 (SK 2843)

A Number of Useful Extracts, Selected from the Amazing Secrets of Albertus Magnus . . . [*Nekotoryia poleznyia stat'i, vybrannyia iz udivitel'nykh sekretov velikago Alberta . . .*], trans. N. Sumarokov, St P.: Kleen at the Artillery and English Cadet Corpus, 1783 (SK 4543)

Omens, Spells and Fortune-Telling [*Primety, zagovory i gadaniia*], Kharkov: Mitets', 1995

The Oracles for the Current and Following Year [*Orakuly na nyneshnii i budushchii god*], [St P.: Academy of Sciences, 1774] (SK 5020)

A Pocket Dreambook, Revealing the Secrets of the Albertus Magnus [*Karmannyi sonnik, otkryvaiushchii sekrety velikago Al'berta*], Mw: [?], 1829

The Popular Dreambook for 1915 [*Populiarnyi sonnik na 1915 god*], Petrograd: [?], 1915

The Prediction Worthy of Note of the Renowned Martyn Zadek, Which He Revealed to his Friends in his 106th Year near Solothurn in Switzerland on the 20th December, 1769. With the Addition to that Interpretation of the Interpretation of Dreams According to Astronomy by the Movement of the Moon [*Primechaniia dostoinoe predskazanie slavnago Martyna Zadeka kotoroe on na 106-m godu ot rozhdeniia, v Shveitsarii pri Zoloturne, priateliam svoim otkryl 20 dekabria 1769 godu. S prisovokupleniem ko tomu istolkovaniiu istolkovaniia snov po astronomii proiskhodiashchikh po techeniiu luny*], Mw: Reshetnikov at the Provincial Administration Press, 1807

Predictive Tarot or the Key to Cartomancy of All Kinds. A Complete Reconstruction of the 78 Cards of the Egyptian Tarot, and the Methods of Interpreting Them [*Predskazatel'nye Taro ili Kliuch ko vsiakogo roda kartochnym gadaniiam. Polnoe vosstanovlenie 78 kart egipetskago Taro, i sposoby ikh tolkovaniia*], comp. G. Encausse, St P.: Naumov, 1912

The Reference Guide and Encyclopedic Lexicon of Dreams. More than 3000 Explanations of the Phenomena of Sleep, Collected over Sixty Six Years by the Kindly Old Man of Duck Street . . . [*Spravochnyi entsiklopedicheskii leksikon snovidenii. Bolee 3000 ob"iasnenii iavlenii sna. Sobiral v techenii 66 let dobryi starichok iz Utinoi ulitsy . . .*], St P.: Strauf, 1863

Russian Sorcery, Witchcraft and Folk Healing [*Russkoe koldovstvo, vedovstvo, znakharstvo*], St P.: Litera, 1994

Russian Yuletide, or Diverting and Pleasant Amusements from 25th December to 6th January for Amiable Girls, Delightful Young Married Women and Bachelors [*Russkie sviatki ili Zabavnye i priiatnye uveseleniia s 25-go dekabria po 6-e genvaria dlia liubeznykh devushek, milykh molodushek i kholostykh mushchin*], Mw: Reshetnikov, 1814–5

A Secret Microscope, or The Mirror of Magical Secrets [*Tainstvennyi mikroskop ili zertsalo volshebnykh tainstv*], St P.: Glazunov, 1817

The Seer and Prophet in Your Drawing Room . . . [*Komnatnyi veshchun i propritsatel' . . .*], Mw: Presnov, 1874

The Shop of All Delights . . .

(1) *The Shop of All Delights. The Rules of Physiognomy and Chiromancy* [*Magazin vsekh uveselenii. Pravila fiziognomii i khiromantii*], Mw: Stepanov, 1830

(2) *The Shop of All Delights. 1. The Fortune-Teller 2. The Famous Magician with Beans 3. The Reader of Coffee Grounds 4. Reading the Cards* [*Magazin vsekh uveselenii 1. Vorozheia 2. Znamenitaia volshebnitsa bobami 3. Kofeinitsa 4. Gadat' na kartakh*] Mw: Stepanov, 1831; Mw: Moscow University Press 1836; Mw: Nazarov, 1866

(3) *The Shop of All Delights or A Complete and Most Detailed Oracle and Magician . . .* [*Magazin vsekh uveselenii ili Polnyi i podrobneishii orakul i charodei . . .*], Mw: Kirillov, 1850

The Sibyl or Morning Teller of Dreams, Selected from the Works of Many Foreign Men Skilled in the Science of Dream Divination . . . [*Sibilla ili utrenniaia razkashchitsa snov, vybrannaia iz sochinenii mnogikh inostrannykh i vo snogadatel'noi nauke iskusnykh muzhei* . . .], 2 pts, Mw: Kirillov, 1839

Sleep and Dreams: A Scientifically Based Interpretation of Dreams, Compiled by the Famous Medium Miss Hussey [*Son i snovideniia: nauchno obosnovannoe tolkovanie snov sostavlennoe znamenitym mediumom Miss Khasse*], Warsaw: Rassvet, 1912; Mw: Red Line Moscow, 1990

Soothsay, Do not Jest, Tell the Whole Truth that Lies in your Heart, the Wizard does not Lie and You will feel Easier [*Vorozhi, ne shuti skazhi vsiu pravdu, chto u tebia na serdtse est', koldun ne solzhet a tebe legche budet*], comp. I. Kurbatov, 3 pts, Mw: Reshetnikov, 1808 (pts 1 and 2), 1827 (pt 3)

Stars and Fates: Antologiia goroskopov [*Zvezdy i sud'by: Antologiia goroskopov*], comp. G. L. Murav'ev, Mw: Lira, 1994; Ekaterinburg: Lekton, 1994

The Systematic Astrologer or Scientific Divination [*Sistematicheskii astrolog, ili Uchenoe zagadyvanie*], comp. I. Stolb-Rapinskii, Smolensk: Provincial Administration Press, 1802

Talking Stars: Practical Astrology [*Govoriashchie zvezdy: Prakticheskaia astrologiia*], Mw: MKPShP Izbor, 1992

Torot (sic!). The Secret Gypsy Art of Fortune-Telling with 52 Cards and the Joker [*Torot. Tsyganskoe iskusstvo gadaniia na 52 kartakh s dzhokerom*], Mw: MKhPiIZO 'Art' [1990]

A True and Most Simple Method of Reading the Cards [*Vernyi i legchaishii sposob otgadyvat' na kartakh*], St P.: Artillery and Engineering Cadet Corpus, 1782; St P.: [n. publ.], 1785 (SK add. 24, 940)

The Truest Astronomical Telescope, Or a General Astronomical, Physical, Political and Economic Calendar for 336 Years . . . [*Samoverneishii astronomicheskii teleskop, ili vseobshchii astronomicheskii, fizicheskii, politicheskii i ekonomicheskii kalendar' na 336 let* . . .], attr. M. Brankevich, Mw: Stepanov, 1829; Mw: Lazarev Institute of Oriental Languages, 1839

The Wizard, No Idle Babbler or the Genuine Fortune-Teller, Supplying Everyone with Correct Answers . . . [*Koldun ne boltun ili Nastoiashschii vorozheia daiushchii kazhdomu na voprosy spravedlivye otvety* . . .], 2 pts, St P.: Sytin, 1792

B. BIBLIOGRAPHY OF SECONDARY SOURCES

Afanas'ev, A. N., *Poeticheskie vozzreniia slavian na prirodu*, 3 vols., Mw, 1994 (reprinted from the Mw edn. of 1865–69)

Alchevskaia, Kh. D. et al., *Chto chitat' narodu*, 2 vols., St P., 1884–9

Bakhtiarov, A., *Briukho Peterburga*, St P., 1888

Baklanova, N. A., 'O sostave bibliotek moskovskikh kuptsov vo vtoroi chetverti XVIII veka', *Trudy otdela drevnerusskoi literatury*, vol. 14, 1958, pp. 644–9

Balov, A., 'Son i snovideniia v narodnykh verovaniiakh', *Zhivaia starina*, no. 4, 1891, pp. 208–13

Balzer, M. M., *Russian Traditional Culture: Religion, Gender and Customary Law*, Armonk, NY–London 1992

Bernshtam, T. A., 'Budni o prazdni: povedenie vzroslykh v russkoi krest'ianskoi srede XIX–XX vv.', *Etnicheskie stereotipy povedeniia*, ed. A. K. Baiburin, Ld, 1985, pp. 120–53

Bibliograficheskie pribavleniia k Zhurnalu Ministerstva narodnogo prosveshcheniia. Ukazatel' knig, vyshedshego v Rossii i v Tsarstve pol'skom, supplement to the *Zhurnal Ministerstva narodnogo prosveshcheniia*, 5 vols., St P., 1837–55

Blium, A.V., 'Russkaia lubochnaia kniga vtoroi poloviny XIX veka', *Kniga. Issledovaniia i materialy*, vol. 42, Mw, 1981, pp. 94–114

Blum, C., *Studies in the Dreambook of Artemidorus*, Uppsala, 1938

Bokova, V., ed., *Moskovskie legendy, zapisannye Evgeniem Baranovym*, Mw, 1993

Bollème, G., *La Bibliothèque bleue*, Paris, 1971

Les Almanachs populaires aux XVIIe et XVIIIe siècle, Paris, 1969

Brackertz, K., *Das Traumbuch des Achmet ben Sirin*, Munich, 1986

Brooks, J., *When Russia Learned to Read. Literacy and Popular Literature, 1861–1917*, Princeton, NJ, 1985

Büchsenschütz, B., *Traum und Traumdeutung im Altertum*, reprinted from the ed. of 1868, Wiesbaden, 1967

Bukhalov, N., *Snovideniia i prívideniia*, Mw, 1901

Burke, P., 'L'Histoire sociale des rêves', *Annales*, vol. 28, 1973, pp. 329–42

Popular Culture in Early Modern Europe, London, 1978

Capp, B. S., *Astrology and the Popular Press: English Almanacs in 1500–1800*, London–Boston, 1979

Chartier, R., *The Cultural Uses of Print in Early Modern France*, trans. Lydia C. Cochrane, Princeton, 1987

Chechulin, N., *Russkoe provintsial'noe obshchestvo vo vtoroi polovine XVIII veka*, St P., 1889

Chicherov, V. I., *Zimnii period russkogo zemledel'cheskogo kalendaria XVI-XIX vekov*, Mw, 1957

Chulkov, M., *Slovar' russkikh sueverii, idolopoklonicheskikh zhertvoprinoshenii svadebnykh, prostonarodnykh obriadov, koldovsta, shamanstva i proch.*, Mw, 1782, and reprinted as *Abevega russkikh sueverii, idolopoklonicheskikh zhertvoprinoshenii svadebnykh, prostonarodnykh obriadov, koldovsta, shamanstva i proch.*, Mw, 1786

Cross, G., *A Social History of Leisure since 1600*, State College, PA, 1990

Crowe, D. M., *A History of the Gypsies of Eastern Europe and Russia*, London–New York, 1995

Curry, P., *A Confusion of Prophets: Victorian and Edwardian Astrology*, London, 1992

Prophecy and Power: Astrology in Early Modern England, Cambridge, 1989

Dal', V. I., *Tolkovyi slovar' zhivogo velikorusskogo iazyka,* 4 vols., Mw, 1956, (reprinted from 2nd edn. of 1880–2)

O pover'iakh, sueveriiakh, i predrassudkakh russkogo naroda, 2nd edn., St P.-Mw, 1880

Derunov, S. 'Materialy dlia narodnogo snotolkovatelia. III. (Iaroslavskoi gubernii)', *Etnograficheskoe obozrenie,* vol. 36, no. 1, 1898, pp. 54–72

Descola, P., 'Head-shrinkers versus shrinks: Jivaroan dream analysis', *Man,* vol. 24, 1989, pp. 439–50

Devlin, J., *The Superstitious Mind: French Peasants and the Supernatural in the Nineteenth Century,* New Haven–London, 1987

Dinershtein, E. A., *I. D. Sytin,* Mw, 1983

Dummett, M., *Twelve Tarot Games,* London, 1980

Dushechkina E., 'Russian calendar prose: the Yuletide story', *Elementa: Journal of Slavic Studies and Comparative Cultural Semiotics,* vol. 1, no. 1, 1993, pp. 59–74

Egorov, B. F., 'Prosteishie semioticheskie sistemy i tipologiia siuzhetov', *Trudy po znakovym sistemam,* vol. 2, Tartu, 1965, pp. 106–15

Ezhegodnik. Obzor knig dlia narodnogo chteniia v 1891, 1892 gg. (Literacy Committee of the Imperial Agricultural Society), Mw, 1893

Ezhegodnik. Obzor knig dlia narodnogo chteniia v 1893 (Literacy Committee of the Imperial Agricultural Society), Mw, 1894

Fischer, S. R., 'The Dream in Middle High German Epic', *Australian and New Zealand Studies in German Language and Literature,* 10), Berne–Frankfurt–Las Vegas, 1978

Fishman, O. F., 'Sotsiokul'turnyi status i ritual'noe povedenie "znaiushchikh" v Tikhvinskom krae', *Zhivaia starina,* no. 4, 1994, pp. 24–5

Gattey, C. N., *Visionaries and Seers,* Bridport, 1988

Geneva, A., *Astrology and the Seventeenth-Century Mind: William Lilly and the Language of the Stars,* Berkeley, CA, 1993

Georgievskii, M., 'Sviatki v derevniakh Olonetskoi gub. i razlichnye gadaniia', *Olonetskie gubernskie vedomosti,* no. 46, 1898, pp. 495–7; no. 48, pp. 514–16

Goody, J., *The Interface between the Oral and the Written,* Cambridge, 1987

Goscilo, H., and Holmgren, B., eds., *Russia–Women–Culture,* Bloomington and Indianapolis, 1996

Gradov, B. A., Kloss, B. M., Koretskii, V. I., 'K istorii arkhangel'skoi biblioteki D. M. Golitsyna', *Arkheograficheskii ezhegodnik,* 1978, pp. 238–53

Graham, L. R., ed., *Science and the Soviet Social Order,* Cambridge, MA–London, 1990

Graham, L. R, *Science in Russia and the Soviet Union,* Cambridge, 1993

Grits, T., Trenin, V., and Nikitin, M., *Slovesnost' i kommertsiia (knizhnaia lavka A. F. Smirdina),* Mw, 1929

Gromyko, M. M., *Traditsionnye normy povedeniia i formy obshcheniia russkikh krest'ian XIX v.*, Mw, 1986

Hammarberg, G., 'Flirting with words: domestic albums, 1770–1840', *Russia–Women–Culture*, ed. Helena Goscilo and Beth Holmgren, Bloomington and Indianapolis, 1996, pp. 297–320

Heier, E., *Studies on Johann Caspar Lavater (1741–1801) in Russia* (Slavica Helvetica 37), Berne–Berlin–Frankfurt–New York–Paris, 1991

Hélin, M., *La Clef des songes*, Paris, 1925

Howe, J. E., *The Peasant Mode of Production, as exemplified by the Russian 'Obshchina-mir'*, Tampere, 1991

Hubbs, J., *Mother Russia: The Feminine Myth in Russian Culture*, Bloomington–Indianapolis, 1988

Ianzhul, I. I. et al., 'Usloviia rasprostraneniia obrazovaniia v narode', *Ekonomicheskaia otsenka narodnogo obrazovaniia*, 2nd edn., St P., 1899, pp. 84–114

Iatsimirskii, A. I., *Bibliograficheskii obzor apokrifov v iuzhnoslavianskoi i russkoi pis'mennosti*, pt I: Apokrify vetkhozavetnye, Petrograd, 1921, pp. 64–75

Iskrin, M., 'Kto takoi Martyn Zadeka?', *Almanakh bibliofila*, vol. 2, Mw, 1975, pp. 169–76

Ivanits, L. J., *Russian Folk Belief*, Armonk, NY–London, 1992

Kaivola-Bregenhøj, A., 'From dream to interpretation', *International Folklore Review*, vol. 7, 1990, pp. 88–96

Kapelus, H., 'Senniki staropolskie. Z dziejów literatury popularniej XVI–XVIII wieku', *Studii z dawniej literatury czeskiej, słowackiej i polskiej*, Warsaw-Prague, 1963, pp. 295–306

Khoteev, P. I., *Kniga v Rossii v seredine XVIII veka. Chastnye knizhnye sobraniia*, Ld, 1989

Khotinskii, M. S., *Rasskazy o temnykh predmetakh*, St P., 1861

Khromov, O. P., ed., 'Astronomiia i astrologiia v Drevnei Rusi. Materialy k bibliografii', *Estestvennonauchnye predstavleniia Drevnei Rusi*, Mw, 1988, pp. 290–310

Kleimenova, R. N., *Knizhnaia Moskva pervoi poloviny XIX veka*, Mw, 1991

Krawczuk, A., *Sennik Artemidora*, Wrocław, 1972

Krinichnaia, N. A., *Domashnii dukh i sviatochnye gadaniia (po materialam severnorusskikh obriadov i mifologicheskikh rasskazov)*, Petrozavodsk, 1993

Lesnye navazhdeniia (mifologicheskie rasskazy i pover'ia o dukhe-"khoziaine" lesa), Petrozavodsk, 1993

Nit' zhizni: Reministsentsii obrazov bozhestv sud'by v mifologii i fol'klore, obriadakh i verovaniiakh, Petrozavodsk, 1995

Krupianskaia, V. P. and Polishchuk, N. S., *Kul'tura i byt rabochikh gornozavodskogo Urala kontsa XIX-nachala XX veka*, Mw, 1971

Kufaev, M. N., *Istorii knigi v XIX veke*, Ld, 1927

Lavrov, V., 'I snitsia chudnyi son . . .', *Moskva*, no. 6, 1989, pp. 168–71

Lekomtseva, M. I. and Uspenskii, B. A., 'Opisanie odnoi semioticheskoi sistemy s prostym sintaksisom', *Trudy po znakovym sistemam*, vol. 2, Tartu, 1965, pp. 94–105

Lewis, I. M., *Ecstatic Religion*, 2nd edn., London–New York, 1989

Lewis, N., *The Interpretation of Dreams and Portents*, Toronto–Sarasota, 1976

Liatskii, E., 'Materialy dlia narodnogo snotolkovatelia. II. (Minskoi gubernii)', *Etnograficheskoe obozrenie*, vol. 36, no. 1, 1898, pp. 139–49

Lipinskaia, V. A., 'Narodnye traditsii v sovremennykh kalendarnykh obriadakh i prazdnikakh russkogo naseleniia Altaiskogo kraia', *Russkie: semeinyi i obshchestvennyi byt*, ed. M. M. Gromyko, T. A. Listova, Mw, 1989, pp. 111–41

Lotman, Iu. M., *Besedy o russkoi kul'ture. Byt i traditsii russkogo dvorianstva (XVIII-nachalo XIX veka)*, St P., 1994

Luckman, T., *The Invisible Religion*, London, 1967

Luhrmann, T. M., *Persuasions of the Witch's Craft: Ritual Magic in Contemporary England*, Cambridge, MA, 1989

L'vovskii, A., 'Piatnitsa v zhizni russkogo naroda', *Zhivopisnaia Rossiia*, 1902, vol. 2, pp. 19–98

MacDonald, M., *Mystical Bedlam. Madness, Anxiety and Healing in Seventeenth-Century England*, Cambridge, 1981

Makarenko, A., *Sibirskii narodnyi kalendar' v etnograficheskom otnoshenii. Vostochnaia Sibir', Eniseiskaia guberniia* (Zapiski Imperatorskogo russkogo geograficheskogo obshchestva 36), St P., 1913

Maksimov, S.V., *Nechistaia sila. Nevedomaia sila. Krestnaia sila*, 2 vols., Mw, 1993 (reprinted from *Sobranie sochinenii*, vols. 17 and 18, St P., 1908–13)

Marakuev, V. N., *Chto chital i chitaet russkii narod* (Publichnoe chtenie 9 marta 1884 g. v Politekhnicheskom muzee), Mw, 1886

Marker, G., *Printing, Publishing and the Origins of Intellectual Life in Russia, 1700–1800*, Princeton, NJ, 1985

Marquiset, A., *La célèbre Mlle Lenormand*, Paris, 1911

McReynolds, L., *The News under Russia's Old Regime: The Development of a Mass-Circulation Press*, Princeton, NJ, 1991

Meier, C.A., 'The dream in Ancient Greece and its use in temple cures (incubation)', *The Dream and Human Societies*, ed. G. E. von Grunebaum and R. Caillois, Berkeley–Los Angeles, 1966, pp. 303–19

Mezhov, V. I., *Piatoe pribavlenie k sistematicheskoi rospisi knigam, prodaiushchimsia v knizhnykh lavkakh Ivana Il'icha Glazunova. Sostavleno za 1883–1887 vkl.*, St P., 1889

Minasian, M. M., *Preferans ili kartiny domashnei zhizni*, Mw, 1993

Min'ko, L. I., *Magic Curing (Its Sources and Character, and the Causes of its Prevalence)*, trans. W. Mandel, *Soviet Anthropology and Archaelogy*, vol. 12, no. 1 (Summer 1973), pp. 3–33; vol. 12, no. 2 (Fall 1973), pp. 34–60; vol. 12, no. 3 (Winter 1973–4), pp. 3–27

Minyonok, E. V., 'The role of women in traditions of exorcism', unpublished paper given at the International Conference on Options for Woman and Freedom in the World of Tradition and Changes, 1993, Institute of Ethnology and Anthropology, Russian Academy of Sciences, Moscow

Nechaenko, D. A., *Son zavetnykh ispolnennykh znakov*, Mw, 1991

Nekrasova, E., *Narodnye knigi dlia chteniia v ikh 25-letnei bor'be s lubochnymi izdaniiami*, Viatka, 1902

Nikiforovskii, N. Ia., 'Materialy dlia narodnogo snotolkovatelia. 1. (Vitebskoi gubernii)', *Etnograficheskoe obozrenie*, vol. 36, no. 1, 1898, pp. 133–9

O vere v snovideniia. Izd. russkogo Sviato-Il'inskogo skita na Afone, no. 41, St P., 1896

Oberhelman, S. M., 'The Oneirocritic Literature of the Late Roman and Byzantine Eras of Greece: Manuscript Studies, Translations and Commentaries to the Dream-Books of Greece during the First Millennium AD, with Greek and English Catalogues of the Dream Symbols and with a Discussion of Greek Oneiromancy from Homer to Manuel the Palaeologian', PhD thesis University of Minnesota, photocopy version Ann Arbor, MI, 1983

Obol'ianinov, N., *Katalog russkikh illiustrirovannykh izdanii 1725–1860 gg.*, 2 vols., Mw, 1914 and 1915

Oinas, F J., 'The devil in Russian folklore', *Essays on Russian Folklore and Mythology*, Columbus, OH, 1985, pp. 97–102

Okenfuss M. J., *The Rise and Fall of Latin Humanism in Early-Modern Russia: Pagan Authors, Ukrainians, and the Resiliency of Muscovy* (Brill's Studies in Intellectual History 64), Leiden–New York–Cologne, 1995

Ol'khin, M. D., *Sistematicheskii reestr russkim knigam s 1831 po 1846 god*, St P., 1846

Oppenheim, A. L., 'Mantic dreams in the ancient Near East', *The Dream and Human Societies*, ed. G. E. von Grunebaum and R. Caillois, Berkeley–Los Angeles, 1966, pp. 341–50

The Interpretation of Dreams in the Ancient Near East with a Translation of an Assyrian Dream-Book (Transactions of the American Philosophical Society, vol. 46, pt 3), Philadelphia, 1966, pp. 179–373

Otshel'nik, *Peterburgskie gadalki, znakhari, iurodivye i pr. (Ocherki petersburgskoi zhizni)*, St P., 1894

Ovsiannikov, Iu., ed., *Russkie narodnye kartinki XVII-XVIII vv.*, Mw, 1968

Palmenfeldt, U. and Kaivola-Bregenhøj, A., eds., *Drömmar och kultur*, Stockholm, 1992

Pina-Cabral, J. de, *Sons of Adam, Daughters of Eve*, Oxford, 1986

Pokrovskii, A., *Kalendari i sviattsy*, Mw, 1889

Pomerantseva, E.V., *Mifologicheskie personazhi v russkom fol'klore*, Mw, 1975

Prugavin, A. S., *Knigonoshi i ofeni (Vstrechi, nabliudeniia i issledovaniia*, 2 vols., 7 pts, n.p., n.d.

Purcell, K., *More in Hope than Anticipation: Fatalism and Fortune-Telling amongst Women Factory Workers* (Studies in Sexual Politics 20), Manchester, 1989

Pypin, A. N., *Lozhnye i otrechennye knigi russkoi stariny (Pamiatniki starinnoi russkoi literatury izdannye G. Kushelev-Bezborodko)*, pt 3, St P., 1862

Ramer, S. C., 'Traditional healers and peasant culture in Russia, 1861–1917', *Peasant Economy, Culture and Politics in European Russia, 1800–1921*, ed. E. K. Mann and T. Mixter, Princeton, NJ, 1991, pp. 207–32

Reay, B., *Popular Culture in Seventeenth-Century England*, London, 1985

Reestr rossiiskim knigam Ivana Glazunova, n.p., 1829

Reestr rossiiskim knigam prodaiushchimsia v Sanktpeterburge u Vasil'ia Plavil'shchikova, St P., 1815

Reestr rossiiskim knigam, landkartam, planam, portretam i notam, prodaiushchimsia, sverkh mnogikh drugikh knig, v Kieve, na Pecherske i Podole v knizhnoi lavke Ivana Ivanovicha Busheva, Mw, 1817

Remizov, A., 'Gadal'nye karty', *Rossia v pis'menakh*, vol. 1, Mw–Berlin, 1922, pp. 111–21

Romanov, E. P., 'Opyt belorusskogo narodnogo snotolkovatelia', *Etnograficheskoe obozrenie*, no. 3, 1889, pp. 54–72

Roper, L., *Oedipus and the Devil: Witchcraft, Sexuality and Religion in Early Modern Europe*, London, 1994

Rosslyn, W., 'Anna Bunina's "Unchaste relationship with the Muses": patronage, the market and the woman writer in early nineteenth-century Russia', *Slavonic and East European Review*, 74, 1996, pp. 223–42

Rovinskii, D. A., *Russkie narodnye kartinki*, 5 vols., St P., 1881

Rubakin, N. A., 'K kharakteristike chitatelia i pisatelia iz naroda', *Severnyi vestnik*, 1891, no. 4, pt 1, pp. 111–45

Etiudy o russkoi chitaiushchei publike. Fakty, tsifry, nabliudeniia, St P., 1895

Ruud, C. A., *Russian Entrepreneur, Publisher Ivan Sytin of Moscow, 1851–1934*, Montreal–Kingston–London–Buffalo, 1990

Ryan, W. F., 'Alchemy, magic, poisons and the virtues of stones in the Old Russian *Secretum Secretorum*', *Ambix*, vol. 37, no. 1, 1990, pp. 46–54

'Alchemy and the virtues of stones in Muscovy', *Alchemy and Chemistry in the 16th and 17th Centuries*, ed. P. Rattansi and A. Clericuzio, Dordrecht, 1994, pp. 149–59

'The onomantic table in the Old Russian *Secreta secretorum*', *Slavonic and East European Review*, vol. 49, 1971, pp. 603–6

'The passion of St Demetrius and the secret of secrets. An onomantic interpolation', *Cyrillomethodianum*, vols. 8–9, 1984–5, pp. 59–65

'What was the *Volkhovnik*? New light on a banned book', *Slavonic and East European Review*, vol. 68, no. 4, 1991, pp. 718–23

Ryan, W. F. and Wigzell, F., 'Gullible girls and dreadful dreams:

Zhukovskii, Pushkin and popular divination', *Slavonic and East European Review*, vol. 70, 1992, pp. 647–69

Sakharov, I. P., *Skazaniia russkogo naroda, sobrannye I. P. Sakharovym*, Mw, 1990 (reprinted from the Mw edn. of 1885)

Sanders, A., *A Deed without a Name: The Witch in Society and History*, Oxford–Washington, DC, 1995

Shcherbina, N. F., 'Sonnik sovremennoi russkoi literatury, raspolozhennom v afavitnom poriadke i sluzhashchii neobkhodimym dopolneniem k izvestnomu "sonniku Martyna Zadeki"', *Polnoe sobranie sochinenii*, St P., 1873, pp. 325–36

Shklovskii, V., *Chulkov i Levshin*, Ld, 1933

Skabichevskii, A. M., *Ocherki istorii russkoi tsenzury: 1700–1863*, St P., 1892

Smilianskaia, E. B., '"Suevernaia" knizhitsa pervoi poloviny XVIII v.', *Zhivaia starina*, no. 2, 1994, pp. 33–6

Smith, R. E. F. and Christian, D., *Bread and Salt: A Social and Economic History of Food and Drink in Russia*, Cambridge, 1984

Snegirov, I., *Lubochnye kartinki v moskovskom mire*, Mw, 1861

Sobolevskii, A., *Perevodnaia literatura Moskovskoi Rusi XIV-XV vekov*, St P., 1903

Speranskii, M. N, 'Odin iz starykh rukopisnykh sbornikov snotolkovanii i pesen', *Etnograficheskoe obozrenie*, nos. 1–2, 1906, pp. 98–101

Rukopisnye sborniki XVIII veka, Mw, 1963

Stewart, C., *Demons and the Devil: Moral Imagination in Modern Greek Culture*, Princeton, NJ, 1991

Svodnyi katalog russkoi knigi grazhdanskoi pechati XVIII veka, 1725–1800, 6 vols., Mw, 1962–75

Sytin, I. D. et al., *Illiustrirovannyi katalog knig knigoizdatel'stva T-va I. D. Sytina*, Mw, 1910

Katalog knigoizdatel'stva T-va I.D. Sytina v Moskve 1914, Mw, 1914

Ocherk izdatel' skoi deiatel'nosti T-va I. D. Sytina, Mw, 1910

Talbot Rice, T., *Tamara: Memoirs of St Petersburg, Paris, Oxford and Byzantium*, ed. E. Talbot-Rice, London, 1996

Tereshchenko, A. V., *Byt russkogo naroda*, St P., 1848

Thomas, K., *Religion and the Decline of Magic: Studies in Popular Beliefs in Sixteenth- and Seventeenth-Century England*, London, 1971

Thompson, E. M., *Understanding Russia. The Holy Fool in Russian Culture*, Lanham–New York–London, 1987

Tiutcheva, A. F., *Pri dvore dvukh imperatorov. Vspominaniia, dnevnik 1853–55*, trans. from French E.V. Ger'e, ed. S.V. Bakrushin, 2 vols., Cambridge 1975 (reprinted from the Mw edn. of 1929)

Tolstaia, S. M., 'K sootnosheniiu khristianskogo i narodnogo kalendaria u slavian: Schet i otsenka dnei nedeli', *Iazyk kul'tury i problemy perevodimosti*, ed. B.A. Uspenskii, Mw, 1987, pp. 154–68

Tolstoi, N. I., 'Slavianskie narodnye tolkovaniia snov i ikh mifologicheskaia osnova', *Son – semioticheskoe okno. Snovidenie i sobytie. Snovidenie i iskusstvo. Snovidenie i tekst* (XXVI-e Vipperovskie chteniia Moskva, 1993), ed. D. Iu. Molok, Mw, 1994, pp. 89–95

Etnolingvisticheskii slovar' slavianskikh drevnostei. Proekt slovnika. Predvaritel'nye materialy, ed. N. I. Tolstoi et al., Mw, 1984

Trevor-Roper, H., 'The invention of tradition: the highland tradition of Scotland', *The Invention of Tradition*, ed. E. Hobsbawm and T. Ranger, London, 1983, pp. 15–42

Turilov, A. A. and Chernetsov, A. V., 'Otrechennaia kniga Rafli', *Trudy otdela drevnerusskoi literatury*, vol. 40, 1985, pp. 260–344

Uspenskii, B.A., 'Antipovedenie v kul'ture drevnei Rusi', *Izbrannye trudy*, 2 vols., Mw, 1994, vol. 1, pp. 320–32

'K simvolike vremeni u slavian: "chistie" i "nechistie" dni nedeli', *Finitis duodecim lustris: Sbornik statei k 60–letiiu prof. Iu.M. Lotman*, ed. S. G. Isakov et al., Tallinn, 1982, pp. 70–5

Vassiltchikov, M., *The Berlin Diaries of Marie ('Missie') Vassiltchikov 1940–1945*, London, 1985

Vinogradova, L. N., 'Devichi gadaniia o zamuzhestve v tsikle slavianskoi kalendarnoi obriadnosti (zapadno-vostochnoslavianskie paralleli)', *Slavianskii i balkanskii fol'klor*, Mw, 1981, pp. 13–43

Virtanen, L., 'Dream-telling today', *Studies in Oral Narrative*, ed. A-L. Siikala (Studia Fennica 33), 1990, pp. 137–45

Vowles, J., 'The "feminization" of Russian literature: woman, language and literature in eighteenth-century Russia', *Women Writers in Russian Literature*, ed. T. W. Clyman and D. Greene, Westport, CT, 1994, pp. 35–60

Watt, T., *Cheap Print and Popular Piety, 1550–1640*, Cambridge, 1991

Weber, E., *Peasants into Frenchmen: The Modernization of Rural France (1870–1914)*, Stanford, CA, 1976

Weiss, H. B., *Oneirocritica Americana. The Story of American Dream Books*, New York, 1944

White, R. I., *The Interpretation of Dreams by Artemidorus*, Park Ridge, NJ, 1975

Zabylin, M., *Russkii narod. Ego obychai, obriady, predaniia, sueveriia i poeziia*, Mw, 1992 (reprinted from the Mw edn. of 1880)

Index

CAMBRIDGE STUDIES IN RUSSIAN LITERATURE

In the same series

Novy Mir
EDITH REGOVIN FRANKEL

The enigma of Gogol
RICHARD PEACE

Three Russian writers and the irrational
T. R. N. EDWARDS

Words and music in the novels of Andrey Bely
ADA STEINBERG

The Russian revolutionary novel
RICHARD FREEBORN

Poets of modern Russia
PETER FRANCE

Andrey Bely
J. D. ELSWORTH

Nikolay Novikov
W. GARETH JONES

Vladimir Nabokov
DAVID RAMPTON

Portraits of early Russian liberals
DEREK OFFORD

Marina Tsvetaeva
SIMON KARLINSKY

Bulgakov's last decade
J. A. E. CURTIS

Velimir Khlebikov
RAYMOND COOKE

Dostoyevsky and the process of literary creation
JACQUES CATTEAU

The poetic imagination of Vyacheslav Ivanov
PAMELA DAVIDSON

Joseph Brodsky
VALENTINA POLUKHINA

Petrushka – the Russian carnival puppet theatre
CATRIONA KELLY

Turgenev
FRANK FRIEDBERG SEELEY

From the idyll to the novel: Karamzin's sentimentalist prose
GITTA HAMMARBERG

The Brothers Karamazov *and the poetics of memory*
DIANE OENNING THOMPSON

Andrei Platonov
THOMAS SEIFRID

Nabokov's early fiction
JULIAN W. CONNOLLY

Iurri Trifonov
DAVID GILLESPIE

Mikhail Zoshchenko
LINDA HART SCATTON

Andrei Bitov
ELLEN CHANCES

Nikolai Zabolotsky
DARRA GOLDSTEIN

Nietzsche and Soviet Culture
edited by BERNICE GLATZER ROSENTHAL

Wagner and Russia
ROSAMUND BARTLETT

Russian literature and empire
Conquest of the Caucasus from Pushkin to Tolstoy
SUSAN LAYTON

Jews in Russian literature after the October Revolution
Writers and artists between hope and apostasy
EFRAIM SICHER

Contemporary Russian satire: A genre study
KAREN L. RYAN-HAYES

Gender and Russian literature: new perspectives
edited by ROSALIND MARSH

The last Soviet avant-garde: OBERIU – fact, fiction, metafiction
GRAHAM ROBERTS

Literary journals in Imperial Russia
edited by DEBORAH A. MARTINSEN

Russian Modernism: the transfiguration of the everyday
STEPHEN C. HUTCHINGS

Reading Russian fortunes
Print culture, gender and divination in Russia from 1765
FAITH WIGZELL

Lightning Source UK Ltd.
Milton Keynes UK
UKOW040627050613

211785UK00001B/44/A

9 780521 024792